1/98
TIM

THE CIVILIZATION OF THE AMERICAN INDIAN SERIES

OKLAHOMA SEMINOLES
MEDICINES, MAGIC,
AND RELIGION

PLATE 1. A Seminole dance leader of yesteryear. Pencil sketch by Willie Lena.

OKLAHOMA SEMINOLES

MEDICINES, MAGIC,

AND RELIGION

BY JAMES H. HOWARD

In Collaboration with **WILLIE LENA**

UNIVERSITY OF OKLAHOMA PRESS : NORMAN AND LONDON

OTHER BOOKS BY JAMES H. HOWARD:

(translator and editor) *The Warrior Who Killed Custer: The Personal Narrative of Chief Joseph White Bull* (Lincoln, Nebraska, 1968)

North American Indian Cultures (Stillwater, Oklahoma, 1978)

The Dakota or Sioux Indians, A Study in Human Ecology (Lincoln, Nebraska, 1980)

Shawnee! The Ceremonialism of a Native American Tribe and Its Cultural Background (Athens, Ohio, 1981)

(with Victoria Lindsay Levine) *Choctaw Music and Dance* (Norman, 1989)

Library of Congress Cataloging-in-Publication Data

Howard, James Henri, 1925–1982.
  Oklahoma Seminoles.

  (The Civilization of the American Indian series; v. 166)
  Bibliography: p. 261.
  1. Seminole Indians—Religion and mythology.
2. Seminole Indians—Medicine. 3. Seminole Indians—Rites and ceremonies. 4. Indians of North America—Oklahoma—Religion and mythology. 5. Indians of North America—Oklahoma—Rites and ceremonies. 6. Indians of North America—Oklahoma—Medicine. I. Lena, Willie, 1912–   . II. Title. III. Series: Civilization of the American Indian series; no. 166.
E99.S28H69   1984   299'.78   83–40328
ISBN 0–8061–2238–2

3   4   5   6   7   8   9   10   11   12

CONTENTS

ILLUSTRATIONS

FIGURES

PREFACE

Mention the name Seminole, and most Americans immediately think of the Florida segment of the tribe—Indian men in colorful shirts poling dugouts through the black waters of the Everglades or wrestling alligators for tourists, and women tending babies and sewing patchwork in palmetto-thatched *chickees*. Most of these same Americans are surprised to learn that another Seminole population lives in the prairie and scrub oak hill country of central Oklahoma. This part of the tribe, though their geographical environment may not be as exotic as the semitropical savannah of Florida, has retained a great deal of its traditional Southeastern American Indian life-style and is fiercely proud of its Seminole identity. It is also the larger part of the tribe. In 1977 the Oklahoma Seminoles were estimated by the Bureau of Indian Affairs to number over 9,000, a population more than four and a half times greater than that of the Florida Seminoles, who number perhaps 2,000 in all, including the Miccosukees. The Oklahoma and Florida segments of the tribe, of course, hold much of their culture in common, since they were a single people before the ancestors of the Oklahoma group were forcibly removed to their present location after the Seminole wars. However, many differences have grown up between the two groups since the "Trail of Tears."

It is generally assumed, and is probably true in great part, that the Florida Seminoles and Miccosukees are more traditional than their Oklahoma kinsmen, having through their relative isolation retained more elements of aboriginal Southeastern culture. Yet when one considers that the Florida Seminoles in 1880 were reduced to no more than 208 individuals,[1] and that this tiny group was ancestral to all present-day Florida Seminoles, and when one notes that the majority of the tribe, including the political and religious leaders, went west to Indian Territory carrying their knowledge of tribal customs and beliefs with them, it is certainly naïve to assume that the Florida group is the more conservative in every instance, or that they represent an aboriginal baseline against which Oklahoma Seminole acculturation may be measured. It is quite certain, in fact, that in many instances the Oklahomans are the more traditional in that they retain cultural forms mentioned in early sources but long forgotten in Florida.

Studies of the Oklahoma Seminoles are relatively few, and this fact has probably contributed to the notion that they are highly acculturated as compared to the Floridians. Thus in Murdock and O'Leary's *Ethnographic Bibliography of North America* we find 325 listings under "Seminole."[2] Of these, only 50 are primarily concerned with the Oklahoma Seminoles, while 270 are concerned with the Florida group, and 5 are concerned about equally with both. This tally is not completely fair, of course, since before the removal the two groups were one and shared a common history—in Florida. It does indicate, in a very rough manner, that there has been considerable neglect of the Oklahoma Seminoles by anthropologists. This book, though it may not completely rectify the imbalance in coverage, will, it is hoped, give some idea of the richness of Seminole culture in the West, and of how much can still be learned if one deigns to inquire.

My objective in undertaking this work was to secure and present to the reader a cognitive view of Oklahoma Seminole culture; to be more specific, to present that culture as it is seen and interpreted by its more traditional members. Several Seminoles, Creeks, and persons of mixed Creek and Seminole descent contributed to its content, but the greatest amount of information by far comes from Willie Lena, a Seminole of Wewoka, Oklahoma.

Unless otherwise credited, descriptions of various aspects of Seminole life given here are paraphrased from his accounts. Although not formally trained, Lena is a talented artist, and the sketches and watercolors used as illustrations are his as well. Interpretive and comparative statements are my own, and I am likewise responsible for any errors in transcribing information provided by my friend and collaborator. Plant specimens collected by Willie Lena and myself were identified (in terms of the white man's botany) by Ronald J. Tyrl, of the department of General and Evolutionary Biology, Oklahoma State University, and James McPherson, of the department of Ecology, Fisheries and Wildlife at Oklahoma State. My thanks to both of them.

My study of the Oklahoma Seminoles began, on a desultory basis, in 1975, and has continued since that time. The bulk of the field work, that involving the gathering of plant specimens for my "Seminole herbarium" and the intensive interviewing of Willie Lena, took place in the summer of 1980 with the assistance of the Smithsonian Institution Urgent Anthropology Small Grants Program (contract number SF0025100000). Since Willie Lena speaks excellent English, interviewing was done in that language. Willie was quick to note, however, when he felt that the customary English term or phrase did not accurately convey the weight or nuance of his native Muskogee, and I have recorded this difference in each case.

Since this is largely a view of Seminole culture as seen through the eyes of one informant, one might ask just how representative of his culture that individual may be. In answer, I would reply that today's Oklahoma Seminoles range from ultra-conservative traditionalists to those who favor 100 percent assimilation to white culture. Each Seminole in his or her life-style and attitudes represents a constellation of points along this acculturation scale. On this scale Willie Lena, in almost every respect, reflects the conservative, native-oriented, point of view—that of the Seminoles who customarily worship at an Indian "square-ground" (tribal ceremonial ground) rather than at a Christian church and whose interests and associations are primarily Indian. Willie was reared by his ultra-conservative grandparents, and they attempted throughout his childhood to shield him as completely as possible from the white man and white culture, while at the same time taking great pains to inculcate in him Seminole culture and values. As a result, he was recognized when still a youth as a traditionalist leader and became a *heniha* or assistant town chief while still in his twenties. He was later elevated to the chieftain-ship of Tallahassee town, a position he holds today.

On the other hand, because of his warm and outgoing nature, his high intelligence and lively curiosity, Willie is anything but the withdrawn and taciturn guardian of an obsolescent culture. In spite of his grandparents' interdiction he managed to learn English and to gain a few years of schooling. He has made his own "anthropological" study of the white man's world and has reached a comfortable accommodation to it. A drive through his home town of Wewoka, Oklahoma, with Willie as a passenger is an unforgettable experience and reveals his cosmopolitan nature. It seems that nearly everyone in Wewoka, whether his skin is red, white, or black, knows "Uncle Willie" and understands his habit of "kidding around." This joking pattern involves Willie's con-struction of verbal scenarios designed to put a person in a highly embarrassing position. Teenage girls blush, their mothers scold, and men and boys grumble, but each one secretly enjoys the joke as much as Willie. Acquaintances seen while driving by, Willie greets with a derisive hoot if there is not time to stop for a visit. In the summer the front yard and porch of Willie's little house at 317 West 19th street are the scene of constant comings and goings of visitors. Some are Indians seeking small loans (expected of him since he is town chief), advice on family problems, herbal reme-dies for various ailments, and, sometimes, counters against sus-pected witchcraft. There are also both Indians and whites seeking information on traditional Seminole culture or wishing to pur-chase some of Willie's fine craftwork, such as a pair of ballsticks or a Seminole baby cradle. Although he has a sign above his work table reading "Please Don't Waste My Time," I have never observed him being abrupt with a visitor, and even half-drunk young bores are heard out with patience. Willie is certainly a "culture broker" and hence, to a certain degree, distinct from his fellow traditionalists, who are renowned for being close-mouthed. One must admit that his artistic ability and skill in articulating knowledge of his own culture in this way also make him atypical to some degree. What he appears to enjoy most is serving as an ambassador of his own culture, both to the younger generation of Seminoles and Creeks and to non-Indians. I consider myself fortunate to have been one of those persons with whom he shared part of his knowledge and called "friend," and I hope that in the following pages I can pass along to the reader some of this lore.

JAMES H. HOWARD

FOREWORD

The Life and Times of a Seminole Chief:
Willie Lena's Autobiography

Dictated by Willie Lena, May 31, 1980

My name is Willie Lena. Our family name, Lena, is not a Seminole word. It is Spanish, and comes from my great-grandfather, who was a Spaniard named Luna. I am sixty-eight years old now, or will be on July 23. I was born on that date in 1912, at one o'clock Sunday morning. I was born at the old place—you were there with me—two miles south of here [This farmstead is located just south and east of the Seminole Indian Clinic, on Highway 270 south of Wewoka, Oklahoma.—JH]. My mother was only sixteen or seventeen years old when I was born, and she had another very young child to care for, so I was placed with my grandparents to raise.

They were old-time Seminoles and didn't believe in the white man's education or ways. They raised me in Indian ways. I was taught that Ipofvnka (God, Providence) watched over us all. Sometimes authorities would come to check on Indian children who were not in school. My grandparents bought me a pony and told me to ride it over the hill whenever any wagon or buggy came near our place. My brother and I spent our time out in the woods hunting when we should have been in school. We hunted rabbits, squirrels, and other game. Bobcats we did not kill, we just got up in

xxi

a tree and threw stones at them. Wolves we didn't mess with. My grandpa said "Don't bother wolves." We saw them, and learned their ways, but we kept away from them.

Sometimes older people would come and visit my grandparents. I would sit and listen to what they said. Sometimes grandpa would take me around in the fields and woods and show me Indian medicines and their uses, just like I take you around.

Finally, both of my grandparents died, and I had no place to go. My mother wanted me to come and stay with her. She had a good place and a big family, but I didn't want to go. Even when I finally did, I spent most of my time out in the country hunting and fishing. My brother and I would make *abadaga* [bannock.—JH] to go with the game and fish we took. We would use devil's shoe-string to catch fish in ponds.

I often think of different things my grandparents taught me. They said that the martins don't like their young to see Indian kids scratched at Green Corn. They fly south with them about that time so they won't see. My grandpa would often take me aside and point at the clouds and tell me what he saw there. He saw pictures there, buffalo, birds, Indians on horseback. Years later I told white people, "When I was little I saw cartoons in the sky. My grandpa taught me how to see pictures in the clouds."

He taught me how to make bows and arrows, and even how to poison arrows. Poisoned arrows are used only on animals you don't eat. There is a little hole in the side of the arrow and that's where you put the— the— [Q. Venom?—JH] Yes, the snake venom. These poisoned arrows were used only on wolves, bobcats, and screech owls [considered to be witches in bird form by the Seminoles.—JH].

I finally went to school when I was eleven or twelve. I went to Justice school. My grandpa didn't want me to go to school. He took me out in the woods and showed me where he had his money, in the form of silver dollars and gold pieces, hidden. There was $17,000 in all. He said I could have it if I didn't go to school. I wanted to attend school real bad by that time, though, so I told my uncle where the money was hidden and in return I was allowed to go to school. I never got past the sixth grade.

PLATE 2. Willie Lena and his daughter Bonnie, May, 1980. Photograph by J. Howard.

My grandpa was a famous match ball game player. He was known all around here for his skill. He taught me how to make ballsticks and how to play—various tricks of the game. The game was really rough in those days. He taught me how to handle bigger men. If they are following you too closely, you reach around behind you and hit them with your ballsticks, still carrying the ball. I played my first match ball game when I was twelve years old.

I took medicine for the first time in 1925 [Willie would have been thirteen that year.—JH]. I was given the name Fus-hatci, "Single eagle feather." In 1936 I was appointed *heniha* [second chief.—JH] of Tallahassee ground. When I started out Ciban hajo was chief, and Sunday Davis was second chief. Ciban hajo died, and Sunday took his place. Then he died too. For a while we had no chief, so we borrowed the Okfuskee chief. About this time they discovered oil in this area and set up a drilling rig near our ground. They had all kinds of equipment and made lots of noise, so we moved our ground. Then my uncle Crazy Fish (Łało), who was of the Beaver clan, became chief.

I went to Bacone in 1929, but I didn't learn anything there. In 1935 I met my first wife. Her name was Elsie Smith, and she was Seneca and Cherokee. We had one child, a girl, Rosetta. We separated, and I married my second wife, Ella May Scott. We had one child, Carol, before we separated. My third wife was Lucille, you knew her. We had four children, Ella, the oldest, Bonnie, Amos, and Jimmy. I have eleven or twelve grandchildren now. Bonnie graduated from East Central State College in Ada this year. Ella graduated from Bacone. Amos graduated from New Lima high school, and Jimmy will graduate from high school next year if he goes back.

In all my life I was never in any bad trouble. I was crippled in 1934 when I was trying to break up a fight between two Indian boys and I got stabbed in the knee. Before then I was a fast runner. I ran the 100-yard dash in 9.9. Nineteen-thirty-four was the last year I played stickball. In 1935 I was stabbed again. I was on crutches. I was trying to stop a fight and I got stabbed in the right arm and in the back. Since that time I have supported myself making ballsticks and other trinkets to sell.

OKLAHOMA SEMINOLES
MEDICINES, MAGIC,
AND RELIGION

1

A SYNOPSIS
OF SEMINOLE HISTORY

Before examining Oklahoma Seminole culture as it is viewed by
Willie Lena and other conservatives, it is appropriate to take a
brief look at the origins of this interesting tribe and the tangle of
historical circumstances that resulted in its being plucked up by
the federal government and then set down again hundreds of miles
from its ancestral territory. In comparison with other American
Indian groups the Seminole tribe is a rather recent development.
Its membership derives principally from elements of certain Lower
Creek towns that separated themselves from the main body of the
Creek Confederacy during the eighteenth century plus a later,
early nineteenth-century, increment of Upper Creek refugees
from the Creek War of 1813–14. Even the tribal name, Seminole,
is a modern historic artifact, coming from the Spanish *cimarron*
meaning "wild." It referred originally to the fact that these Indians
had moved into wild, unoccupied territory, and were thus distin-
guishable from both the missionized Florida Indian remnants at
Saint Augustine and also the main body of the Creeks. Since the
Muskogee language has no "R" sound, the Spanish "Cimarrones"
became to the Indians "Simalones," soon changed to "Seminoles," their present name.[1]

The nucleus of the group that ultimately came to be known as
Seminoles were Lower Creeks who had established tribal towns

3

apart from the main settlements of that tribe in what is now northern Florida, then Spanish territory. In moving from Georgia into Florida these Lower Creek pioneers were taking up land vacated by the native Timucua, Apalachee, and Guale tribes. These original Floridians had been missionized by the Spanish beginning in 1573, but by 1711 had largely disappeared because of a combination of European diseases and raids by the Yamasees and Creeks, sometimes under English leadership.[2] The first move into Florida by Creek Indians followed the Yamasee War of 1715. In that conflict the Yamasee tribe of Georgia, instigated by Emperor Brim of the Creeks, rose against the South Carolina colony, seriously threatening that British outpost. The uprising might have succeeded, but the Cherokees failed to join in the attack, and the move collapsed. As a result of the failure of this revolt, there was an influx of Lower Creeks into northwest Florida.[3]

In 1716, 1717, and 1718 the Spanish sent emissaries to the Lower Creeks in an attempt to persuade them to resettle the now vacant Apalachee region and serve as a buffer against the English.[4] The Creek towns of Apalachicola, Oconee, Hitchiti, Sawokli, and Yuchi agreed to move, and all five are identifiable later as components of the early proto-Seminoles. These immigrants established settlements in the Tallahassee area, the former Apalachee territory, and near present Gainesville in what had been Timucua country.[5] They had with them a small number of refugees from the original Florida tribes who had fled to the Lower Creeks and were now returning to Florida as Creek allies.

With the possible exception of these small remnant groups of Indians from central and southern Florida and the Yuchi, the proto-Seminoles at this period were representatives of two divisions of the Muskhogean linguistic family, the Hitchiti and the Muskogee or Creeks proper. The Hitchiti languages (Hitchiti proper, Mikasuki, and Alachua) although related to Muskogee or Creek, are not intelligible to Creek speakers. Today one of these Hitchiti languages, Mikasuki, is still spoken by a large number of Florida Seminoles. Other Florida Seminoles, those of the Cow Creek group, speak Muskogee. Almost all of the Oklahoma Seminoles at the present time are Muskogee speakers, though both

Hitchiti and Mikasuki speakers were represented among the Seminoles who were removed from Florida in the nineteenth century, and a recent investigation revealed one remaining Mikasuki speaker, an elderly man, in the Oklahoma group.

There was a gradual accretion to these initial Lower Creek or proto-Seminole settlements as the eighteenth century advanced. A conference at Saint Marks in 1764 listed five Creek villages in the neighborhood: Tallahassee, Mikasuki, Chiskataloofa, Tamathli, and Ocklocknee.[6] By 1764 there were Creek settlers in the area between Saint Johns River and Alachua from the towns of Oconee, Apalachicola, Sawokli, and Chiaha, as well as some Yamasee.[7] All or most of these were Hitchiti speakers. A colony of Muskogee-speaking Creeks from Eufala was established in central Florida by 1767, and in 1778 there is reference to settlers from three additional Muskogee-speaking towns, as well as from two Alabama-speaking towns.[8] In 1799 Hawkins listed seven Seminole towns and said that they were derived from the Creek towns of Oconee, Sawokli, Eufala, Tamathli, Apalachicola, and Hitchiti.[9] The first use of the word Seminole so far found comes from this period, and is in an English document of 1765.[10] It was applied specifically to Cowkeeper's Alachua group, but as time passed the term was gradually extended to cover all Florida Indians as well.

For a long period these Indians resident in Florida did not regard themselves as distinct or set off from the main body of the Creek Confederacy. The Confederacy, after all, had always been a rather shadowy entity, and an individual's primary loyalty and concern was to his or her tribal "town," a residential and political unit that had much the same meaning for a Creek Indian as "tribe" did elsewhere in North America. The gradual development of a political as well as geographical separation of the proto-Seminoles from the Creek Confederacy is well illustrated by a statement made by Cowkeeper, one of the first important chiefs of the Florida group, when he visited Savannah in 1757. On this occasion, Cowkeeper reported "that he had not been in the [Creek] Nation These four Years, nor had he received any Instruction from thence whereon to Talk."[11]

Spain relinquished control of Florida to Great Britain in 1763. In 1765 the British, in an attempt to organize their relationships with the tribes on their borders, met with the Lower Creeks from southern Georgia and those resident in northern Florida at Picolata, near Saint Augustine. The Picolata Congress resulted in a substantial grant of land by the Creeks to the British. Though representatives from the Florida towns attended the Congress, they did not sign the treaty which described the grant. In 1771 when the British and Creeks again met at Pensacola to redefine the boundaries of the grant, representatives of the proto-Seminoles were not in attendance. In all later formal or treaty relationships between Creeks and European colonists, including Georgians, and between Creeks and Americans, the Seminoles either had no part or refused to be bound by Creek commitments. The Creek chief McGillivray, negotiating for the Creek Confederacy, often claimed to speak for the Florida settlements in international affairs, but with his death in 1793 separatism accelerated. Negotiations in 1804 over land cessions and debt payments show the Seminoles acting almost entirely independent of the Creeks.

As early as 1700 many blacks had arrived in Florida, mostly runaway slaves from the Carolinas. With the settlement of Georgia the number of escaped blacks increased. These escaped slaves became essentially free under the Seminoles, who tended to treat them more humanely than did the British colonists. In most instances the blacks established their own towns, separate from those of the Seminoles. These towns were made up of both free blacks and slaves. Like their Seminole neighbors, they engaged in farming and cattle raising. These Seminole Negroes played a significant role throughout the ensuing Seminole Wars and the removal to Indian Territory and were fiercely loyal to their Seminole allies. This loyalty was reciprocated by all Seminole leaders. Until quite recently Negroes continued to reside among the Seminoles, acting as interpreters and liaison with whites. There was some intermarriage, but in almost all cases the mixed offspring became a part of the black communities rather than of the Seminole towns. Blood group frequencies, for example, prove that the modern Florida Seminoles have almost no Negro ancestry, and observations of Oklahoma Seminole phenotypes indicate this is true for that portion of the tribe as well.

In 1783 the Treaty of Paris returned Florida to Spanish rule. The Spaniards realized that the most effective way to control the Indians was to supply them with trade goods. This Spain could not do, and therefore British traders were allowed to remain in the colony. They did so until the Treaty of 1819, by which Spain ceded Florida to the United States.

Before the Creek War of 1813–14 the Florida Creek or proto-Seminole towns were largely composed of offshoots of Lower Creek towns—that is, the eastern towns of the Creek Confederacy in Georgia. Because of their geographic position, close to the English settlements on the Atlantic Coast, the Lower Creeks were quite acculturated to white ways and served as a buffer against white contacts with the Upper or Western Creeks in central Alabama. Following the American Revolution, however, this situation quickly changed as American settlers and traders erupted into the Upper Creek territory in Alabama. This invasion of their territory led to a nativistic and anti-American rising of the Upper Creeks against the Americans that has come to be known as the Creek War of 1813–14 or, more popularly, as the Red Stick War. White Georgians and Tennesseans aided by many Lower Creeks and Cherokees, all under the command of Andrew Jackson, ultimately defeated these conservative Upper Creeks. Many of the survivors fled to Florida to escape the Americans and their Lower Creek allies. Some arrived as individuals or family groups, others as organized Upper Creek towns.

Some of the refugees joined the existing Florida settlements, while others moved beyond them to establish their own towns to the south and west toward Tampa Bay. These refugees usually abandoned all ties with the Creek Confederacy and immediately became Seminoles. For example, the noted Seminole war leader Osceola (Assi Yaholo) was one of these Upper Creek immigrants who entered Florida as a child or young man after 1814. This influx of Muskogee-speaking Upper Creeks contributed to the separatism of the Florida Indians. The Upper Creek refugees, of course, were bitterly antagonistic to the Lower Creeks who had aided Jackson. Their feelings were reciprocated by the Lower Creeks in Georgia, who were incensed that their Florida relatives should harbor these "Red Stick" Upper Creeks. Now the Lower Creeks had even more justification for regarding all of the Florida people as *isti simanoli*—"wild people" in the sense of outlaws or runaways.[12] This last and greatest immigration increased the Seminole population from somewhere in the vicinity of thirty-five hundred or four thousand to as much as six thousand and set the stage for the forthcoming Seminole Wars.[13]

The First Seminole War (1817–18) can be interpreted as an outgrowth of the Creek War of 1813–14. In 1812–13 the Seminoles in northeastern Florida had supported the British and Spanish against the Americans, drawing a counterattack by Georgia and Tennessee militia. Those in northwestern Florida, including Red Stick Creeks and Negro refugees, supported the British in 1814 during the latter part of the War of 1812. British influence continued strong after the war had officially ended, the British encouraging the Indians to raid into Georgia. The Georgians retaliated by stealing livestock and Negroes. Finally, in 1818, Andrew Jackson, with an army of two thousand Americans and friendly Lower Creeks crossed into Florida, destroying Seminole and Negro forts on the Apalachicola River. He then moved east to the Suwanee River, burning villages and crops. Most of the Seminoles and their black allies eluded capture and destruction but were forced to migrate south and east of their old locations.[14] The net result was that the First Seminole War firmly established Seminole independence from the Creek Confederacy. Following this conflict, there were thirty-two Seminole towns spread over most of peninsular Florida from the Apalachicola River east and south. Nineteen of these towns—including two of Yuchis— derived from settlements antedating the Creek War, eight were made up of Red Stick refugees, three were of Seminole Negroes, and two were of unknown derivation.[15] In south Florida, the Everglades and Big Cypress Swamp were not occupied at this period, but were used for hunting, fishing, and gathering.

In 1823 the United States government attempted to restore

peace to the area at the Treaty of Camp Moultrie. The Seminole chiefs came in reluctantly, and most of the influential ones refused to sign the treaty, for it ceded to the government all of the good land on which their villages stood. Finally, six chiefs were induced to sign the treaty after they were given plantations along the Apalachicola River. The rest had to move.[16]

Under the terms of the Camp Moultrie treaty, a reservation for the "Florida Tribes of Indians" was to be established in central Florida in the area east of Tampa Bay, and the Seminoles, in return for $6,000 in farming implements and livestock and an annuity of $5,000 for twenty years, were to remove to the reservation. The treaty was a failure from the outset. It proved to be impossible for the government to locate the reservation or move the scattered Seminole bands within it, much less to protect the Indians from depredations by frontier whites. Annuities promised in the treaty were withheld, allegedly to compensate whites for the loss of slaves and for Seminole attacks on white settlers. The Seminoles, meanwhile, discovered that the reservation assigned to them was generally a swamp country worthless for farming. Soon most of them were experiencing an acute shortage of food, in some cases actually starving. They were also subjected to continual raids by frontier whites ostensibly seeking runaway slaves, this with the permission of the United States secretary of war.

To add to their miseries, Andrew Jackson, their old tormentor, became president of the United States in 1829, and in 1830 he signed into law the Indian Removal Act. This document provided for the cession of all Indian lands in the Southeast and the removal of the resident tribes to points west of the Mississippi. Pursuant to Jackson's removal policy, on May 9, 1832, fifteen Seminole leaders were induced to sign the Treaty of Payne's Landing, which provided that all claims to Florida lands be relinquished, that the Seminoles remove west of the Mississippi, that the Creeks and Seminoles "reunite" on the Creek lands in the west should the Creeks be of "favourable disposition," and that the Seminoles remove within three years of the ratification of the treaty, with such immigration to commence "as early as practicable" in the year 1833.

An exploring party of seven of the Seminole signers came west to find a location in the Creek nation. They were accompanied by their agent, John Phagan, and "their faithful interpreter" a Negro named Abraham. Among this delegation were Jumper, Black Dirt, Charley Emathla, Coa Hadjo, and Holahte Emathla. They arrived at Fort Gibson (now Fort Gibson, Oklahoma) in November, 1832. The party examined the western part of the Creek country, but were not happy with the cold climate. They also objected to settling so near the Plains Indians, who were engaged in continual tribal warfare.[17]

While this party was still in the Creek country, United States Commissioners Montfort Stokes, Henry L. Ellsworth, and J. F. Schermerhorn secured a treaty with the newly-removed Creeks at Fort Gibson (dated February 14, 1833) purporting to settle the boundary lines of the Creek country west and agreeing that the Seminoles should henceforth be considered a constituent part of the Creek Nation and be located in some part of the Creek country to be selected by the commissioners. Agent Phagan maneuvered the Seminole exploring party into signing a treaty with these same commissioners at Fort Gibson two months later (March 28, 1833), despite the fact that it was an exploring party only, and had not been authorized by the tribe to enter into treaty negotiations.

The new treaty stated that this Seminole delegation was satisfied with the Creek country the commissioners designated and assigned the "Seminole tribe of Indians, for their separate and future residence, forever," a tract of country between the main Canadian and the North Fork rivers, extending west to a line twenty-five miles west of the Little River. When the exploring party arrived home in Florida and reported what had taken place, there was great agitation among all the Seminoles. Not only was there objection to being merged with the Creek Nation, itself torn by factional disputes, but there was fear that in settling in the new country they would be antagonizing the Plains Indians who resided there and would be drawn into war with them. The upshot was that the Seminoles refused to recognize the Fort Gibson treaty as valid and urged Agent Phagan to convene a council where all the people, including chiefs, could confer on the difficulties confronting them. This request was refused, Agent Phagan stating that nothing could be done and that the Seminoles must leave Florida for the west immediately.[18]

The treaties of Payne's Landing and Fort Gibson were both ratified by the Congress on April 12, 1834. Although the terms of the former specified a period of three years subsequent to the ratification before the removal was to take place, government officials interpreted it to mean three years after the signing of the treaty by the Seminoles; hence 1835 was declared the year for the removal rather than 1837. When United States Agent Wiley Thompson announced this fact to the Seminole chiefs it was evident that most of them were bitterly opposed to such a course of action. In a council at Fort King in April, 1835, Jumper, one of the signers of the 1832 treaty, renounced it and, speaking for Micanopy, the head chief, declared that the Seminoles would not move west. After being rebuked by Agent Thompson and General Duncan Clinch, some of the chiefs backed down, but Micanopy, Jumper, Alligator, Black Dirt, and Sam Jones all refused to change their position, whereupon Thompson declared that they were deposed as chiefs.[19] It was at this time that the youthful Osceola, until then not known to the whites, emerged as a public figure in his opposition to removal. There is a tradition (probably apocryphal) that Osceola stalked to the front of the room where the proceedings were taking place and plunged a knife through the paper tendered by Agent Thompson to the chiefs for their signatures, saying "This is the only way I sign!"[20]

All these circumstances led to the Second Seminole War, which began in 1835 and did not end until 1842. In November, 1835, Charley Emathla, who was a strong supporter of removal, was killed by a war party led by Osceola. Agent Thompson then issued an ultimatum that if the Seminoles were not ready to leave Florida on the date set, troops would be sent to enforce the order. Soon afterward (December 28, 1835), he, Lieutenant Constantine Smith, and three agency employees were fired upon and killed by a band of Mikasukis led by Osceola. This inaugurated the seven years of hostilities.

The Second Seminole War is reputed to have been the most

costly Indian war ever fought by the United States Army. It cost the lives of nearly 1,500 soldiers and many civilians and twenty million dollars in money. For the Seminoles it meant, in addition to those killed in battle and those who died of disease and hardships while being pursued by the army, a total of 4,420 Seminoles captured and surrendered who were deported to the Indian Territory, present Oklahoma. At its conclusion only 500 Seminoles, more or less, remained in Florida.

Because of their small number, as compared to the armies sent against them, the Seminoles waged the war as a guerrilla campaign. Young Osceola, who emerged as the principal leader of the tribe, relied upon harassment and ambush to defeat the government forces. Seminole families scattered, hiding deep in the swamps while their warriors fought with coolness and courage. On the same day that Agent Wiley Thompson and Lieutenant Smith were killed, Major Francis L. Dade and his detachment were cut off and almost wiped out by a party of warriors under Micanopy, Jumper, and Alligator, only three men escaping. Then beginning with General Clinch, and continuing with generals Scott, Gaines, and Call, one after another officer was placed in charge of the army sent against the Seminoles. Each was successively baffled, owing to the Seminole ability to hide in the swamps and forests they knew so well.

As the war dragged on, there was increasing pressure from the general public of the United States to bring the war to a successful conclusion. Responding to this pressure, frustrated military commanders resorted to ever more questionable tactics to achieve their ends. In the campaign carried on in the fall of 1837 under the command of General Thomas Jesup, Indian towns and provisions were burned and destroyed, cattle were killed, and ponies were confiscated. Seminole slaves who were captured were promised their freedom if they would help track down the Indians. Finally General Jesup, maddened by the public outcry, directed his second in command, General Joseph Hernandez, to seize Osceola and his attendants while holding a parley with them under a flag of truce. Osceola, suffering from malaria, eventually died in prison.[21]

Head chief Micanopy signed articles of capitulation at Fort Dade on March 6, 1837, and Alligator and Jumper surrendered the following spring, but hostilities continued for years. As various small bands of Seminoles surrendered or were captured they were sent west to Indian Territory. Their descendants are the Oklahoma Seminoles of today. In August, 1842, the Second Seminole War was declared to have ended with the removal of a large group of Seminoles.

The first group removed to the west, 116 captives, arrived in the Indian Territory in June, 1836. From that time until 1843, Seminoles and Seminole Negroes in groups ranging from a dozen or so to larger parties numbering in the hundreds were on various occasions transported to the west. Many perished while awaiting passage at embarkation points. Others died on the march. According to present-day Seminole informants, the soldiers did not permit a halt even for the burial of the dead. In the spring of 1842, General Zachary Taylor reported a total of 2,833 Seminoles, including their Negroes, in what is now Oklahoma.[22]

The five hundred Seminoles still remaining in Florida at the end of the Second Seminole War were in the far south of the peninsula, in practically inaccessible hiding places in the Everglades and the Big Cypress Swamp. Since this country was very difficult for the Army to scour out, and since these few were too far away and too weak to pose any military threat or serve as a refuge for runaway slaves, they were allowed, for the time being, to remain.

In 1849 and 1850, troubles broke out between these remaining Seminoles and local whites. A white man named Barker was killed on Indian River on the east coast of Florida in January, 1849. Although the Seminoles delivered up seven men allegedly involved, together with the hand of a man they killed when he resisted arrest, the Florida legislature immediately demanded that the remaining Seminoles be removed to the west. Not wishing to touch off another costly campaign, the federal government responded by hiring a "removal expert" to persuade the remaining Seminoles to leave the state. To assist him, the expert brought with him to Florida a delegation of Seminoles from the west. He then proceeded to take them, together with Billy Bowlegs, the principal Florida chief, and some of his followers on a grand tour of Washington, Baltimore, Philadelphia, and New York, a tour designed to impress the Seminoles with the might of the United States. By this and other means thirty-six more Seminoles were persuaded to emigrate, at a cost of over $50,000.[23] Because of the high cost to the governnment, the expert was summarily discharged.

The Third Seminole War (hardly deserving of the name) broke out in 1855, and in the next three years the Florida militia and a few federal troops killed perhaps 20 Indians in the Big Cypress Swamp area and finally managed, in 1858 and 1859, to deport 240 more. Billy Bowlegs and other chiefs emigrated in the 1858 group, and the noted Black Warrior in the 1859 group. This was the last of the removal efforts.

The first party of immigrant Seminoles to arrive in the Indian Territory was led by Chief Holahti Emathla, who died en route a few miles west of the Choctaw Agency in the summer of 1836. His party, which had lost many of their number by death during the two months' journey, located north of the Canadian River near Little River, in present Hughes County. In June, 1836, soon after the arrival of Chief Micanopy and his party at Fort Gibson, a friendly council was held with the Creeks of the Lower towns, headed by Chief Roly McIntosh. Micanopy and the Seminole leaders refused to settle in any part of the Creek Nation other than the tract assigned them between the Canadian and the North Fork under the treaty of 1833. Since the Upper Creek towns were occupying the best locations in this tract, the Seminoles remained near Fort Gibson, some of them in the Cherokee Nation.[24]

The Seminoles at this time not only were impoverished but also lacked the solidarity of their old tribal organization. In addition, there were difficulties with the Creeks, who claimed some of the Negro slaves and free blacks who had accompanied the Seminoles from Florida. In 1845, a treaty signed by United States commissioners and delegations of Creeks and Seminoles paved the way for adjustment of the trouble that had arisen between the two tribes. Provision was made for the settlement of the Seminoles in a compact body, if they desired, anywhere in the Creek country, where they could have their own town government under the general laws of the Creek Nation.[25]

The Seminoles, however, were never reconciled to being part of the Creek Nation. Their wishes were finally considered in a treaty between the United States and the Creeks in 1856 , which ceded to the Seminoles part of the Creek country in which they were to establish their own government and laws. The tract assigned to the Seminoles lay due north from the mouth of Pond Creek to the North Fork of the Canadian, thence up said North Fork to the southern line of the Cherokee country, thence with that line, west, to the hundredth meridian, thence, south to the Canadian River, and thence, down that river to the mouth of Pond Creek. The area thus defined, when surveyed, provided to be almost 2,170,000 acres in extent.[26]

Settlement of the Seminoles on this tract, the reestablishment of the tribal economy, and the organization of their tribal government were well under way by 1859. The new agency for the tribe, with Samuel Rutherford as agent, was erected that year at a location that approximates the present site of Wanette, Oklahoma, in Pottawatomie County. Unfortunately, the outbreak of the American Civil War put an end to this progress and plunged the tribe into another period of turmoil.

The Seminoles, like the Creeks and Cherokees, were divided in their loyalties during the Civil War. An estimated three-fourths of the tribe favored a neutral stance. The withdrawal of federal troops from the region, however, placed the tribe in an extremely vulnerable position. In addition, all the principal officials of the United States in the Indian country were Southerners, in sympathy with secession. Therefore, when the very able Confederate commissioner Albert Pike appeared in the Nation, he was able to conclude a treaty (August 1, 1861) signed by John Jumper, principal chief of the Nation, and nine town chiefs. Town chiefs Billy Bowlegs and John Chupco refused to sign the Confederate treaty, and before the close of the year they and their followers joined forces with the pro-Union Creek leader Opothleyahola and other loyal Indians and attempted to flee to Union protection in Kansas.

Their flight was soon discovered by Confederate forces in the area, and a large Confederate force, composed of both regular Confederate troops and Confederate Indian units, set out in pursuit. Although their warriors managed to turn back two Confederate attacks, the Seminoles were finally overwhelmed. The pitiful survivors reached Kansas with little more than the clothes on their backs. Seminole men served in both the Union and Confederate forces until the end of the war. The "Loyal" Seminoles served in the Indian Home Guard Brigade of the Union Army, while those with pro-Southern sympathies joined the Seminole Battalion of the Confederate Army with Chief John Jumper in command. Historians agree that the losses suffered during the Civil War by members of the Five Civilized Tribes, including the Seminoles, were greater, proportionally, than those suffered by the population of any Southern or border state.

At the close of the war the northern and southern factions of the tribe selected delegates separately and were hurried off to Washington to sign a new treaty with the federal goverment. The government took the position that the tribe as a whole must be punished because a part of it had aided the Confederacy. John Chupco, of the loyal or northern faction, was recognized as principal chief of the tribe and signed the new treaty on March 21, 1866. John F. Brown, son-in-law of Chief John Jumper, who had served as a lieutenant in the Confederate Indian forces, represented the southern faction and signed the treaty in their behalf.[27]

The treaty provided for the cession to the United States of the entire Seminole domain (1856 lands, estimated at 2,169,080 acres), for which the Indians received about fifteen cents per acre, or a total of $325,362. Out of this sum, they were to pay fifty cents an acre to the Creek Nation for a 200,000-acre tract. Through an error in the government survey of the western boundary of the Creek Nation, many Seminoles discovered some years later that they had settled and made improvements in the Creek country. This necessitated the purchase of approximately 175,000 additional acres from the Creeks, adjoining the first tract, at one dollar per acre, making a total of 365,851 acres. This tract comprised the lands of the Seminole nation until 1907, when Seminole County was organized under the Oklahoma constitution. The treaty of 1866 also renewed the annuities due the Seminoles under earlier treaties and provided that the Negro slaves of the Seminoles be admitted as citizens of the Nation. Certain sums were apportioned out of the tribal funds to establish the Seminole people in their new country, $50,000 to be used to reimburse the "Loyal" or northern Seminoles for losses sustained during the war.

By 1868, the various Seminole bands had left their refugee locations elsewhere in Indian Territory and settled in the area that became known as the Seminole Nation. Here, finally, they were allowed to settle in peace, and they began to rebuild their shattered tribal structure. A council house was erected at Wewoka, which was designated the capital of the Nation. The government consisted of a principal chief, a second chief, a national council of forty-two members, and a company of lighthorsemen (mounted police). The principal chief and the second chief were elected every four years by a majority vote of the male citizens. The council of forty-two members, three for each of the fourteen bands or tribal towns in the Nation, constituted the legislative and judicial departments, all civil and criminal cases being tried in the latter. Homicide and larceny were the two capital offenses. All other offenses were punishable by whipping.[28]

Famous in the early history of the Oklahoma Seminoles was the company of lighthorsemen. This group of ten mounted policemen, headed by an elected captain, was the law-enforcing body of the tribe and won distinction as the best police force among the nations of Indian Territory. The chiefs, judges, and lighthorsemen took pride in the speed with which cases brought before them were brought to a conclusion. When measured against today's standards, Seminole justice was harsh. The punishment might be by whipping, with the payment of damages in cases where Seminole citizens were involved. The death penalty, administered by a firing squad, was also quite common.[29]

Until the building of the first railroad in their country about 1895, the Seminoles were more isolated than any other of the Five Civilized Tribes. They nonetheless had the reputation of being a law-abiding, peaceful people. There were twelve Indian towns in

the Nation and two separate towns for Negro freedmen, these
people having full rights as citizens of the Nation through the
treaty of 1866. Allotment of lands in severalty was completed
among the Seminoles by 1907, under an agreement between the
Dawes Commission and the Nation signed on December 16,
1897.

The most important event in the history of the tribe after
statehood was the opening of the Greater Seminole oil field near
Wewoka in 1923. Within three years Seminole County was world
famous for the production of oil. Drilling for oil and gas had been
carried on without appreciable results as early as 1902 by the
Wewoka Trading Company. At the opening of the Greater Seminole field, only about a fifth of the original Seminole lands were
owned by tribal members. Most of this land was in small acreages,
but brought good returns, even great wealth in some instances, to
the Indian owners. Many Seminoles also made money in other
enterprises during the industrial development that followed the oil
boom.

Many Seminoles today are members of Christian denomina-
tions, the Baptist and Presbyterian churches having the most
adherents. Other Seminoles maintain the ancient tribal religion,
which is centered at various square grounds or ceremonial centers.
All Seminoles, whether Christians or followers of the old religion,
have a strong commitment to education for their children and full
participation in the economic life of the larger society.

The annual tribal holiday, "Seminole Days," is held each year
in mid-September at the old Mikasuki Mission, southwest of
Seminole, Oklahoma (September 12, 13, and 14 in 1980). This
celebration, to which members of other tribes and whites are
cordially invited, combines sporting events with Indian dances
and dramatizations of aspects of Seminole history. Stickball
games, Stomp and animal dances, and other "tribal" events share
time with a generalized Oklahoma "Pan-Indian" powwow with its
selection of a Seminole princess, "straight" and "fancy" War
Dance contests, and Gourd Dancing. An outstanding feature of
the second day of the 1980 celebration was a chilling re-enact-
ment of both a flogging and an execution by a group representing

the Lighthorsemen of the pre-statehood era. This drama was narrated by an announcer from a prepared script with a piano accompaniment composed by a young Seminole musician. In true Indian fashion, all visitors to Seminole Days are fed, free of charge, each day of the event.

Today's Oklahoma Seminoles are friendly, hospitable folk. They are intensely interested in athletics, both traditional games such as single-pole and "match" stickball and softball and basketball from the non-Indian world. They are dedicated to improving their own situation and preparing their young people to compete in the economic world of the whites, but equally determined to maintain their own Seminole identity and the best parts of their native culture.

2

SEMINOLE
HERBAL REMEDIES

In common with most native groups in eastern North America, the Oklahoma Seminoles possess an extensive knowledge of the flora of their region. Some of these plants, or portions thereof, are used as foods. Others are steeped or boiled in water to produce infusions that are drunk as a tonic or medicine, or applied externally to wounds or sores. Still others are simply carried in buckskin pouches as counters to "bad medicine" or witchcraft, or are burned and their smoke used to exorcise malignant influences.

During the spring and summer of 1980, Willie Lena and I, sometimes assisted by other Seminole men, collected specimens of fifty-one different plants, each of which had at least one use as a food, medicine, or magical substance. Willie also mentioned and described several others that were known to him but were unavailable locally. Many of the plants had multiple uses and several were employed in combinations of two or more.

From descriptions of the uses of the medicinal plants supplied by Willie during and after our collecting trips, the outlines of the Seminole theory of disease and its prevention or cure gradually emerged. It came as no surprise to learn that this doctrine was virtually identical with the disease theory reported for other Southeastern groups such as the Cherokees,[1] Chickasaws,[2] Creeks,[3] and Florida Seminoles.[4] Most disease, in the Seminole view, occurs because of the ill will of the spirit prototype of some species of animal or bird. The Cherokees have an ingenious myth to back up this theory, which states that the various diseases were invented by different animal species in revenge for the injuries inflicted upon them by the human race.[5] The Creeks and Seminoles apparently lack this myth, and though they attribute most diseases to animals, they also credit them with originating their cures.

Often there is a resemblance, both in the symptoms of the illness and in the substance used to treat it, to some aspect of the animal species considered responsible for the disease. Many animals therefore have a plant that is specified as a remedy for the particular illness identified with them. Thus the rabbit spirit is considered to be the cause of kidney stones, which is therefore termed "rabbit sickness." This "rabbit sickness" is treated by drinking an infusion of *hvtki kafka*, which is known as the "rabbit medicine." Though Seminole curers do not expound on this theory, the idea is apparently that because the patient abused or slighted the "rabbit people" in some way, they have visited their sickness upon him. Having caused the illness, they can also cure it through their particular plant, properly administered.

While the great majority of diseases are caused by revengeful animal spirits, some are caused by ghosts, witches, or the violation of ceremonial regulations.

The proper administration of the herb is extremely important in effecting a cure. Many herbal remedies are considered more efficacious when a particular verbal formula is recited or sung during their administration. Indeed, formulas alone are often employed to secure a desired result. These formulas are the stock in trade of Seminole doctors, ranked equal to a knowledge of herbs. Medicine men are often quite jealous of their formulas and conceal them from others. On more than one occasion, Willie Lena mentioned that he knew that a certain herb could be used for a particular purpose, but that he did not know the accompanying formula. Sometimes medicine men make long trips to visit other practitioners known to possess a certain useful formula, and two medicine men may exchange formulas as marks of mutual esteem.

PLATE 3. A Seminole medicine man of the old school. Watercolor by Willie Lena, 1975. Note the bubbling tube in his right hand.

PLATE 4. A Seminole medicine man "bubbling" a liquid medicine. Pen and ink sketch by Willie Lena, 1982.

The use of a "bubbling tube" is likewise important for many herb medicines that are steeped or boiled in water. Not only does the blowing of the medicine man's breath into the "tea" mix the potion, but the act itself adds strength to the brew. The bubbling tube, a two-foot length of hollow native cane, is considered a sacred instrument. Like the doctor's black bag in Euro-American culture, it is the badge of an Indian doctor. It is so imbued with "power" that when it is not in use its ends are carefully plugged with a twist of the holy plant *mikko hoyvnijv* (*Salix humilis* Marsh.) to prevent its profanation. The Florida Seminoles, and formerly the Oklahoma Seminoles as well, tie short strips of red cloth around the bubbling tube to indicate its sacred nature.

To treat an illness, the medicine man must first determine, from an examination of the patient and a recital of his or her symptoms, what is causing the problem. Once this has been accomplished the second step is to find the appropriate remedy, say a particular herb or other substance, and then apply it in the correct manner.

The relationship between a Seminole doctor and his patient is equally important in effecting a cure. As Willie Lena remarked, "A Seminole doctor doesn't treat just anyone." When a would-be patient comes and asks for treatment the doctor, before he accepts that individual as his patient, asks a number of questions, such as, "Do you think I can help you?" and "How much can you pay me?" The latter question should not be interpreted to mean that the medicine men are totally venal, but instead refers to the pervasive Creek and Seminole belief that a treatment will not be beneficial unless the doctor is well paid. Thus, even in the Green Corn Ceremony, the most sacred event in the native religious year, before the communicants "take medicine," the speaker cries out "*Malatka tagis!*" meaning "Get your donations ready!" A collection is then taken up to "pay" the medicine man for his services. One gives the medicine man *malatka* in the firm belief that doing so will make the treatment more efficacious, and that without gifts the treatment will probably be of little value. The *malatka* can be money, yard goods, whatever one wishes. Usually the doctor doesn't ask for a specific sum, but simply leaves it up to the patient and his or her family.

The following plants were collected and their uses described by Willie Lena in 1980. In each case the plant involved was later identified from field specimens by botanists James McPherson or Ronald J. Tyrl of Oklahoma State University. Except for two specimens (Nos. 30 and 31) all of these herbs were gathered within ten miles of Willie's home in Wewoka, Oklahoma. In our collecting it was obvious that Willie knew from previous experience just where certain "stands" of a particular herb were likely to be found. The summer of 1980 was unusually dry, and often it was quite difficult to secure good specimens, but almost invariably Willie guided us unerringly to a place where a particular plant species was known to grow. The plants are listed in the order in which they were collected. In each case the native Muskogee name (or names) is given first, then its scientific or Latin name, then its common English name or names, and finally data supplied by Willie regarding its characteristics and use plus, in some cases, comparative data from other Southeastern tribes.

1. *Tawá łakko*

   "weed" "big"

   Rhus glabra L., Smooth sumac

The root of this plant (*yalv́mga*) is gathered and its outer skin (*hałpe*) is removed and boiled in water. The infusion is taken four times a day, once before each meal and once at bedtime, as a specific for back trouble, particularly the back pain experienced by women. The infusion is also good for headache in either sex, and for gonorrhea. the stem of the plant is employed in a rite of ceremonial placation of the Giant Horned Snake, to be described later in this work. The fruit can be rubbed under the arm as a deodorant. It can also be touched to the lips to awaken someone who is drowsy.

Comparative notes: Smooth sumac was widely used in the Southeast, and for a variety of purposes, the Creeks, who call the plant *tawa cati* or "red weed," boil the roots and take the infusion internally for disentery.[6] The leaves of the plant were formerly mixed with tobacco as a smoking additive, and Pope says "this preparation of *Sumach* and *Tobacco* the *Indians* constantly smoke, and consider as a sovereign Remedy in all cephalic and pectoral Complaints."[7]

2. *Hiluk haka*

   Bumelia lanuginosa (Michx.) Pers., Chittam wood. Willie called it "Gum tree" in English.

The leaves and stem of this plant are boiled and the tea is drunk as needed to cure diarrhea. The tea is also drunk as a general tonic and "cleans your system," according to Willie.

3. *Pałko łakko*

   "grape" "big"

   Vitis palmata Vahl., Missouri grape, Red grape, Catbird grape. Willie called it simply "Wild grape" in English.

The leaves and stems are gathered and boiled to make a tea that is taken four times a day, once before each meal and at bedtime as a specific for diabetes. The tendrils are chewed by children to prevent cavities in their teeth. A cloth soaked in the tea made from the leaves and stems, or a bunch of the crushed leaves are put on the head by Seminole men to promote hair growth and prevent baldness. *Pałko łakko* leaves and stems can be boiled together with roots of the *mikko hoyvnijv* (*Salix humilis* Marsh.) to make it more effective. The mixture of the two herbs is taken four times a day as well, as a specific for the treatment of diabetes.

Willie also noted that the tendrils of the grape, which will "hold on to" anything, are used in a form of sympathetic magic by a husband to "hold on to" his wife, and vice versa. A lock of the spouse's hair is secured and wrapped in a grape tendril that has been doctored with a certain medicine. This device is then buried in the ground before the couple's front door. Just as the grape tendril "holds on to" the branch or bark of a tree, the wandering spouse will be "held on to" by his or her husband or wife through this magic.

Comparative notes: Swanton notes that the *pałko łakko* was used by the Creeks as an alternative cure for the "snake disease," or snake bite. The tendrils and soft, succulent ends of the vine were boiled thoroughly and the infusion afterward given to the patient to drink.[8] He later notes that it was employed in cases of tonsilitis, when the tendrils were steeped in hot water and cloths put into this solution and then bound around the throat. With it must be little parings of ginseng.[9]

4. *ſmpvkpvki holati tihvs łakita*

   "blossom" "blue" "penis" "makes-big"

   Tradescantia ohiensis Raf., Spiderwort. Willie Lena called it "Blue flower" in English.

This plant exudes a slimy sap when the stem is broken. This sap was rubbed onto the penis by Seminole men who were not blessed with a large membrum. The sap caused the penis to swell to a size which would "satisfy any woman." The tumescence later subsided with no ill effect.

5. Ijó pakánoji

"deer" "plums"

Prunus gracilis Engelm. & Gray, Oklahoma plum. Willie called it "Deer plum" in English, a direct translation of the Muskogee name.

The root is boiled in water and the tea drunk for headache. The tea can also be used as a mouthwash. It is drunk warm as a treatment for short-windedness.

6. *Opaga*

Passiflora incarnata L., Maypop, Passion flower, Passionaria, Apricot vine.

This plant is distinguished by its three-pronged leaf. It has an orange-yellow fruit that has a pleasant, citrus-like taste when ripe, though it is full of seeds. The Seminoles boil the stem and leaves and drink the resulting tea to "clean the system." A stronger tea can be used as an emetic.

Comparative notes: Speck notes that the Houma Indians of Louisiana crushed the root of *P. incarnata* and placed it in their drinking water for a "blood tonic," an employment of the plant similar to that of the Seminoles.[10] Vogel notes that *P. incarnata* has been called antispasmodic and sedative.[11]

7. *Adakła ho·ma*

"weed" "bitter" or "strong"

Artemesia ludoviciana Nutt., Sage

The leaves of this sage are crushed and rolled in the hand and inhaled as a sort of tonic to cure headache. The leaves may be dried and saved for winter use in the same way.

Comparative notes: Milligan notes that the Chickasaws brew "bitterweed" stalks and blossoms into a tea used to reduce fever.[12] The women of the Arikara tribe of the Upper Missouri used *A. ludoviciana* to overcome delayed menstruation, to control profuse menstruation, or to relieve pain.[13]

8. *Kado ho·mi*

"wood" "bitter" or "strong"

Amorpha fruticosa L., Bastard indigo

This plant grows about four feet tall. It grows in clusters, but not thickly. The leaves and stems are boiled, then the resulting tea is left to stand overnight. The following day it is reheated and is ready for use. It is taken four times a day, before meals and at bedtime, as a general tonic. Willie also noted that the Seminoles made arrowshafts of the stems.

9. *Mabilanoji*

Polytaenia nuttalli DC., Prairie parsley

This plant is the traditional war medicine or wound medicine of the Seminoles. The heads of the plant are chewed and then stuffed into a bullet or arrow wound to stop the bleeding. Willie's grand-father, who was a Seminole scout with the United States Army, reported seeing a bullet "fall out" of a wound several hours after the application of this medicine. The wound then healed with no further treatment.

10. *Hoyvnijv łakko*

"red loafers" (referring to the roots) "big"

Rhus aromatica Ait., Lemon sumac, polecat bush

The skin of the root of this plant is applied to diabetes sores, also syphilis chancres. The dried skin can be powdered and applied to sores in the same way.

This is one of several related plants which the Seminoles identify by color: *hoyvníjv hvtki*, white *hoyvníjv*; *hoyvníjv la·ni*, yellow *hoyvníjv*; *hoyvníjv okcati*, pink *hoyvníjv*; and *hoyvníjv cati*, red *hoyvníjv*. Any one of these can, in a pinch, be sub-stituted for the *míkko hoyvníjv* (*Salix humilis* Marsh.) in the Green Corn or Busk Ceremony.

11. *Hvtki kafka*
   "white" "milk-exuding"
   also called
   Tuji hflfswa
   "kidney" Medicine"

   Asclepius viridis Walt., Milkweed (sp.?)

The root of this milkweed is boiled and the tea is drunk for kidney trouble. Kidney stones are believed by the Seminoles to be caused by rabbits. This medicine, being the treatment for kidney stones, is therefore the "rabbit" medicine. In addition to drinking a tea made of the stem and leaves of this plant the patient must avoid greasy foods, butter, and milk, and must not lift heavy things.

12. *Pasa*

   Eryngium yuccifolium Michx., Button snake root, Rattle-snake master. Willie called it simply "Black root" when speaking English.

This is the most important Creek and Seminole medicine. It takes precedence over even the *mikko hoyvnijv* (*Salix humilis* Marsh.) It is drunk before the *mikko hoyvnijv* in the Busk or Green Corn, and is always prepared separately. The crushed leaves, stem, and top of the plant are simply stirred in a crock of cool water, then "bubbled" by the medicine man with his cane bubbling tube. This is done in a very reverential manner, accompanied by prayers.

The men who are taking medicine during the Green Corn approach the pot containing an infusion of *pasa* in pairs. As each one reaches the pot an official seated behind it offers a dipper of its contents to him. The recipient kneels, and using the first two fingers of the right hand, offers a small amount to the spirits of each of the four sacred winds or directions, using a flipping motion. Then, still using the same two fingers, he applies a small amount to his tongue four times in succession. He then drinks the remainder of the medicine in the dipper.

Though *pasa* has often been referred to in the literature as an emetic, I am certain that it is not, at least in the strength in which it is prepared at Creek and Seminole Green Corn ceremonies. I have taken it myself on many occasions and have never experienced the slightest discomfort. It is true that the communicants at the Green Corn *do* vomit immediately after drinking the *pasa* and the *mikko hoyvnijv*, but this is because they are *expected to do so* as a ritual act, not because of any emetic effect of either medicine. My fellow medicine-takers assure me that their reaction to the medicines is the same as my own, namely, that if they wished to do so, they would have no difficulty in keeping the liquids down.

Willie Lena commented that the *pasa* is regarded as a strong masculine stimulant by the Creeks and Seminoles. It is a medicine for men only, and is thought to promote virility. At the Green Corn Ceremony it is served only during the first of the four rounds of medicine taking.

Comparative notes: The Button snake root was widely employed by Southeastern Indians, both in ceremonies and privately for various maladies. The medicine is mentioned in the Creek migration legend that was delivered by Chekilli, "Head-chief of the Upper and Lower Creeks," in a talk held at Savannah in 1735 as follows:

> Here [at the King of Mountains] they also found four *herbs* or roots, which sang and disclosed their virtues: first Pasaw, the *rattlesnake root*; second Micoweanochaw, *red-root*; third Sowatchko, *which grows like wild fennel*; and fourth Eschalappotche, *little tobacco*. These herbs, especially the first and third, they use as the best medicine to purify themselves at their Busk.[14]

Writing in 1798 and 1799, Benjamin Hawkins notes that an infusion of the plant was drunk by warriors before setting out on the warpath[15] and also by youths undergoing the initiation into manhood at the age of fifteen to seventeen.[16]

Swanton's Creek informant Caley Proctor said that the plant was pounded up, mixed with water, and drunk cold in cases of neuralgia and for kidney troubles.[17] It was also administered in cases of snake bite, and Jackson Lewis, another of Swanton's Creek informants, gave this as its principal use,[18] in which he is

PLATE 5. A Seminole medicine man gathering herbs. In his hand he has a supply of *pasa*, and he is looking at a stand of *hoyvnijv*. Pencil and crayon sketch by Willie Lena, 1980.

confirmed by as venerable an authority as James Adair.[19] Lewis added that it was used in conjunction with the "deer potato" [*Liatris aspera* Michx.] in cases of rheumatism. Zachariah Cook, another of Swanton's Creek informants, said it was used for diseases of the spleen.[20] Another Creek informant said that it was a great medicine to cleanse the system and purify the blood, and still another declared that its function at the Green Corn Ceremony was not so much to combat positive diseases as to produce a feeling of peace and tranquility, a sort of access to good health.[21] Caleb Swan, however, echoing Hawkins, describes it as "the war physic."[22] Adair states that Southern Indians frequently drank it to such excess as to impair their health.[23]

Swanton reports that the Alabamas and Koasatis swallowed small sprouts of this plant in spring, in order to prepare themselves for the ensuing year.[24] Later in the same source he notes that the Natchez-Cherokees employed the Button snake root as a remedy for nosebleed. The leaves and stem were chewed and the flow of blood ceased. A tea made of parched plants was used by the same group for flux. After imbibing, the patient would fast until sundown and then make himself vomit. His Natchez-Cherokee informants also told him that the plant was used in former times as a substitute for salt.[25]

Greenlee notes that among the Florida Seminoles "Snakeroot is sometimes boiled in a pot and taken internally as a specific for stomach ache."[26]

The plant, as its English name would indicate, was widely regarded as both a preventive and a cure for snake bite. James Adair mentions that upon one occasion he saw "the Chikkasah Archimagus chew some snakeroot, blow it on his hands, and then take up a rattlesnake without damage."[27] He also mentions the Chickasaws using the snakeroot as a remedy for snake bite.[28]

13. Ahá lvbvkca

Gnaphalium obtusifolium L., Cat-foot, Fragrant cudweed.

The small white flowers and stem material of this plant have a distinct butterscotch odor.

As a counter to bad medicine (witchcraft) and illness one may have picked up in a crowd, a mixture of *ahá lvbv́kca* and cedar leaves is put on top of coals or on a hot stove top. As the smoke rises, one fumigates his or her hands in it and rubs the smoke on limbs and body. One should also inhale the smoke from the ritual four times.

The same procedure is followed if one believes that someone has entered the house during one's absence and left "bad medicine" about. According to Willie, inhaling the smoke is also a fine way to relieve stress and worry . Many of today's Seminoles are distraught by worries about losing their land through the machinations of conniving whites. If such an individual inhales the Cat-foot and cedar incense he can go to bed and "sleep like a baby." Willie also commented that the smoke "kills germs," indicating a syncretism of native belief with the white man's germ theory.

Willie customarily carries a mixture of *ahá lvbv́kca* and cedar leaves with him, and provided me with such a dried mixture contained in a small plastic envelope on May 7, 1980, from which the identification of the plant was made. *Ahá lvbv́kca* is also one of the several ingredients in the Seminole "cooling off" medicine described later in this chapter.

Comparative notes: Swanton's Creek informant Jackson Lewis stated that this plant was employed in the treatment of mumps. A great many leaves were collected, even in winter when they were dried up, a strong infusion was made by boiling them in water, cloths were dipped in this, a little lard added, and the whole tied around the throat. According to Caley Proctor this substance was put with several other medicines to add a perfume. The leaves were boiled by themselves and the infusion drunk when one was unable to keep anything upon the stomach. The patient also bathed in the liquid. To cure bad colds the tops were boiled, the odor inhaled, and the infusion drunk. The faces and heads of old people were bathed in it and some drunk when they could not rest well and woke up with a start as soon as they had fallen asleep.[29]

The Alabamas also frequently mixed this herb, which they called *Ahisi láksa*, "bitter or strong medicine," with other medicines. It was used when a man was nervous, woke up frequently, and wanted to run away . It was boiled in water along with cedar, and the face of the patient was washed in it until he got well. This sickness was believed to be brought on by ghosts, and the medicine was intended to drive them off. Another way to effect the same end was by burning this plant and cedar together.[30]

All of these practices are quite reminiscent of the Seminole uses of this plant.

14. *Wajaje hitci*

"Osage" "tobacco"

Verbascum thapsus L., Mullein, Mullen

The leaves of this plant are boiled together with the finely shaved inner bark of the cottonwood (*Populus deltoides* Marsh.). A sprained ankle is soaked in this tea. A towel soaked in this infusion is wrapped around a broken limb to reduce the pain and swelling. A towel soaked in the same infusion can be put on the head to relieve a headache.

Comparative notes: Swanton writes that the Creeks boiled mullein roots together with those of the "button willow" for a drink used internally for coughs. The leaves were also boiled and the patient bathed in the infusion while it was hot.[31] Speck writes that the Choctaws put the leaves on the head as a headache poultice.[32] The use of mullein leaves to reduce swelling is noted for the Chickasaws.[33] The Catawbas boiled the root and sweetened it to make a syrup for croup in children. The leaves were mashed and applied as a poultice for pain and swelling, sprains, bruises, and wounds.[34]

15. *Tʃkacok lofka*

"fragments"? "sticks-on"

Xanthium strumarium L., Cockleburrs

An infusion of this plant makes a good eyewash. The burrs themselves are sometimes boiled in water and the infusion drunk as a general tonic.

16. *Ofa·la ahagi*

"climbing" "imitation"

Campis radicans L., Trumpet-vine, Trumpet-creeper, Cow-itch

The leaves and stem are boiled in water. The doctor drinks some of the resulting tea first, then gives it to the patient. This is a specific for sore back. It is also good for the treatment of gonorrhea.

17. *Kowakoji hʃlʃswa*

"Bobcat" "medicine"

No specimen collected

This plant grows a little taller than a wildcat, hence its name. Boil some of this medicine in water. When it has cooled, bathe your baby in the infusion. This will prevent the baby from catching colds, pneumonia, etc. A bobcat has thick fur and can stand the cold, hence a baby bathed in an infusion of bobcat medicine will have the same ability. A smaller plant of the same type is called *Puze hʃlʃswa* or "Pussycat medicine."

18. *Lało nʃski*

"Fish"?

Tephrosia virginiana (L.) Pers., Goat's-rue, Cat-gut, Rabbit's pea. Willie Lena called it "Devil's shoestring" in English.

This is the famous fishing medicine of the Southeastern Indians. It contains rotenone, a chemical that temporarily stupefies fish. The Seminoles pounded up the plant and put it in ponds in order to catch fish. The plant can also be boiled and the resulting tea drunk by humans as a treatment for general malaise.

Comparative notes: This is a famous Indian herb that recently has come into prominence again following the discovery of its insecticidal properties and the isolation of rotenone and tephrosia from it.

Swanton's Creek informant Zachariah Cook noted that Sassafras and *Tephrosia virginiana* were used in treating the *perch disease*. The symptoms of this illness are very acute attacks of coughing that the patient can hardly stop. The two plants are boiled together in water and about a tablespoonful given at a dose.[35] His informant Jackson Lewis, also Creek, said that the roots were employed in cases of pulmonary consumption. Caley Proctor, another of Swanton's Creek informants, said that eight roots were pounded up, mixed with water, and the resultant infusion drunk cold in case of bladder trouble. It was also combined with Queen's-delight (*Stillingia sylvatica* L.) in cases of male impotence, prepared in the same manner.[36] Elsewhere he notes that a Creek woman suffering from irregular periods bathed in an infusion compounded of the same two medicines.[37] His Creek informants also noted the use of *Tephrosia virginiana* to stupefy fish.[38]

His Natchez-Cherokee informants noted that *Tephrosia virginiana* was good for coughs, and, as among the Creeks, they employed it for poisoning fish.[39]

Mooney reported that the Cherokees drank a decoction of this plant for lassitude. The Cherokee women washed their hair in a decoction of its roots to prevent their hair from falling out, because they believed the toughness of the roots would be transfered to their hair. For the same reason Cherokee ballplayers rubbed the decoction on their limbs to toughen them. At that time (1885) the United States Dispensatory described the plant as a cathartic and the roots as tonic and aperient.[40]

Milligan describes an interesting Chickasaw cure involving this plant, related to her by her informant Melvin Worcester:

> I remember a man who was having a bad hurting in his chest. The Indian doctor felt around on the chest and apparently located the source of the trouble. (Doctor just nodded and grunted like he had found what he was looking for, at any rate.)
>
> The Indian doctor went out in the yard, dug a hole about a foot and a half or two feet in diameter and probably six or eight inches deep. He got some boiling water in a pan and set the pan down in the hole. Then he laid a blanket over the hole and told the man to lie down over the hole. The man lay face down with his chest over the pan of hot water for several minutes. When the doctor told him to get up, we could see a black spot on his chest.

The the doctor went out and picked a plant that we always called 'Devil's Shoestring.' It's a whitish fern-like weed. He got a cow horn, put the Devil's Shoestring inside it, just sort of wrapped it around inside the horn.

Next he got some brown glass, broke it into sharp pieces, and pierced the skin where the black mark was on the man's chest and left it there quite a while. There's something in the plant that has a drawing action, and it just drew out the poison inside. We could see that his chest wasn't black or sore any more.[41]

19. *Cofe mvsɛ*

"rabbit" "tea"

Panicum oligosanthus (?), Scribner's panicum

Here we have another example of sympathetic magic. The plant is boiled and the infusion used to bathe the head to make the hair thicker and stronger." Because rabbits have thick hair (fur) a head bathed in "rabbit tea" will also grow thick hair.

Comparative notes: Hawkins writes that "Cho-fe-mus-see" was one of the fourteen "physic plants" employed by the eighteenth-century Creeks on the eighth day of their Green Corn Ceremony.[42]

20. *Tadalaka łakko*

"Stings" "big"

Circium altissimum (L.) Spreng., Nettle. Willie Lena called it "Bull nettle"

Boil the plant and apply the infusion to sore joints, or a sore back. The infusion can also be taken internally for upset stomach. This is a powerful medicine and should not be taken in too concentrated a form.

21. *Colakko ʃngeska*

"Horse" "imitation"

Vernonia Baldwinii Torr.

This plant derives its Indian name from the sharp angle the root makes just below the surface of the earth, which resembles the angle of a horse's head to its neck. This plant is boiled, together with *Rhus glabra* L., and the tea applied externally for a sore back.

Comparative notes: This may be the same as the plant known to the Natchez-Cherokee as *Cāxwåł*, popularly known as ironweed. A tea was made out of the whole plant and drunk in cases of dysentery.[43]

22. *Tulani*

Maclura pomifera (Raf.) Schneider, Osage orange, Bois d'arc

A Seminole contemplating a journey secures four "stickers" from the bois d'arc and puts them under the band of his hat, in front. This should be done as one faces the direction one is going to travel. This will cause dangerous snakes to get out of one's path.

Comparative notes: I have been unable to find any use of the Osage orange by Southeastern tribes. The Comanches sometimes boiled the roots to make an eyewash.[44]

23. *Hʃlʃs hili*

"medicine" "good"

Psoralea tenuiflora Pursh., Scurf pea

This medicine is boiled in water and when it is cooled used as a baby's bath. The doctor puts a little bit on his finger and touches it to the baby's lips. Next the doctor washes his own face and head in the medicine and wets his own lips. He then calls the baby's mother, saying: "Come on, it's your turn," and she does the same. The bath is thought to improve a baby's appetite. Wesley Green, a Seminole man who lives near the Justice School south of Wewoka, was observed to have a large supply of this plant in dried form in an outbuilding near his home when I visited him in 1980. Wesley said that it was used in treating colic in infants.

24. *Yalvng cati*

"root" "red"

Stillingia sylvatica L., Queen's-delight, Queen's root

The root of this plant is boiled in water and the resulting tea is drunk by women as a preventive and cure for diabetes. According to Willie the treatment is sex-specific and simply does not work for men. It can also be taken by women to cure a sore back, a headache, and for kidney infection.

Comparative notes: This is a plant native to the pine barrens of the South and was reported by Barton to be used by whites in that region as a cathartic and by southern Indians as a venereal remedy.[45] Bartram indicates that it was used by the Creeks of his day as a cathartic.[46] Swanton says that the roots were mashed and boiled by the Creeks to prepare a medicine drunk by a woman who had just given birth.[47] As noted earlier, he also reports that a woman suffering from irregular periods bathed in an infusion compounded of this plant and devil's shoestring, *Tephrosia virginiana.*[48] Note that the uses of the plant reported by Swanton for the Creeks are, like the Seminole uses reported by Willie Lena, limited to the female sex.

25. *Kofutcka łakko*

"fragrance" "strong"

A good specimen of this plant could not be secured for identification during the period of my field work in the spring and summer of 1980, since it had not yet flowered, but it was clearly some member of the *Labiatae* or mint family. Swanton indicates that it is horsemint, a species of *Monarda.*[49]

Mints are often mixed with other herb medicines by the Seminoles and Creeks to make them taste good, just as pills in the white man's culture are given a sugar coating. According to Willie, a Seminole patient will often say to his doctor: "Be sure to put *kofutcka* in the medicine!"

Comparative notes: Swanton reports that among the Creeks the entire plant was used in an infusion designed to induce a perspiration. When one was delirious he could be cured by the use of horsemint and everlasting (probably *aha lvbvkca*, Gnaphalium obtusifolium L. is meant) boiled together and administered internally. According to Caley Proctor it was boiled with *Mikko hoyvnijv* (*Salix humilis* Marsh.) to cure dropsy and swellings in the legs. The patient drank it hot and also bathed in it. He reports that the Alabamas used it after a person had died, to ward off the rheumatism which was likely to ensue and also to cure all kinds of rheumatism. It was mixed with cold water, conjured by the doctor, and then each member of the household washed his body in it up to the ears, besides drinking some. It was used on the morning or evening after the death and was for protection against the ghost of the dead, which otherwise might afflict one with deafness.[50]

26. *Kazasa*

Schrankia uncinata Willd., Catclaw sensitive brier

There is no medicinal use of this plant, but the Seminoles have two interesting beliefs concerning it. One is that if you touch its leaves they "get mad" at you and contract (The leaves in fact do react to the touch). The other is that if this brier scratches you, you must not say "Ai!" (the Seminole for "Ouch!") but rather be silent and take no notice. Otherwise the wound will get bigger and more inflamed.

27. *Kaputcka*

Teucreium canadense L., American germander, Wood-sage

This is another common mint. It is regularly used by the Seminoles as a perfume. Seminole men would frequently tie some of the leaves into a small sachet at the back of their neckerchief when attending Stomp Dances, just as Prairie and Plains Indian "straight" War dancers and peyotists tie sachets of Indian perfume to their dance bandoliers.

28. (no Seminole name known)

Desmodium rotundifolium (Michx.) DC, Tick-trefoil, Beggar's ticks. Willie Lena called this plant "Quail beans" in English, but did not know the native term.

There is no medicinal use for this plant, but the Seminoles recognize that quail feed on its seeds, hence the name.

29. Hvtki kafka mabijadi

"white" "milk-exuding" "stem-red"

Asclepius viridiflora Raf., Green milk weed

This plant is distinguished from No. 11 by the fact that it has a red stem. Tony Holata, a Seminole man who lives near the Justice School south of Wewoka, identified this plant and called it to my attention. He said that the plant is boiled in water, then a towel is soaked in the infusion and placed on a sore navel to reduce the soreness.

Comparative notes: Swanton reports that the Natchez-Cherokees cut up the roots of a species of *Asclepius* for a tea used in kidney trouble, including Bright's disease. During treatment, the patient was required to take nothing containing salt.[51] Milkweed was also used by this group in the treatment of syphilis.[52]

30. Šawanogi hſlſswa

"Shawnee" "medicine"

Acorus calamus L., Sweet-flag, Flag-root, Calamus-root, Belle angelique (Fr.), Redote (Fr.)

This plant is extemely rare in Seminole County. To find some, Willie Lena, Tony Holata, and myself had to drive to a small lake a mile and a half south and two and a half miles east of Prague, Oklahoma, on the property of Tony Bruner, another Seminole. The lake was ringed with the plant, which grew in the water near the shore, standing from a foot to two and a half feet in height. Willie waded into the water to secure good specimens. The plant is quite scarce in Oklahoma, and James McPherson, who later identified the plant, reports that this is only the second recorded occurrence in the state. He suggested that it may have been propagated by the Seminoles.

The plant is used by the Seminoles for swiftness and agility in sports. The root, which is quite aromatic, is chewed and then spit on the hands, which are then rubbed on the legs for speed in foot racing, on the arms, legs, and shoulders by basketball, football, and Indian stickball players. It is also used on race horses. They are fed a small bit of the root and the masticated root is rubbed on their shoulders and legs. It is also used, in the same way, on bucking horses at rodeos. Willie says that the plant's use was learned from the Shawnees by the Seminoles, hence the name.

Comparative notes: This marsh plant is said to be common to both hemispheres and has been used for medicine since ancient times. I was, frankly, quite surprised to learn of the rather restricted use of the plant by the Seminoles in view of its extensive use by both whites and Indians elsewhere in North America. Plains Indians used it as a carminative: a decoction was drunk for fever, and the rootstalk was chewed to relieve toothache and to stop coughing. An infusion of the pounded root was drunk for colic. For a cold remedy Indians chewed the rootstalk, drank a decoction, or used it in the smoke treatment. In fact, for Plains Indians, the plant seems to have been regarded as a panacea.[53] Calamus was official in the *Pharmacopeia of the United States of America*, 1820–1916, and in the *National Formulary*, 1936–50. It was considered effective as a carminative, stimulant, and aromatic bitter tonic, besides being used as a flavoring agent.[54]

31. *Hoyvnijv* (Seminole name)

"spreading (?)," "loafers (?)," evidently referring to the rhizomatous nature of the roots

Mikko hoyvnijv

"chief " "wild"

Salix humilis Marsh., Small pussy willow

This plant, or tree, is one of the two most important in the Green Corn ceremony of the Seminoles, Creeks, and Yuchis. Some informants rank it first in importance, even above the *Pasa (Eryngium yuccifollium)*, No. 12, but most rank it second. To employ it, the roots are first washed, then beaten with a wooden mallet on a section of log, and then steeped in cool water. Those "taking medicine" at the Busk, both men and women, bathe their faces, arms, and legs with great dipperfuls of the medicine. The women drink only small amounts of the liquid, but the men drink great quantities, after which they retire to a spot just east of the square ground and regurgitate what they have just drunk. The active ingredient in this medicine is acetylsalicylic acid, the same ingredient found in aspirin.

Since this medicine looms so important in the culture of the Seminoles and other Southeastern tribes, I should like to emphasize that it is *not* an emetic. I have, as an adopted member of a Creek Indian tribal town, "taken medicine" each year at the Green Corn Ceremony for the past ten years. In no instance has the ingestion of either the *pasa* (*Eryngium yuccifolium*) or the *mikko hoyvnijv* induced nausea, and questioning of my fellow Creek and Seminole initiates, including Willie Lena, indicates that it does not operate as an emetic with them. The vomiting which follows the imbibing of the medicine is a *cultural*, not a *biological* act. Several of my fellow medicine takers commented that they could, if they wished, "keep it down." The fact that *hoyvnijv* is used in other contexts by the Creeks and Seminoles, sometimes in conjunction with other medicines, likewise demonstrates that it is not employed as an emetic.

The Creeks and Seminoles are very particular to seek out and use only the roots of *Salix humilis*, not just any sort of willow. This willow is rather rare in Oklahoma, and Willie Lena, in fact, did not know where it could be found. He therefore enlisted the help of Tony Holata, who took us to an area near Boley, Oklahoma. According to Tony this stand of *Salix humilis* had previously been known only to himself and the late Harry Bell, chief of Fishpond square ground. The location of stands of *hoyvnijv* are generally kept secret by the Seminoles and Creeks.

Comparative notes: As noted in connection with the *pasa* or Button snake root, the *mikko hoyvnijv* is mentioned in the Chekilli legend, delivered in 1735.[55] It is also mentioned in almost every other account of the Creek Busk where medicines are specifically identified, and this is true for other Southeastern groups as well. Concerning the Creek use of this important medicine Swanton writes:

1. Miko hoyanīdja (a species of *Salix*, willow), "passer by of the chiefs," the medicine being supposed to pass by of its own power (G. W. G.) or perhaps "sovereign purgative." This is one of the two great busk medicines and as a remedy seems to have been thought more of than the pasa. It is known colloquially as the "red root," the roots of some being blood red and others pale red. Jackson Lewis said that it was used as part of the medicine in a great many complaints, such as fever with nausea and vomiting. According to Caley Proctor it was put in water and drunk by the patient, either cold or hot, in cases of internal fever, malaria, and biliousness. According to another informant it was used as "a graveyard medicine"—as he explained it, a medicine for dropsy—and also to cure the deer sickness. The patient was also bathed in it. It was used in conjunction with the spicewood (*kápapāska*) in cases of rheumatism and swellings. According to another informant the miko hoyanidja and pasa will cure "the clap" almost immediately.[56]

Speck reports that the Creeks employed the plant in treating headaches, believed to be caused by the deer. He also notes its ceremonial use by the Yuchis.[57] Eakins, also writing of the Creeks, says simply that it was used in fevers.[58]

The Chickasaws employed the roots of the "red willow" (*Salix humilis*) in treating "head sickness," the symptoms of which were headache and sometimes nosebleed. This tribe also employed the plant ceremonially. They drank it toward morning, after a dance, and vomited it out in order to make themselves feel strong and healthy.[59]

The Alabamas boiled willow roots in water and kept a supply of the infusion in the house in the summertime so that the family might bathe in it and drink it and thereby ward off fever. The Texas Alabamas used this to cure fevers as well. The roots were put in cold water and the doctor came every morning for four mornings and blew into the infusion, after which the patient drank of it and bathed in it all over.[60]

The Natchez-Cherokees also used the *Salix humilis* for fevers.[61]

The Houma Indians made a decoction of the roots and the bark of black willow (*Salix nigra* Marsh.) or *S. langipes* for fever and for feebleness attributed to "thinness of the blood."[62] The Catawbas made a root tea of water willow for swellings on the back.[63]

The anodyne properties of the salicin in willow have been recognized in the Old World since ancient times, as well as by American Indians. Salicin, the well-known pain killer, which is present in all willows, was official in the USP, 1882–1926, and the NF 1936–55. Aspirin and other synthetic substitutes have become popular since the later years of the previous century.

Although Greenlee, in his account of Florida Seminole medicines, notes only that the *hoyvnijv* was used to bring good luck in the hunt,[64] Fairbanks reports that it is used in brewing a ceremonial drink on Court Day of the annual Busk, as with the Oklahoma Seminoles.[65] Its companion "black drink," the *pasa*, is also employed by the Florida Seminoles at this time.

32. *Hvtki kafkoji*

"white" "little-milk-exuding"

Milk purslane (var.)

This plant is boiled in water and the infusion is drunk by men afflicted with "slow leak" (i.e., older men who cannot retain the urine). This illness is associated with dogs by the Oklahoma Seminoles, since dogs are continually urinating here and there.

33. *Adakla ho·ma łakko*

"weed" "bitter" "big"

or

Ta wohoga

"low ground"

Ambrosia trifida L., Giant ragweed

To treat a bleeding nose, one boils the root of this plant, then cools the infusion. The patient inhales the vapor from the infusion, sniffs it up his nose and blows it out. It is likewise useful to put a cloth soaked in the infusion on the top of the head and the back of the neck.

Willie pointed out that when injured the juice of this plant is blood red, hence the connection with the human blood and its use in treating nosebleed.

Comparative notes: I have found no reference to the use of this plant by other Southeastern tribes. The Cheyennes drank a tea brewed from the leaves and stems of *Ambrosia psilostachya* to treat cramps in the bowels and bloody stool.[66]

34. *Pʃngeska*

"turkey-weed"

Cacalia plantaginea (Raf.) Shinnners, Indian plantain

This plant takes its Muskogee name from the fact that its leaves resemble the tail of a turkey. The root is boiled and the infusion applied to the top of the head and the neck of a person who suffers fainting spells. The patient also takes a small amount of the infusion on the end of his finger and touches it to his lips, repeating the ritual four times. This is called *sapkidv* or "sipping."

35. *Owisa*

Vaccinium arboreum Marsh., Farkleberry or Sparkleberry

The root of this shrub is boiled and the infusion is put on the head of someone who is deranged or "out of his head" and talking or behaving irrationally. Willie noted that deer are fond of the berries on this bush, which turn purple when ripe, and Seminole hunters often look for deer near stands of *owisa*.

36. *Hiluk haka* (the second plant with this same Muskogee name, see No. 2., above)

Antennaria plantaginifolia (L.) Richards, Everlasting, Ladies tobacco

Pussy's toes

Boil this plant in water. Make an infusion of one or two gallons. Drink it all and throw it up to relieve gas on the stomach.

37. *Otci tofkv*

"hickory" (?)

Carya cordiformis (Wang.) K. Koch, Bitternut hickory, called "white hickory" by Willie Lena in English

The roots of this tree are boiled in water to make an eyewash to cure blurred eyesight. The infusion is cooled, then applied to the eyes and head. Willie cautioned that one should not use too strong an infusion. Both Willie and Wesley Green later mentioned that the same infusion may be applied to sore joints.

38. *Takko*

Arisaema dracontium (L.) Schott, Green dragon or Dragonroot

Willie called this "Indian tacos" in jest. The leaves and tender shoots are boiled and eaten as greens in the spring before the plant is six inches tall. A curious belief associated with this plant by the Seminoles is that if one has had a bowel movement shortly before eating the plant it will taste like fecal matter. This may be related in some way to the fact that the plant contains calcium oxylate, a substance which numbs the tongue and palate.

39. *Hſlſs hvtki*

"medicine" "white"

Solanum nigrum L., Black nightshade. Willie called it "Indian ginseng" when speaking English

This is another very famous medicine of the Seminoles and Creeks, and it is used in many ways. A bit of it is placed under the lip, with "words" or a sacred forumla if possible, to cure nosebleed. It is also thought of as a "woman catcher" medicine, perhaps because the root occasionally resembles a woman's hips and thighs. The root is boiled and the resulting infusion is used as a hair tonic and to wet the sweatband of a man's hat. The man thus prepared then simply strolls through a crowd and is soon surrounded by attractive women who attempt to engage him in conversation. Willie cautioned that the man must choose only one from this bevy of beauties, lest the medicine "turn back on him." This is a common American Indian attitude in regard to love medicines.

For one who has difficulty breathing, a large amount of "tea" is brewed, using the root of this plant. The patient drinks and vomits up a large amount of the medicine and soon is breathing better.

In 1970, I purchased a small medicine box from Willie Lena, one of the various types of craft items he makes for sale. On either end of this particular box he had painted native medicine plants in flower. One of these plants is definitely *Solanum nigrum*. It is interesting to note that Willie's favorite spot for digging *hʃlʃs hvtki* is a vacant lot at the north end of Wewoka's main street, and this is where he dug the specimens used for identification in this report, oblivious to the stares of non-Indian passersby.

James McPherson informs me that the leaves and fruit of this plant are poisonous.

Comparative notes: The Muskogee name of this plant is also applied to ginseng (*Panax quinquefolium* L.), and reported uses of ginseng by the Creeks are much the same as those for the black nightshade, described by Willie above. For this reason, and because Willie called this plant "Indian ginseng" in English, I rather suspect that the two plants are considered equivalents by the Oklahoma Seminoles.[67]

Speck notes that the Houmas boiled the roots of *Solanum nigrum* for an infusion given to babies with worms. The green leaves were crushed and mixed with grease to produce a poultice used on sores.[68] The Rappahanocks used a weak infusion of the leaves to cure insomnia.[69] Vogel reports that the black nightshade is naturalized from Europe and is related to the plant providing belladonna, the leaf of which has been official in the USP since 1820. It is used as a stimulant for the central nervous system and for several other purposes.[70]

40. *Ito-ʃliko*, commonly abbreviated *Toʃliko*

   Phoradendron serofinum (Raf.) M. C. Johnston, Mistletoe

An infusion of mistletoe leaves and berries is used as a wash for ringworm sores. To treat hemorrhoids, the plant is boiled and the rectum is exposed to the vapor. Mistletoe is also boiled in water, and the infusion, laced with sugar, is given to children for whooping cough.

Comparative notes: Speck writes that the Creeks used mistletoe to treat the "raccoon" sickness:

> Sleeplessness and sadness are caused by the raccoon, *wótko*, who is himself always roaming about at night and grieving, as is shown by the white circles around his eyes. The plant used to cure the trouble is *tohíligo*, 'plant without feet,' or mistletoe . . . which grows high up on trees near the rivers. The raccoon is thought to associate with this plant.[71]

Swanton reports that the Creeks used mistletoe leaves and branches as one of the ingredients in medicines for lung trouble, consumption, and similar ailments.[72] He also notes that the Chickasaws used mistletoe to treat the "red squirrel disease," the symptoms of which are toothache or swollen jaws and sometimes nosebleed.[73]

41. Svtv

Diospyros virginiana L., Persimmon

Willie Lena mentioned that the rootstock of the persimmon is boiled by the Seminoles and the infusion drunk to halt diarrhea.

Comparative notes: John Lawson called the persimmon fruit "the greatest astringent I ever met withal," and asserted that it was good for cleansing "foul wounds."[74] The Cherokees boiled the persimmon fruit for a medicine taken in bloody bowel discharges.[75] The Alabamas and Koasatis boiled the roots for a tea used in "bowel flux" in a baby or child.[76] The Catawbas boiled the bark for an infusion used to wash a baby's mouth to cure thrush.[77]

42. Lvtakvpi

Cercis canadensis L. Redbud

Willie stated that the root of the redbud is boiled and the infusion drunk for diarrhea.

Comparative notes: The Alabamas put the roots and inside bark of the redbud into a small bucket of water where they were sometimes conjured by the doctor and sometimes not. The mixture was drunk four to six times a day to cure a kind of "congestion" which causes one to become hot all over and is soon fatal if not checked.[78]

43. *Tvffo ohlikitv*

"butterfly" "chair"

Asclepias tuberosa L., Butterfly milkweed, Willie called it "Butterfly's bed" or "Grasshopper's bed" in English.

One boils the plant and drinks the infusion, also bathes in it, as a general tonic.

Comparative notes: Benjamin Barton believed that this was the plant employed by southern Indains in treating chancre.[79] The Natchez-Cherokees believed this plant to be the best remedy for pneumonia and "winter fever." They boiled the roots and took a teacupful at a time. "If one sick with a hot dry fever drank this and wrapped himself up well in bed he would soon perspire freely."[80] The Catawabas made a decoction of the roots for dysentery.[81] *Asclepias tuberosa* was official in the USP 1820–1905 and the NF, 1916–36. The dried roots of this and other members of the milkweed family were regarded officially as diaphoretic and expectorant, and in large doses, emetic and purgative.[82]

44. *Tvl łakko*

"?" "big"

Opuntia macrorhiza Engelm., Prickly-pear

The root is boiled and drunk "by the gallon" by one who is suffering back pain as the result of an infected kidney. When taking this medicine one must avoid eating greasy food for ten days. This medicine is said to be pleasant to the taste, as Willie said "like *sofki.*" It cleans out the kidney and also the bladder.

45. Taltvhkv

Populus deltoides Marsh., Cottonwood

The inner bark is removed from the east side of the tree. Strips of the bark are then wrapped around a sprained or broken ankle or knee. They are held in place by a cloth tied over the joint. Then a warm infusion of the bark is poured over the joint repeatedly.

Willie Lena gathered a quantity of cottonwood bark to treat his own crippled knee on our July 11, 1980, collecting trip. Wesley Green, who accompanied us on this trip, cut the bark for Willie, using a small axe.

Comparative notes: The Creek use of the cottonwood is exactly the same as that of the Oklahoma Seminoles.[83] The Chickasaws also use it in this way.[84] They also boiled cottonwood and willow roots together for a drink taken internally for dysentery. Unstated parts of the cottonwood were also used by them, in a manner not described, for fevers.[85] Bushnell reported that the leaves and bark of "Carolina poplar" (*P. angulata* Mich., syn. *P. balsamifera* L., cottonwood) were boiled in water by Louisiana Choctaws to create a steam for treating snakebite.[86]

46. Catv falódv

"blood" "grinder"

Symphoricarpas orbiculatus Moench., Buckbrush

This plant is used to treat high blood pressure. The entire plant and root is boiled. The infusion is drunk three times a day.

Comparative notes: The Chickasaws used "ice weed" (probably *Pluchea camphorata*) for a high blood pressure treatment.[87]

47. Pvkan-vpi

Prunus persica, Peach tree

Willie said that new twigs from a peach tree are boiled and the infusion drunk as a treatment for diabetes. The best twigs for this purpose are those which have grown where old limbs have been cut away. Four such twigs are boiled in a quart of water.

Comparative notes: The Alabamas and Koasatis treat tired legs by scratching them with a pin until blood is drawn and then rubbing peach leaves on the scratches.[88]

48. *Wilanv*

"in the water yellow"

Chenopodium ambrosioides L., Mexican tea, Wormseed, Jerusalem oak

This plant is used during the Green Corn ceremony to "kill the green wood" just after the arbors at the square ground have been rebuilt or repaired and covered with a new roof of willow boughs. Twelve sprigs are used. One is placed in the fork of each of the three front posts of each arbor, beginning with the chief's arbor at the west, and proceeding counter-clockwise. Before doing this, the assistant medicine man makes a circle of the arbors, sweeping the benches with these same sprigs. I suspect that this plant is used for this purpose because of its strong scent, which would lead to the belief that it "overpowers" or "kills" the power of the green wood and boughs used to make the arbors.

A second use of the plant is to kill intestinal worms, especially in children. The leaves, stem, and root are boiled and the infusion is drunk.

This plant was identified for me by James Stritzke, professor of Agronomy at Oklahoma State University.

Comparative notes: The importance of this plant is indicated by Hawkins's mention of it as one of the fourteen employed by the eighteenth-century Creeks in their Busk.[89] Speck writes that the bear, *nokusi*, is thought by the Creeks to cause nausea and diarrhea, symptoms of a disease called *nokusi aleja*, "Bear the cause." The plant used by the shaman is *wilanv*. The whole plant is steeped in water and the decoction given to the patient. Speck gives a medicine song employed during the treatment, ending in a deep *ho* imitating a bear's grunt.[90] Swanton notes the Creek use of this plant in purifying the busk ground and the final cleansing of the fasters at that time. His informant Caley Proctor said it was a kind of family medicine, apparently a sort of spring tonic, and was also used in cases of fever. Jackson Lewis said it was employed in a great many ailments.[91] Folsom-Dickerson calls the plant "fish bait weed" and states that the Alabamas and Koasatis used it for treating worms. The leaves are boiled, sugar is added to the mixture, and it is drunk.[92] The Catawbas beat the whole plant to a mash and bound it on as a poultice to draw out poison, especially in snakebite. They also applied it to sores.[93]

49. *Locv lupi*
    "turtle" "liver"
    No specimen collected
The leaves and stem and root are boiled and the infusion drunk to relieve chest pains.

50. *Ijo maha*
    "deer" "potato"
    Liatris aspera Mich., Gay feather

This is a famous plant among the Seminoles and Creeks. Its root is boiled by the Seminoles and eaten to cure short-windedness.

Comparative notes: Speck records that swellings on the body and limbs are believed among the Creeks to be caused by the deer. The shaman prepares a mixture of cedar leaves and the deer potato, using both the bulbous root and leaves of the latter. Speck obtained several medicine songs employed when this medicine is used.[94] Swanton writes that the "deer's potato" was used to cure the deer disease, rheumatism, by the Creeks. The roots were pounded up and boiled, and the infusion rubbed on the affected parts. Some was also drunk. According to his informant Jackson Lewis *pasa* was used in connection with it and a little sprig of cedar was also added. Caley Proctor did not mention these accessories.[95] The Koasatis used the deer potato in a similar manner. The roots, mixed with certain others, were boiled and drunk for rheumatism.[96]

51. *Yaha mileka*

"wolf " "rucksack"

Baptisia leucophea Nutt., Cream wild indigo

This is a man's medicine. A man who has sore testicles, pain when he urinates, and cloudy urine boils the roots of the plant and drinks the infusion.

Comparative notes: Swanton says that the roots of a species of *Baptisia* were boiled in water and administered to children who seemed drowsy and lifeless and on the point of coming down with some sickness. They were bathed in it and a little was given to them to drink.[97]

52. *Taka·jv*

Cirsium undulatum (Nutt.) Spreng., Wavy leaf thistle

Every culture, including that of the Seminoles, is plagued by guests who overstay their welcome and linger on, consuming the hard-earned provender of their hosts. The Seminole solution to this universal problem is to sprinkle bits of this plant, dried, on the guest's bedclothes, which causes an intolerable itching. The weary hosts may be accused of harboring bedbugs, but at least their unwelcome visitors finally move out. The same trick is sometimes used by a jealous third party to break up a marriage.

53. Oak galls

A certain species of wasp deposits its eggs under the bark of an oak. The chemicals deposited with the eggs react with the oak and its growth to produce the gall, a nut-like excrescence which encapsulates the egg and provides a place for the wasp larvae to develop. The gall appears as a round ball attached to the twig of the tree. When sufficiently developed the larvae bores its way out of the gall. The black powder in the gall which gives it its astringent quality is tannic acid.

The Seminoles make use of these oak galls in various ways, both internally and externally. For treating high blood pressure a number of galls are boiled in water and the infusion drank four times a day. To treat hemorrhoids, sixteen galls are boiled in a dishpan of water. The patient then squats in the water. This is done four times daily. Another use of oak galls is to heal sores. The gall is cut open and the black powder inside is collected on a piece of paper or buckskin. This powder is then applied to the sore. According to Willie Lena, this even works to cure skin cancer. In all of these treatments it is undoubtedly the tannic acid in the gall that is the active agent.

54. *Cafokna*

No specimen collected

This is a grape vine producing grapes intermediate in size between the "possum" grape and large wild grapes. The vine is boiled and the infusion drunk to treat diabetes. Willie stated that the Cherokees know and use this medicine as well, and that a lot of it grows in the Cherokee country around Tahlequah, Oklahoma.

55. *Wʃso*

Sassafras officinalis Nees & Ebermaier, Sassafras

Sassafras tea, made by steeping the root in water, is used in treating pains in the chest. The medicine is administered together with a sacred formula, as follows:

> *Cʃfi·ki nok'kati*
> "big-heart" "hurts"
> *Cʃfikoji nok'kati*   } Both repeated four times
> "small-heart" "hurts"

followed by the words

> *fʃnuk, fʃnuk*
> "beats" "beats"

After you have said the formula four times, blow into the vessel of water in which the sassafras root has been steeped with your blowing tube. This enlivens the medicine, which is then drunk.

Comparative notes: Sassafras had been a famous medicinal

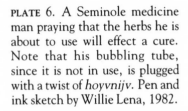

PLATE 6. A Seminole medicine man praying that the herbs he is about to use will effect a cure. Note that his bubbling tube, since it is not in use, is plugged with a twist of *hoyvnijv*. Pen and ink sketch by Willie Lena, 1982.

plant since earliest Colonial times, and once loomed as an important commercial trade item. It was regarded as almost a cure-all by both Indians and whites, and was used in some way by virtually all Indians living in its range, which is mainly south of 42 degrees latitude.[98] Greenlee notes that the Florida Seminoles use sassafras for coughing, gall stones, and pain in the bladder.[99] Speck states that sassafras roots were steeped in water as a medicine for a disease the Creeks attributed to the spirit of the "underwater wolf." Its symptoms were nausea, gripes, and dysentery. As with the Oklahoma Seminoles, the medicine was administered with a sacred formula and "bubbled before use.[100] Swanton notes that the Creeks employed sassafras in a treatment for the "dog disease," the symptoms of which were severe pains in the bowels and stomach, accompanied by vomiting. Parings of the roots were boiled in water together with a handful of a fine grass known to the Indians as "dog's bed." The infusion was given to the patient to drink warm. A formula was employed in which the points of the compass were successively addressed.[101] The same symptoms and treatment were associated with the "wolf disease."[102]

The Alabamas made a strong tea of sassafras roots, which was drunk frequently to alleviate stomach trouble or pain of any kind. The same treatment was used by them for pneumonia. For both of the above a variant method of treatment was to grind up the leaves

PLATE 7. A Seminole medicine man who is planning to use the roots of a certain tree as a medicine walks around the tree four times in a counter-clockwise direction. His hands dangle loosely, to permit the transfer of power, and as he walks he prays. Pen and ink sketch by Willie Lena, 1982.

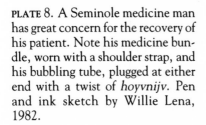

PLATE 8. A Seminole medicine man has great concern for the recovery of his patient. Note his medicine bundle, worn with a shoulder strap, and his bubbling tube, plugged at either end with a twist of *hoyvnijv*. Pen and ink sketch by Willie Lena, 1982.

like black pepper and make a soup, which was eaten or drunk. The Koasatis boiled the roots and drank the decoction for heart trouble. The same tribe treated bee stings by applying a mash of sassafras leaves.[103]

The Louisiana Choctaws boiled the roots and drank the extract "to thin the blood."[104] The Houma Indians living in the same state boiled the fresh or dried roots for an infusion which was drunk for measles and scarlet fever.[105] Sassafras tea is highly regarded as a spring tonic by the Oklahoma Cherokees, and, in fact, by both Indians and whites in eastern and southern Oklahoma. On a number of occasions I have purchased bunches of sassafras root from small children who peddle them on street corners in Oklahoma towns, and it is regularly stocked in some groceries. The dried root bark of sassafras was official in the USP 1820–1926, and remained official in the NF 1926–65.[106]

56. *Sfcv*

Quercus marilandica Muench., Blackjack oak

The leaf of the blackjack oak can be trimmed into a rectangular shape and employed, together with tobacco, in rolling a "medicine cigarette" for use in love magic. Special "doctored" tobacco must be used in such cigarettes. Willie Lena, though he knew the proper procedure, did not know the sacred formula employed in "doctoring" the tobacco. When the cigarette is rolled, the user lights it and faces the direction where the desired woman lives. He takes four drags on his cigarette and blows the smoke toward her, at the same time pronouncing her name, drawing out the last syllable thus: Mary–y-y: Mary–y-y. This will make the woman "lonesome," according to Willie.

Comparative notes: Blackjack oak leaves are commonly employed as cigarette "papers" in the Peyote religion by all Peyote-using groups. Such oak leaf cigarettes are not the principal "prayer" cigarettes, which are rolled in cornhusks, but a secondary type rolled by the individual peyotist for his own use during the meeting without applying to the Road man or leader.

57. Hici pvkpvki

"tobacco" "foam"

No specimen collected.

This is an extremely rare and valuable plant among the Seminoles and Creeks, Willie did not own any, but on a number of occasions he mentioned that a friend of his had promised him four seeds, which he planned to plant in order to assure his own future supply. He noted that it was one of the four important medicines in the Seminole Green Corn Ceremony. He also commented that a small amount of hici pvkpvki tied in a small buckskin pouch and suspended from a thong around the neck is a powerful protective medicine.

Comparative notes: This is probably the same as the "Es-chalapootche" (hici lapucki) or "little tobacco" mentioned in the Chekilli legend of the Creeks.[107] Its leaves were prepared as a ceremonial physic on the first day of the Kasihta town Green Corn and other Creek Green Corn ceremonies, and distributed in the square ground on the last day. An idea of its great importance can be gained from Hawkins's description of the proceedings:

Two men appointed to that office, bring some flowers of tobacco of a small kind, (Itch-au-chu-le-puc-pug-gee,) or, as the name imports, the old man's tobacco, which was prepared on the first day, and put in a pan in the cabin of the Mic-co, and they give a little of it to every one present.

The Micco and counsellors then go four times round the fire, and every time they face the east, they throw some of the flowers into the fire. They then go and stand to the west. The warriors then repeat the same ceremony.[108]

Later, after the entire group of celebrants has left the square and marched to the bank of a nearby river:

> . . . they all put a grain of the old man's tobacco on their heads, and in each ear. Then, at a signal given, four different times, they throw some into the river, and every man at a like signal plunges into the river, and picks up four stones from the bottom. . . . . "[109]

Swanton, who identifies *hici pvkpvki* as "native tobacco, some species of lobelia (?)," says that it is said to grow to a height of about ten inches, but otherwise to resemble the common tobacco exactly and to have the same kind of flower. His informant Jackson Lewis told him that the Creeks, Yuchis, and Shawnees all had the plant, but he was not aware of its existence among any other Indians. It was reported as of rare occurrence and very highly valued. Traditionally, the plant was with the Creeks from the very beginning and was supposed to be older than the smoking tobacco. The plant derives its name from the fact that the flowers were the part used in medicine, four of them being generally placed in the pot. It was used in all kinds of cases, sometimes when a person was sick to the point of delirium, and it was used to ward off ghosts.[110] The Tuggle manuscript, quoted by Swanton in the same monograph, states that the Tuckabatchee Creeks obtained their first examples of this important medicine growing from the grave of an *Ispokogi*, a messenger from the Life Controller or Source of Life itself.[111]

58. *Kapvpockv*

No specimen collected but probably *Lindera benzoin* [L.] Blume

Spicebush

FIGURE 1. Shape of a *kapvpockv* leaf, a Seminole beadwork design.

This plant was identified by Willie Lena as one of the four important medicines employed in the Green Corn Ceremony. Its leaves are shaped as shown in figure 1. Sometimes the Seminoles used a design element derived from the shape of the *kapvpockv* leaf in the their beadwork. This medicine was considered to be so "powerful" that it was customarily kept in a special medicine pouch closed off with stitching at the bottom so that the medicine enclosed would not "breathe," that is, dissipate harmful vapors, as shown in Willie's sketch in figure 2.

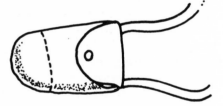

FIGURE 2. A medicine pouch used to store *kapvpockv*.

Comparative notes: The historical importance of this plant is indicated by its mention as one of the fourteen "physic plants" employed by the Creeks on the eighth day of their busk in the period 1798–1800.[112] Swanton writes that among the Creeks when pains and aches were experienced an infusion was made of the branches of *kapvpockv* and taken internally or the body steamed in the liquid in order to produce a perspiration. It was also taken in conjunction with *mikko* hoyvnijv to produce vomiting, "which after some time purifies the blood greatly." Sometimes it was also used as we use tea.[113] Loughridge, in his dictionary, identifies *kapvpockv* as "hackberry," which is undoubtedly erroneous.[114]

59. *Hoyvnijv la·ni*

"loafers" "yellow"

No specimen collected

This plant was described by Willie Lena as a specific for nosebleed and headache. Nothing further was learned of it.

60. *Notosa*

No specimen collected but probably *Angelica atropurpurea* L. [115]

Willie said that his grandfather kept a supply of this important medicine in a medicine bag. It was used to calm people who were over-excited or disoriented. A cloth soaked in an infusion was placed on the patient's forehead.

Comparative notes: William Bartram calls this "the Angelica lucida or nondo," and says "its aromatic carminative root is in taste much like that of the Ginseng (Panax) though more of the taste and scent of Anise-seed: it is in high estimation with the Indians as well as white inhabitants, and sells at a great price to the Southern Indians of Florida, who dwell near the sea coast where this never grows spontaneously."[116] In another place he remarks: "its friendly carminative qualities are well known for relieving all the disorders of the stomach, a dry belly-ache and disorders of the intestines, colic, hysterics, etc. The patient chews the root and swallows the juice, or smokes it when dry with tobacco. Even the smell of the root is of good effect. The Lower Creeks (Seminole), in whose country it does not grow, will gladly give two or three buckskins for a single root of it."[117] Swanton's Creek informant Jackson Lewis states that it was given to children as a vermifuge and to adults to alleviate pains in the back.[118]

61. *HſlſS hvtki* (the second plant with this same Muskogee name)

"medicine" "white"

Panax quinquefolium L., Ginseng

Homer Emarthle, a Seminole native minister and a man acknowledged to know a great deal about herbal remedies, said that there are two plants called *hſlſs hvtki* by the Seminoles. One of these is the Black nightshade (*Solanum nigrum*), the plant that Willie Lena had secured and identified for me, the other is ginseng (*Panax quinquefolium*). Both are used in the same way by the Oklahoma Seminoles (see No. 39), that is to cure nosebleed, a "woman catcher," and to treat shortness of breath. Willie Lena, who was present during my interview with Homer, agreed with him concerning the equivalence of the two plants.

Homer added that ginseng sometimes grows to a large size, and that it sometimes has the form of a human body with two legs. He remarked that it can be purchased at some drugstores but is very expensive. He mentioned that he recently had visited the Florida Seminoles and found that they would pay $300 for a "cigar-box full" of ginseng.

Comparative notes: Capron writes, in his discussion of Florida Seminole medicines, that "There is also used a root that does not grow in Florida but has to be brought from Oklahoma. It is known in each language as 'white medicine'—*hil-eesh-hat-kee* (Cow Creek), *ai-yicks hat-kee* (Miccosuki). I am convinced this is ginseng."[119]

Speck notes that the Creeks of his day recognized an illness caused by various kinds of fish (*Łało aleja*, "Fish the cause") which resulted in sleeplessness. To cure it a decoction of ginseng root was drunk or a portion of the root chewed. It was administered with a medicine song.[120] Swanton speaks of ginseng used by the Creeks to treat the millipede disease, in which the patient coughs and is so hoarse as to almost lose his voice. An infusion of the plant is drunk very warm.[121] Later in the same work he writes:

> Hilis hatki, "white medicine." This is ginseng and it was a very highly esteemed remedy. Caley Proctor said that when one suffered from shortness of breath the roots of this plant were cut up and put into boiling water and the infusion drunk. It was not used externally. Jackson Lewis also mentioned its use in cases of shortness of breath, and he added croup in children and a very low general condition. It constituted one of the elements in many compound remedies and

generally relieved the patient. When a person was sick with a fever and could not sweat new ginseng was boiled with ginger, then both were mixed with alcohol and a little given to the patient, when sweat would break out all over him. It was also used, according to both Caley Proctor and Jackson Lewis, to stop the flow of blood from a cut. The latter by its means cured a woman who had been shot in the head. Before applying the medicine in such cases the wound was cleaned out by the use of the long wing feather of a buzzard. At that time no one must be near, and above all a woman at the time of her monthly period. Elsewhere I have mentioned its employment to keep away ghosts. . . .[122]

He gives a formula used over this medicine when it is employed in cases of shortness of breath.[123]

Adair notes that ginseng was employed on religious occasions by the Chickasaws and was also a valued remedy.[124]

Swanton remarks that the Alabamas broke off the roots of *ahisi hatka*, "perhaps ginseng," and rubbed the milk that came from them on sores.[125] The same tribe burned the roots and fumigated the area around a man's bed when he was worried, talking out of his head, and thinking about some impending calamity.[126]

The Houmas boiled the roots for a drink to stop vomiting and used the same infusion with whiskey added to abate rheumatism.[127] The Cherokees gathered the root for traders, but also used a decoction of it for headache, cramps, and female troubles. The chewed root was blown on the side for pains in that locality.[128]

62. No Seminole name learned. Willie Lena called it "Needle grass" in English
   Stipa spartea Trin., Porcupine grass, Spanish needles, Needle grass

Needle grass is used in a treatment for hemorrhoids. The awns of needle grass are boiled in water. The afflicted person sits on a chair or stool which has an opening in the seat and exposes the rectum to the vapor. The Seminoles have the curious custom of referring to the dilated veins characteristic of this affliction as *cvncofi*, "your rabbit."

63. *ʃmpvkpvki cadici*

"blossom" "small-red"

Verbena canadensis (L.) Britt., Verbena

This plant is used by the Seminoles to treat what they call "spring itch," which from Willie's description, appears to be what is commonly termed athlete's foot in English. The entire plant is boiled and the feet are soaked in the warm infusion. The verbena can be used alone or together with the inner bark of the cottonwood.

64. *Lupaka*

Ulmus rubra, Slippery elm

Elm sap is employed by Seminole women as a vaginal lubricant before having sexual intercourse. The sap is taken from under the bark, mixed with water, and applied with the hand by the woman herself. It was also used in the same manner when she was giving birth.

Comparative notes: Swanton mentions the use of slippery elm bark by the Alabamas when a woman was in labor and the delivery was delayed, but states that it was boiled in water along with gunpowder. He notes that the reasons assigned involved sympathetic magic. [129] The method of administration is not discussed.

65. *HʃIʃs hvtki* (the third plant with this same Muskogee name)

"medicine" "white"

Callirhoe involucrata Gray, forma *novomexicana* (E.G. Baker) Waterfall, Wine cup, Cowboy rose; Willie Lena called it "Indian ginseng" in English

This plant, which has an attractive red flower, was identified as "another kind of *hʃIʃs hvtki*" by Willie when the two of us observed it growing near the Greenleaf square ground, near Okemah, Oklahoma, in 1981. Like the other two plants that bear the same Muskogee name (Nos. 39 and 61, above) it is used to cure nosebleed, as a "woman catcher," and to treat shortness of breath.

All of the above herbal remedies (with the exception of No. 13, *Aha lvbv́kca*, which is apparently always employed together with cedar leaves) are used singly. There are many compound medicines employed by the Seminoles as well, utilizing these and other medicines in combination. A number of these were described by Willie Lena, as follows.

Adiloga

The *adiloga* is a mixture of different roots and leaves. It can be used on the last night of the Green Corn Ceremony, as with the Florida Seminoles, but also, with the Oklahoma Seminoles, during the last Stomp Dance of the season in the fall. The people at a particular ceremonial ground decide whether it will be served cold or hot. The ingredients of this medicine are: 1. *Hflfs hvtki* (*Solanum nigrum* L. or *Panax quinquefolium* L.); 2. *Pasa* (*Eryngium yuccifolium* Michx.); 3. *Hoyvnijv* (*Salix humilis* Marsh.); 4. Peach leaves; 5. Oak leaves; 6. Yellow thorn leaves; 7. Grape leaves; 8. Willow leaves; 9. *Loca Lupi* or "turtle liver" (no. 49 above); and 10. *Hiluk haka* (*Bumelia lanuginosa*). The *adiloga* is brewed by the medicine man who officiates at the ceremonial ground, who bubbles the medicine with his bubbling tube and recites a sacred formula while doing so. The medicine is a general tonic, with both physical and spiritual benefits accruing to the drinker.

Unnamed compound medicine

One afternoon when Willie and I were afield collecting plant specimens, we had occasion to cross a small creek in Seminole County called *Asina haci* ("Cedar river") which had recently flooded. Several small puddles stood in the now dry creek bed. Some were filled with many dead leaves, which had stained the water in the puddles to a brownish color. Willie retrieved a number of the dead leaves from one of the puddles and commented that the Seminoles frequently secured a large number of such leaves and put them in a tub of water. After the water in the tub had turned brown, they bathed in it to restore "pep" and vitality. The idea is apparently that the great number of medicinal leaves in the mixture provides a good general tonic for the bather. I have heard the same idea expressed by both Eastern and Western Cherokees, who regard the waters of creeks and streams in autumn, when they are full of fallen leaves, as a powerful medicine. Just for curiosity's sake, I had the leaves which Willie retrieved from the puddle identified. They proved to be black oak, sycamore, and hickory.

Hot weather medicine

On July 3, 1980, I attended a Stomp Dance at Tallahassee ceremonial ground, where Willie Lena is chief. Like so many of the days in the summer of 1980, this was a "scorcher." The continued heat and drought had made most Oklahomans, unless they worked in air-conditioned surroundings, quite disinclined to move about any more than absolutely necessary. At Tallahassee ground, however, I watched the male members of Willie's tribal town busily chopping and sawing posts and stringers for cooking arbors and gathering branches for roof covering. Meanwhile the women busily attended large kettles of food over crackling wood fires for the evening meal and children frolicked in the hot sun and 105° F heat. At first I marveled at this apparent insensitivity to the withering heat, attributing it to some metabolic difference between myself and other ordinary mortals and my Seminole friends. I was thoroughly wilted myself, though I had done nothing more strenuous than drive a hundred miles from my home in Stillwater, and had stopped in an air-conditioned restaurant en route for a cool soft drink. Then my eye caught a recurrent activity in all of this bustle which explained the mystery. In the very center of the cluster of cooking arbors stood a galvanized washtub with a drinking gourd hanging above it. At regular intervals each person in the work party would walk over to this tub, drink a large draught, then step back and pour another dipperful over the head and wash his or her face and arms in it. Matrons, likewise, frequently called their

PLATE 9. The snake people are great teachers of medicine. Here a Seminole medicine man plays with a rattlesnake to show his young apprentice that the snake people are harmless when approached in the correct manner. Pen and ink sketch by Willie Lena, 1982.

small children from their play to pour a large dipperful on their heads and backs.

Willie invited me to drink and "freshen up" in the hot weather medicine, and soon, like my Seminole hosts, I was restored and ready for a delicious evening meal and a night of Stomp Dancing. Willie later supplied me with a list of the ingredients in the mixture, which were: *Hoyvnijv* (*Salix humilis* Marsh.), *Kaputska* (*Teucreium canadense* L.), and *Ahá lvbv́kca* (*Gnaphalium obtusifolium* L.). All of these are stirred and "bubbled" in several gallons of cool water. This medicine effectively prevented the Tallahassee Seminoles from succumbing to sunstroke and heat exhaustion, which caused many deaths during the summer drought of 1980.

A compound for high blood pressure

Willie Lena described a compound medicine using various oak barks that was used to treat high blood pressure. The scraped inner bark is secured from four kinds of oak: Black jack oak (*Quercus marilandica* Muench.), Red oak, White oak, and Black oak. In each instance the bark is secured from the east side of the tree. This is true of all Indian medicines—they should be taken from the east side of the tree or, in the case of plants, with the medicine-seeker facing the east. Boil the four oak barks together. Drink half a glassful of the infusion before each meal to treat your high blood pressure.

Comparative notes: Hudson states that the Cherokees collected medicinal barks from the east side of the tree, and roots and branches were likewise taken from the eastern side. The reason given was that they had absorbed the greatest potency from the rays of the sun.[130]

A compound for whooping cough

Hoyvnijv (*Salix humilis* Marsh.) and *hflfs hvtki* (*Solanum nigrum* L. or *Panax quinquefolium* L.) are mixed in a large crock of water. The medicine man blows into the infusion with his bubbling tube, then sings four songs of the Feather Dance, blowing into the medicine after each one. The texts of the four songs, the same songs used during the Feather dance episode of the Green Corn ceremony, are as follows:

1. *Gidahayo, gidahayo,* (repeat twice)
   He-e-e-e
   Ho-o-o-o
   Gidahayo

2. *Gidahayalino, gidahayalino* (repeat twice)
   He-e-e-e
   Ho-o-o-o
   Gidahayalino

3. *Agi^{n}da-ha agi^{n}daha* (repeat twice) (*Agi^{n}da* according to Willie, refers to a type of snake)
   He-e-e-e
   Ho-o-o-o
   Agi^{n}daha

4. *Waku waku he wali yani yo* (repeat twice) (The word *waku* in this
   song refers to the blue crane *wakułakko*, who supposedly taught the
   songs to the ancestors of the Creeks and Seminoles)
   He-e-e-e
   Ho-o-o-o
   He wali yani yo

In the fourth song the word *yasuli*, "turkey vulture," may be
substituted for *waku*. After the medicine is prepared in this manner, the patient is given four draughts of it to drink.

The fact that Feather Dance songs are used in this treatment
probably indicates a connection, in the minds of the Seminoles,
between birds and whooping cough.

NON-HERBAL REMEDIES

In addition to the herbal remedies described in the previous chapter, the Oklahoma Seminoles employ numerous remedies that utilize portions of the bodies of animals, birds, and insects. There are also treatments involving the bleeding, scratching, and "bow and arrow" techniques. Others consist entirely of the recital of a sacred healing formula. As with the herbal remedies, sympathetic magic is often involved in these non-herbal remedies.

Animal, bird, and insect derived remedies

Skunk scent is employed in a treatment for tuberculosis. The skunk must be killed before it gets excited, and the scent sac must be removed. About half a drop of the scent is put into a quart of water. The patient then drinks one large glass of this infusion once a day to treat his or her tuberculosis. Willie explained that the Seminoles learned of the efficacy of skunk scent quite by accident, as follows: "There was an old man who had *ohoket-kvłpe* (lit. "dry cough" or tuberculosis). He coughed and coughed, but nothing came up and he could get no relief. One day he was lying, weak, in his lodge and a skunk wandered in. It saw him and became alarmed and sprayed him right in the face. The poor fellow swallowed some of the scent and soon began to retch violently and to throw up

71

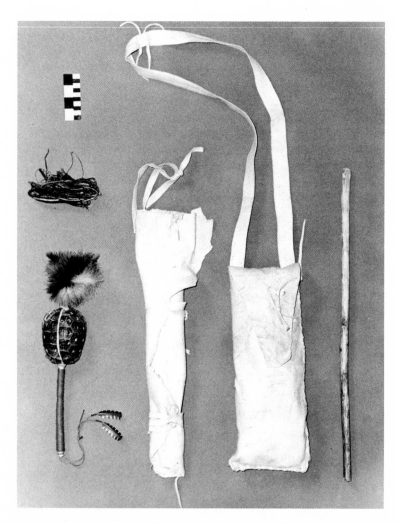

PLATE 10. A Seminole medicine man's equipment. *Left above*: a bunch of *hoyvnijv* roots; *Left below*: terrapin-shell rattle of an archaic type. *Center, left*: model of the type of bundle carried on the wrist by a Seminole medicine man when afield gathering herb medicines. The plants were stored in the bundle until he returned to his home, when they were either used immediately or dried and transferred to his larger "permanent" medicine bundle, of the type shown *center right*. *Right*: medicine man's bubbling tube. All items were made by Willie Lena, 1980–81.

phlegm. He got relief from this, and ever since, the Seminoles have used skunk scent to treat tuberculosis."

A portion of the shell of a certain kind of turtle is used in treating someone with lower back pain (a slipped disk). The shell of a certain type of small turtle which has a sort of "tail" at the rear end of its carapace is secured, and the "tail" of the shell is removed. This sharp shell fragment is used to make four light scratches at the base of the patient's spine, and soon gives him relief.

Pig toes were always saved at butchering. They came off easily when boiled or scorched. These pig toes can be boiled in water and given to children as a treatment for whooping cough.

Buck stones come from inside large cervids, such as deer, elk, and moose. They are black in color, and not every animal has one. Willie suggested that they might be like gallstones in humans. A Seminole who finds one in an animal he has shot is fortunate, for a buck stone has great curative powers. If you have one, rub it in your hands until it is warm, then rub it on a part of your body— such as your hip—that aches, and the aching will disappear.

The dried marrow from old cattle or horse bones, a substance Willie described as "like sand" was saved and used by Seminole medicine men to coagulate the blood in wounds. The bones were sawed part way through and the dried marrow caught in a paper or piece of buckskin and tied up for later use.

The lining from a chicken gizzard has medicinal properties. These linings were always saved and dried for later use in a treatment for hemorrhoids. The treatment is identical with that described in the previous chapter in connection with Needle grass (*Stipa spartea* Trin.), except that the dried gizzard linings are substituted for the needle grass awns. The gizzard linings are boiled in water. The patient sits in a chair or stool that has an opening in the seat to expose the rectum to the vapor rising from the pan of hot liquid placed beneath it.

To cure children of bed-wetting, the Seminoles make the children eat burned chicken feathers.

The feathers of powerful wild birds, especially the eagle, are powerful medicine objects and can ward off evil influences. These feathers can also cause illness if not treated properly before they are used for dance ornaments or other purposes. Therefore, Seminoles and Creeks go through certain procedures to "kill" the power inherent in the feather before using it in a hat roach or other decoration. Ira Bird Creek, a Creek Indian of Shawnee, Oklahoma, cuts off the base of the feather about a quarter of an inch from the end and then stuffs a small bit of red cloth or yarn inside the quill to prevent "eagle sickness." Willie Lena does the same, but first recites the following sacred formula:

> Lvmhi łakko kudułati (repeated twice)
> "Eagle" "big" "?"
>
> Lvmhoji kudułati (repeated twice)
> "Little-eagle" "?"
>
> Kudł, kudł

After reciting this, one blows into the cut-off base of the feather, then stuffs it with the red material.

Various types of bird feathers are used by Seminole medicine men as insignia, to indicate their area of specialization. Thus a yellow-hammer (flicker) feather worn in the hat indicates that the wearer can treat headaches. The symbolism probably derives from the fact that this bird probes beneath the bark of trees to remove insects, much like the Seminole doctor penetrates the skin of his patient in the bleeding treatment for headache, described below. An owl feather worn similarly indicates that the wearer can treat many illnesses, an analogy with the numerous bars on an owl feather. A buzzard feather indicates that the wearer can treat arrow and bullet wounds. The connotation here is the use by Seminole doctors of buzzard feathers as probes in locating bullets and arrowheads.

The spider called "daddy long-legs" is used as a medicine by the Seminoles. Such a spider is caught and its legs are pulled off. The body of the spider is then baked in a biscuit that is eaten by a patient to prevent boils.

Bleeding

Like many other Native Americans, the Oklahoma Seminoles employ the bleeding treatment, using a sharp piece of bottle glass to make the incision and a sucking instrument made from the end of a bison or cow horn to draw out a quantity of blood. The Muskogee name for this treatment is *nokki caukv* (lit. "pains" "sucks out"). The sucking horn is carved from the small end of the bison or cow horn. It is about two and three-quarters inches in length, with a diameter of two or two and a third inches at the large end. It tapers to the small end, but is slightly enlarged at the distal end to provide a mouthpiece. The opening inside the mouthpiece is only about an eighth of an inch in diameter.

The glass sherd used in making the incisions from which the blood is drawn must be from a *brown* glass bottle, perhaps imitating the brown flint or chert chip used in ancient times. Willie did not know why brown glass was necessary but commented that years ago, instead of brown bottle glass, the Seminoles used a fragment of deer vertebra. This practice, he said, was discontinued because fragments of bone sometimes broke off and lodged in the wound, causing it to become infected.

In treating a patient with a swelling, the bleeding practitioner first brushes an infusion of *ido ho·mi* (lit. "bitter wood," an unidentified plant) and *hoyvnijv* (*Salix humilis* Marsh.) on the affected part. He then makes two small vertical incisions, using the piece of bottle glass. As the blood wells from the wound the medicine man applies the large end of the horn so as to cover the wounds and the area around them and sucks the horn full of blood. In his mouth he has a piece of wet animal sinew, and when the horn is nearly filled with blood he maneuvers this sinew with his tongue so as to plug the small hole in the mouthpiece of the sucking horn. This creates a suction which retains the blood in the horn, and it can then be removed from the wound without soiling the patient's clothing or that of the doctor. The medicine man then brushes the wound with the *ido ho·mi* and *hoyvnijv* infusion once again. In a few minutes the wound will have stopped bleeding.

PLATE 11. A Seminole medicine man administering the bleeding treatment. Pen and ink sketch by Willie Lena, 1982.

Willie employs a formula to stop the bleeding after the treatment, thus:

Canvlani catv kvtpetv (repeat twice)
"Green-flies" "blood" "dry"

Canv łakko kvtpetv
"Flies" "big" "dry"

The "power" in this formula derives from the fact that since flies
have "dry" blood, the patient's blood will also "dry up" quickly.

The bleeding treatment, so widespread in North America, may
have been learned from whites in colonial times. Certainly it was

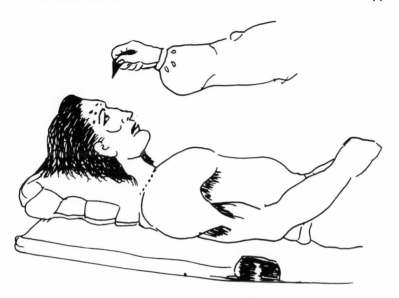

PLATE 12. A Seminole medicine man treating a headache using the bleeding method. Pen and ink sketch by Willie Lena, 1982.

used by both whites and Indians at this period. It is actually a crude form of counterirritation, and in some cases is quite effective. It is still employed in modern medicine, I am told, for the treatment of high blood pressure.

The Seminoles do not always employ the sucking horn in the bleeding treatment. For headaches, for example, the medicine man simply incises a vertical row of holes in the patient's forehead, between the eyes, and then asks the patient to lean forward and let the wounds bleed. After a time the patient is told to sit up straight. Shortly the headache disappears. There is a special formula associated with this headache bleeding treatment but Willie does not know it.

The Seminoles strongly believe in object intrusion witchcraft, a subject that will be discussed at greater length in the following chapter. It is thought that people who use bad medicine (i.e., witches) can blow medicine magically at a victim from a long distance. Shortly a swelling will appear on the patient's body. If this swelling is lanced and sucked in the bleeding treatment a hair or some other small foreign object will be found in the blood inside the sucking horn after treatment. This is the "witches arrow," shot into the patient by the witch, which has now been removed by the bleeding treatment.

Scratching

Scratching the arms, legs, and body by the medicine man using a rattlesnake tooth, thorn, bone or copper splinter, or needle is an ancient Native American therapeutic technique. Most of the early sources on Southeastern Indians mention it, and finds of groups of narrow native copper pins in Mississippian archeological contexts indicate its prehistoric origins.

Among today's Creeks and Seminoles, it is still a prominent feature of the Green Corn Ceremony or Busk, where it is used to promote the general vitality of the communicants. Ballplayers in "match" or men-against-men ball games, are also scratched on their arms and legs to prevent stiffness. In both instances, and when scratching is done for general therapy, the area to be scratched is first moistened with an infusion of *hoyvnijv*. To punish children, however, "dry" scratching, which is much more painful, is the rule.

In the Green Corn, the men are scratched twice on each upper arm, twice on each lower arm, and twice on the back of each calf. The four scratches on each arm were said by Willie to symbolize "eight more years of life." Women are scratched only on the lower arms in the Green Corn. Formerly men were scratched on the chest as well, though today only those who specifically request it are scratched there. Willie said that a diagonal scratch from one shoulder across the chest and down to the opposite hip was often elected by warriors to enable them to carry ammunition in battle because it resembled a bandolier of cartridges.

Scratching may be done at any time of the year to improve

PLATE 13. A Seminole medicine man administering the scratching treatment. Pen and ink sketch by Willie Lena, 1982.

muscle tone. For weak muscles in the arms a ligature of buckskin is fastened above the muscle of the upper arm. Deep vertical scratches are then made on both the upper and lower arm. These are allowed to bleed freely for twenty minutes or so, the blood being wiped away with a small wooden spatula as necessary. The ligatures are then loosened.

When a person has high blood pressure, a condition indicated by a very rapid heart beat, he or she may request the scratching treatment. In this case four vertical scratches are applied to the upper arm and four to the lower arm.

The little bow and arrow treatment

A small bow and arrow are used in treating boils and sties. The person desiring treatment prepares the utensils—a bow about a foot long, an arrow about six and two-thirds inches long, and a clean chip of wood from the woodlot. The afflicted person then secures the assistance of his sister-in-law (her brother-in-law in the case of a woman) to shoot the wood chip, which is placed on the boil or sty, with the little bow and arrow. The in-law shoots four times at close range. Sometimes the boil will break. One must be careful not to injure the eye while using this treatment for a sty.

Miscellaneous remedies

When a child has a pain in its leg a split twig is put on the earlobe. This treatment is of interest in that the area being treated is remote from the area of treatment, as in acupuncture.

To treat high blood pressure, a length of red woolen yarn is worn around the left wrist.

When a person is vomiting blood this formula is recited:

Yamʃndi, yamʃndi, sutv topvɬv

"on this side" "on this side" "sky" "behind"
isti foni

"man" "bones"

The strength of the formula derives from its mention of the fact that in the afterworld there is no bleeding. Only dry bones remain after death. Thus, through the principle of sympathetic magic, the recital of the formula will cause the bleeding to stop.

When a child is cranky and cries all the time, get a bird's nest and burn it. Hold the child in the smoke and it will stop crying.

If you have trouble sleeping because of worry, get up and go east from the house. At the first pond of water wash your face and head. This will clear the worry from your mind.

Another way to accomplish this result is to burn cedar leaves and breathe in the smoke. When there is a bad argument in the home, one should always burn cedar to dispel the bad feelings.

One of the most bizarre remedies described by Willie is the following treatment for rupture of the testicles. An elm tree is stripped of its branches and top to a height of about twenty feet.

The remaining trunk is then split from top to bottom and the two sides are bent out to form a sort of hoop and tied in this position. The ruptured man now walks through this hoop eight times, the first four times circling on the outside in a counterclockwise manner and coming through it from the back, the second four times entering it from the front and circling it counterclockwise from the left. Willie could not explain what sympathetic principle was involved or how this was supposed to cure. Perhaps the magical power of the hoop itself, an important world symbol to the Seminoles and other North American Indians, is involved. Since the hoop is "complete," the notion may be that its "completeness" will be transferred to the patient, making him "complete" again.

To cure stroke, secure several splinters of wood from a tree that has been struck by lightning. Burn some of these and have the patient ingest the ashes. Use other splinters to "scratch" the paralyzed part.

To prevent whooping cough, capture a brown turtle. Pull its hind leg out straight and prick it with a pin to make it bleed. Collect two drops of the turtle's blood in a spoon and give it to your child. This works only on children under twelve years of age.

For impotence, capture a snapping turtle and remove its tail. Use the tip of the turtle's tail to lightly scratch the penis on either side. "This will bring it up every time."

4

MAGIC AND WITCHCRAFT

The traditional Seminole world is a world suffused with magic. There is a type of magic for every occasion, ranging from the simple trick that saves a woodcutter the bother of chopping up a fallen tree, through techniques designed to attract or hold a lover, to the powerful black magic employed by witches who can transform themselves into owls, dogs, or insects to achieve their evil ends.

Every traditional Seminole knows some magical formulas and techniques, and routinely employs these to cope with the uncertainties of life. A few individuals, invariably older persons, know a great deal more, the accumulation of a lifetime of study and experience. These "medicine people" are sought out by younger and by less knowledgeable folk when they need additional help in attaining a goal, or when certain telltale physical or mental symptoms lead them to believe that they have been "witched."

Certain substances have great magical power as well, particularly pieces of the horns of a species of giant horned snake, or the animated stones known as *sapiya*. Medicine people possessing such rare and powerful substances are particularly fortunate, but few remain among today's Seminoles and Creeks.

Everyday magic

When a man finds that his shirt or sweater is buttoned unevenly (the bottom button fastened in the next-to-the-bottom buttonhole) or that his shirt collar has accidentally been turned inside the shirt, instead of out, it is a clear sign that someone is angry with him. By the same token, if a woman discovers that the hem of her dress is turned up in the back, it means the same thing. The correct procedure upon making such a discovery is to face toward the east and recite a magical formula.

Likewise, if a man discovers that he has put his undershirt on backwards it means bad luck. If this happens, one should, as soon as he discovers his mistake, continue on to his destination but then immediately return home and correct the error.

To save yourself work when you are felling a dead tree for firewood, clap your hands four times before the tree hits the ground and the limbs will magically break into short pieces and you won't have to chop them up yourself.

A person who wishes to learn medicine songs must kill a mockingbird and swallow its heart while it is still warm.

To ward off the possible negative effects of someone having put bad medicine in your food or drink, recite this formula:

Łupót hoti (repeat twice)

"Go through (?)"

Łup'ot

Then blow into your cup of coffee, drinking water, etc., four times.

If you suspect that someone has entered your house in your absence and left bad medicine, sprinkle an infusion of cedar leaves and water in the room. Another way of neutralizing bad medicine is to burn a mixture of *aha lvbvkca* (*Gnaphalium obtusifolium*) and cedar leaves on hot coals or on the hot stove top. As the smoke rises, rub your hands in it and rub the smoke on your limbs and body. One should also inhale the smoke, repeating the ritual four times. This procedure is also followed to counter bad medicine one may have picked up in a crowd.

An owl feather tied over the entrance of a house will prevent witches from entering and leaving bad medicine when you are absent or asleep. Owl feathers are used for this purpose because owls do not sleep at night, the time when witches are likely to move about. Willie has such an owl feather tied above his front door with a piece of red yarn. Ashes strewn in the yard are also good protection, because witches cannot step over ashes. Perhaps the best way to protect your house is to secure four red corncobs. Cut off the soft end of each of the four cobs. Bury one of these at a depth of four inches about fifteen feet out from each corner of your house. This should be done early in the morning, before breakfast.

To counter bad medicine when going out in public wear a buckskin pouch containing *ahá lvbv́kca* and cedar leaves on a buckskin thong around your neck. An even more powerful counter against bad medicine at public gatherings is to wear an extended owl's foot on a buckskin thong around the neck, positioned to hang over the throat. This owl's foot should be decorated with blue beads at the top. Willie mentioned that his grandfather always wore such an amulet when appearing in public.

To influence a person's thoughts in a positive way, a small amount of *hſlſs hvtki* (*Solanum nigrum* or *Panax quinquefolium*) is chewed and the breath blown on or near the person to be influenced. Willie said that he had done this to influence the man who owns the land his tribal town wishes to purchase for use as a ceremonial ground. Another town member had used tobacco smoke from a "doctored" cigarette in the same way. Willie has great faith in this magic and boasted that he had been able to secure the release of an Indian girl who had cashed social security checks sent to a deceased family member by entering the courtroom before the hearing and blowing his "doctored" breath here and there. This had influenced the judge favorably in the Indian girl's behalf, and she had been let off without punishment. The same thing could be done, he said, to secure a favorable verdict for Rita Nauni, the Sioux girl then being tried for murder.

Willie said that Tony Hill, town chief of Greenleaf, a Creek square ground, knew a magic formula designed to keep people from gossiping about a person. This, Willie said, is very important for an Indian leader, such as a town chief, and he hoped to learn the formula from Tony.

Love magic

The mourning dove, called *Locv pvci* (lit. "turtle" "dove") in Muskogee is important in Seminole love magic. They have a magical song that refers to the bird and imitates its lonesome call. This song is used by a man who wishes to attract a certain girl or to call back a girl friend who has strayed to the arms of another man. The words of the song are *Pvci ho we, pvci ho we* which may be translated roughly as "Dove, go there (and make me invincible)." The mourning dove, enlisted in the young man's service by means of the magical song, flies to the woman's house and repeats its haunting call, making the woman "lonesome" for the magician.

We have already noted, in chapter 2, how an infusion of *hflfs hvtki* used as a hair tonic or to wet a man's hatband, makes a man irresistible to women. The same is true of Indian paint that has been stored with a *sapiya* or magic stone, as will be described below. Also described in chapter 2 is the use of a "medicine" cigarette rolled in a black jack oak leaf. The man wishing to influence a young lady rolls and lights the cigarette, puffs on it four times and, facing the direction where the woman lives, blows smoke toward her, at the same time pronouncing her name. This makes the woman "lonesome" for him.

A Seminole man who suspects that his wife's or lover's affections are straying to another, secures four small grains of gravel, which he swallows. These four grains are said to *ihunetska*, "make you heavy." The man, now "heavy like stone," now "outweighs" the wandering female, and she is magically compelled to return to his arms.

Throughout Willie's accounts of the use of love magic is the theme that while such magic is good if employed in moderation, its use to excess will redound on the user. There is a strong moral tone pervading even this area of culture. Nevertheless, the knowledgeable man can manipulate things to cover up his peccadillos. For example, the Seminoles strongly believe that if a man

PLATE 14. A Seminole youth "making a woman lonesome" (practicing love magic) using specially "doctored" tobacco rolled in a blackjack oak leaf to make a cigarette and reciting a magical formula. Pen and ink sketch by Willie Lena, 1982.

"cheats" on his wife shortly after she has given birth to his baby, his sin will weaken the child if the man picks up the child and fondles it. To avoid this, some philanderers, returning home from an extramarital encounter, were careful to pet the family dog before touching the newborn. The dog thus carried off the residue of the man's transgression.

Weather-controlling magic

To make it rain the old-time Seminoles caught an old turtle and hung him up by the neck. They then proceeded to scratch him, just as they scratch the men and boys at the Green Corn. While they were scratching him they threatened this powerful emissary of the "water world," telling him that they would cut his throat unless he made it rain. Another way of handling the turtle was to hang him up and whip him in the way that the Lighthorsemen whipped a criminal, threatening him in the same way.

PLATE 15. A Seminole medicine man using magic to avert a tornado. Note the characteristic staff trimmed with eagle, hawk, crow, and owl feathers, which is stuck in the ground before him, and the terrapin shell. Pen and ink sketch by Willie Lena, 1982.

During the hot, dry summer of 1980, I stopped to visit Willie on my way to participate in the Green Corn Ceremonies at Cedar River Tulsa square ground. Willie advised me to "accidentally" spill quantities of the liquid medicine when I drank it and poured it over my head as a part of the ritual. This would, he said, bring a much-needed rainstorm.

Another way to bring rain is to cut off the head of a stag or horn beetle and place it in water.

Tornadoes are a serious threat in Oklahoma, and the Seminoles have magical techniques to cope with them. They conceive of a tornado as a giant old woman carrying an enormous broom or a *sofki* paddle. One way to harness a tornado is to capture a small part of it. To accomplish this one secures an old terrapin shell and drills a hole in either side of it. Using these holes the carapace is lashed to a flat board. The board is placed so that the raised front of the shell, where the terrapin's head formerly came out, is pointed in the direction of the approaching tornado. If even a small portion of the deadly twister enters the shell the tornado is rendered harmless. Willie gave me such a device in 1980, to protect my home, explaining that to protect a dance ground from tornadoes, hailstorms, and other bad weather, four such devices should be used, one at each of the four sides of the square ground.

Another use of a terrapin shell to prevent a tornado is based upon the old tornado woman's habit of going barefoot. One takes the terrapin shell and breaks it into small pieces, which are scattered in the yard, except for the four scutes at the top of the shell. These are saved and put into the fire when a tornado threatens. When they burn they make a loud popping noise. The tornado woman hears this and knows that the Indians have placed fragments of broken shell around their houses, fragments that will hurt her bare feet if she comes near.

Sometimes a medicine man will face the approaching tornado and pray for it to go around. A sketch by Willie (plate 15) shows a Seminole shaman thus engaged. A prayer stick with golden eagle tail feathers atttached is stuck in the ground before him, but Willie offered no explanation of this feature.

The *sapiya*

The Seminoles, like their kinsmen the Creeks, have great respect for a certain type of magic stones called the *sapiya*. These stones, which are colored red, blue, and yellow, bring their owners power in love, the chase, and war.[1] According to Willie Lena, the *sapiya* look like small stones of various colors but have the ability to move around, sometimes hopping like fleas. They are also capable of breeding and producing more of their own kind.

Willie said that his uncle possessed a *sapiya* and knew the

PLATE 16. Feeding the *sapiya* medicine. Pen and ink sketch by Willie Lena, 1982.

procedures and songs necessary to control it, but he refused to teach this lore to Willie. Willie, however, did manage to "catch" one of the songs associated with this powerful medicine and sang it for me: "*Sidio sidio.*" The Creeks keep their *sapiya* stones tied up in circles of white buckskin, but Willie said that the Seminoles use a container made from a small section of river cane with a small buckskin disk tied over the top.

To use the *sapiya* one places powdered Indian paint (vermilion) in the container along with the stone. The user goes out in the woods, away from other humans, and builds a small earthen mound. The container with the *sapiya* and paint is placed on top of this mound. The practitioner then sings the proper songs and carefully removes the buckskin cover from the container. Using a grass stem, he carefully removes a small amount of the paint that has been next to the magic stone and applies it at the outer corner of each eye.

This act immediately transforms the person using the paint. As Willie described it "the paint makes you 'sparkle.' Someone will see you and say to herself 'I want to visit with that person.' They will come and visit with you and you will be popular."

Owning a *sapiya* is a heavy responsibility, because the medicine must be cared for very carefully. If it is not "fed" and "watered" regularly, it will "turn back on you" and give you sores. To feed the *sapiya*, its container is carefully placed on top of a stump and opened. Then, using a grass straw, it is "fed" with squirrel blood and given dew to drink (plate 16). A *sapiya* can be used by a man to catch a woman, or a woman to catch a man. It can also be used to attract deer and other game by a hunter. Some people don't want to keep the *sapiya* because of its potential for "turning back" on the owner. Willie told of a friend who had one and wanted to get rid of it. "I told him to go to a growing tree and drill a hole in it and put the *sapiya* deep inside, then stuff the hole with green stuff [i.e., leaves and twigs]. I told him that he would hear a voice singing from the hole in the tree for four days—a man's voice if it is a *sapiya* used to catch a woman, a woman's voice if it is a *sapiya* used to catch a man. They will sing all kinds of pretty songs. Drunken dance and other kinds of songs, but you must resist and not go over there. After four days the singing will stop, but the *sapiya* won't die completely until four months have passed."

Medicine from the Giant Horned Snake

The Seminoles believe that one of the most powerful medicines for hunting and love magic is a piece of the horn of the Giant Horned Snake. This creature, according to Willie, resembles an ordinary tie snake and, in fact, is called *stvkwvnaya* (lit. tie-snake) in the Muskogee language. The Giant Horned Snake, however, is much larger than a regular tie snake. It is also called *Cftto mikko*, "Snake King." It is blue on its upper surface and yellow underneath. The horns are variously colored. Willie's uncle once saw one with horns which sparkled "like diamonds." The Giant Horned Snake lives underwater, and its home is in the deepest pools in lakes and streams. It is extremely dangerous, drowning and partially eating its victims, but if approached in the correct manner its horns can be scraped to provide a substance giving the possessor a powerful hunting and love medicine and also an ability to learn the uses of all herbal medicines. The presence of the Giant Horned Snake is indicated by a sound resembling the ringing of a small silver bell.

Willie said that his grandfather had secured hunting medicine from the Horned Snake and described the ceremony involved.

PLATE 17. A medicine man performing the ceremony to call and secure medicine from the Giant Horned Snake. Pencil and crayon sketch by Willie Lena, 1980.

The equipment required is a gourd rattle, a short log of green wood, a special knife for scraping the snake's horn, a circle of buckskin to catch the scrapings, and a supply of the freshly cut stems of *tawa łakko* (*Rhus glabra*, smooth sumac) with the hard outer bark peeled off. This last will be used to feed the Horned Snake. The shaman is usually alone, but may bring with him as an observer a young boy whom he is training to become a practitioner (Willie's uncle was in this apprentice role once, but was too frightened, when the Horned Snake appeared, to learn the songs).

When he arrives at the stream or lake where the Snake King lives, the shaman places the short log close to the edge of the water with its long axis parallel with the shore line and kneels behind and a bit to the right of it. Taking up his gourd rattle in his right hand and holding the *tawa łakko* stem in his left, he begins to sing the four magical songs used to call the snake. Soon, with a great boiling and splashing of water, the Snake King emerges from the depths. When it appears, the birds that are flying overhead and perched in nearby trees become much agitated and cry out in distress, for the Giant Horned Snake, as chief of the "Powers below" is their foremost enemy. This time, however, called by the magical songs, the Snake King will do no harm. It swims toward the shore and out of the water just far enough to rest its head on the section of log provided by the shaman. Charmed by the music it calmly takes its food, the *tawa łakko* stems, from the shaman's left hand.

The shaman greets the Snake King and asks it for good health for the coming year. The shaman now has a short time in which to take up his special knife and scrape some fragments from one of the horns of the snake. He catches these precious scrapings in the piece of buckskin he has provided for this purpose, and the Snake King retires once more into the depths. The scrapings from the horn of the Giant Horned Snake are the most powerful medicine of the Creek and Seminoles.[2] The owner of such medicine usually stores it in a hollow tree at some distance from his house, lest it injure his children.

The Muskogee name of the medicine is *cʃtto yvpi isfa·ka* (lit. "snake" "horn" "to-hunt-with"). It is primarily a hunting medicine, but like the *sapiya* it can also be employed to attract women. Paint is placed with the fragments of snake horn, the two being stored in a buckskin pouch. When a man goes hunting he places a small amount of the paint that has been stored with the medicine directly below each eye, simply a short, horizontal line.

Willie Lena has never seen the Giant Horned Snake, but told me a number of stories about it on various occasions.

One time I was walking near a stream by B———— R————'s place. One of these snakes is supposed to live there. I heard a little bell ringing in the water, but I knew what it was and stayed my distance. I just kept walking away. When I finally looked back I saw a big splashing in the water where I had heard the bell. That night we heard a faint voice crying "Help!" from the same place where I had seen the splashing. The next morning we went down to the creek and found the body of a white man. He had been killed by the snake. His nose, eyes, lips, ears, and the fingers of his left hand had been eaten off. These snakes do this when they are hungry. They drown people and then eat those parts. My cousin Wilson Tiger saw the snake once. The male has horns but the female has something like hair.

On another occasion he reported that:

A Negro friend of mine saw one of these snakes once and didn't know what it was. He was out hunting and had his gun with him, so he shot it. It was just a small one, but it had a bad effect on him. He went out of his head and his arms went limp, just like a snake's body. He was in a bad way until an Indian doctor worked him over and restored him. Even then he had bad dreams about snakes and was never quite the same again. I told him "You shouldn't have done that. You are fooling with things you don't understand."

Willie said that some people are "too weak hearted" to look at the Horned Snake and come away unscathed. His brother once saw the snake and became ill as a result. A medicine man was called in and used *Notosa* (probably *Angelica atropurpurea*) to calm him down. Kelly McGirt also saw a Horned Snake once and became ill as a result. Kelly reported that this snake was a female, because it had hairs on its head. There is a magical technique to protect one against the bad effects of seeing the Horned Snake. A thorn of bois d'arc (*Maclura pomifera*, Osage orange) stuck through your hat or cap will prevent you from becoming ill when viewing it.

Willie pointed out a pool in a stream three miles south and one mile west of the Justice school, south of Wewoka, Oklahoma, where the Giant Horned Snake has been seen. There is a cleft in the rocky bank at this point and the pool is just beneath it. Willie plans to go to this place some fine June day, when the time is just right, and perform the ceremony he learned from his grandfather. In this way he will acquire unlimited ability as a curer, or as he put it "If you start out this way, you will learn it all!"

Creek and Seminole belief in the Giant Horned Snake as a

powerful source of magical power almost certainly derives from the prehistoric period. Representations of horned snakes are common in the art of the Mississippian archeological culture. The ceremony of calling the snake, as described by Willie Lena, is mentioned by Benjamin Hawkins in his *A Sketch of the Creek Country*, penned in 1798–99.[3] Discussing the "War Physic, Hoith-le Hil-lis-so-wau (*Hoʈʃ hʃlʃswa*)" he writes:

> . . . They have in their shot bags, a charm, a protection against all ills, called the war physic, composed of chitto gab-by and Is-te-paupau, the bones of the snake and lion.
>
> The tradition of this physic is, that in old times, the lion (Is-te-paupau) devoured their people. They dug a pit and caught him in it, just after he had killed one of their people. They covered him with lightwood knots, burned him and reserved his bones.
>
> The snake was in the water, the old people sung, and he showed himself. They sung again, and he showed himself a little out of the water. The third time he showed his horns, and they cut one; again he showed himself a fourth time, and they cut off the other horn. A piece of these horns and the bones of the lion, is the great war physic.[4]

Magical dolls

In former days murders were common the Seminole Nation. Sometimes a man would be found shot to death and hung on a fence and no one knew who had done it. To apprehend and punish such a murderer the Seminoles employed a ceremony involving a magical doll or effigy of clay.

Four male relatives of the murdered man assembled for this ceremony. One of them had prepared and brought with him a human effigy about nine and a half inches in height made of pottery clay. In a secluded open space in the woods the four men laid a fire of very dry blackjack oak wood. Blackjack was selected because it burns with a hot, even flame. The clay effigy was made to stand up in the center of the fire and it was ignited.

The four men now positioned themselves around the fire and about four feet from it, one at each of the four cardinal points, and seated themselves facing inward. The eldest of the four men sat at

PLATE 18. The ceremony in which a magical clay doll is burned to apprehend and kill a murderer. Pen and ink sketch by Willie Lena, 1982.

the west, facing east. He had brought with him a small clay or stone pipe and a pouch containing a supply of *hici pvkpvki* (native tobacco, *lobelia* ?). Charging his pipe, he lit it, then prayed and smoked, announcing the purpose of the ceremony.

As the four men gazed at the magical doll the fire blazed hotter and hotter, and the clay effigy became red-hot. Sometimes it fell, as if the little man had been shot. When this happened the ceremony was deemed a success, for it meant that the murderer, wherever he was, would die within four days. If it remained standing, however, this indicated that the murderer had powerful counter-magic of his own. In this case he might become ill, but would recover and not die.

A model of such a magical doll made by Willie in 1981 is shown in Plate 19. Willie's illustration of the ceremony in progress is seen in Plate 18.

PLATE 19. Model of the magical clay doll used in the ceremony to apprehend and kill a murderer. Made by Willie Lena, 1980.

Witches

A belief in witches pervades Oklahoma Seminole culture. Most illness, if not caused by offended animal spirits or ghosts, is due to their machinations. Witches can operate at long range, magically sending "medicine arrows" through the air to enter the bodies of their victims, or at close range, introducing "bad medicine" into food or drink. At other times they accomplish their evil work by shapeshifting, changing themselves from human form into that of an owl, a dog, a bear, or even an insect. In this guise they prowl the homes of potential victims.

Witches most often assume the form of a horned owl when on their nefarious errands. For this reason they are usually called *fsti tikini*, "man-owls," or *stikini* for short. Such witches add to their own life span by stealing and eating the hearts of their victims. Each heart stolen and eaten by a witch adds two or three years to the witch's own life. Using black magic the witch can put all of the people in a house into a deep sleep and then work on the intended victim. The heart is extracted through the victim's mouth. It will later be cooked by the witch in a small iron kettle (a standard item of Seminole witch paraphernalia) and devoured.

Once a woman, a relative of Willie's, told of how, as a small child, she accidentally overheard two old women, actually witches, discussing human hearts they were eating: "Mine is tough," said one. "That's because it belonged to an old person. Mine is tender, from a young boy." The little girl, alone in the house, had hidden behind the stove when the old women entered her parents' dwelling. Fortunately she remained unperceived and was too terrified to scream.

A witch, in order to assume the form of an owl or other creature, must retire to the woods or some other secret spot and vomit up his or her inner organs. These they leave behind when on their deadly errands. Returning, they must swallow these parts again in order to reassume their human form. The stink of these entrails sometimes gives away the witch's base of operations. Willie illustrated his point with a story:

A certain Seminole family often left their old grandmother at home

PLATE 20. A female witch. Note the typical kettle used by witches to cook the hearts plucked from their victims. Pen and ink sketch by Willie Lena, 1982.

PLATE 21. Witch disguises. *Above*: a witch who has shapeshifted into the form of a dog. Such dogs can be easily recognized by their eyes, which glow red in the dark. *Below*: a witch who has shapeshifted into the form of a moth. Pen and ink sketches by Willie Lena, 1982.

when they went to town for supplies. One time when they came back from town grandma wasn't in her room and the window was wide open. There was a bad smell in the room. They suspected that grandma was up to something, so the next time they purposely came home early. There was the same open window and bad odor. Grandma was nowhere to be seen, but then someone looked in the closet. It was pitch dark and the bad smell was almost overpowering. Grandma was in there all right. They could see her eyes glowing red in the dark. "What are you doing in there?" "Nothing!" "We think you are doing something bad. You must stop."

Sometimes a witch is shot when in animal form. In this case it always returns home to die, and changes back into human form just before death. Willie told of a man seeing a bear in a place where no bears were usually seen. The man shot the bear, wounding it severely, but it managed to escape into the brush. A few days later he heard an old woman, a suspected witch, had died.

Because a witch must leave his or her insides behind when in bird or animal form, the witch is highly vulnerable if anyone observes the locale where the transformation from human to animal form takes place. Willie told another story to illustrate this:

This is a true story about a witch. You know little boys see lots of things. They are always around playing and seeing things they are not supposed to. One time a little boy of this type came and said to his grandpa "I saw an old man when I was out playing. He walked behind a stump. Then I saw a shadow and an owl flew away from the stump." His grandpa told him to keep a close watch on the stump. Later he saw an owl light on the stump, and shortly the same old man walked out from behind it. Again he told his grandpa. His grandpa said "Did you see him kneeling behind the stump and throwing up?" "Why, yes I did." The grandpa asked "Did you see anything else?" "Well, I saw a bunch of old guts hanging there on the stump." "That was a bad man you saw, grandson." The two of them went out to the stump and surely enough there were the guts and other insides of the old witch. Even the heart was there, still beating. They took all this stuff down and fed it to their dogs. Later the little boy saw an owl come to the stump. It flew around and around in an agitated manner. It was seen doing this for four days. At the end of that time the body of the old witch was found near the stump. Owls were hooting in nearby trees."

PLATE 22. "At the end of that time the body of the old witch was found near the stump." Pen and ink sketch by Willie Lena, 1982.

For obvious reasons, witches usually concealed their ability to shapeshift. But sometimes, for reasons of bravado, a witch would show off his ability. Willie told another story to illustrate this:

One time a Seminole saw a big dog walk up the street. It went over a hill and shortly a man came walking down the hill from the same direction. The Seminole asked him "Did you see that big dog when you came that way?" "That was me," the witch said. "I don't believe you," said the skeptic. "I will prove it to you then," said the witch. The next time the man who had seen the dog was sitting in the yard with several friends. He saw the same big dog walk up the street. "Look at that big dog!" he said to his companions. "What big dog?" the others said. "That's a man walking up the hill!"

Witches can put people to sleep through their evil magic. A

male witch will put all of the people in a house asleep so that he
can enter and have sexual intercourse with the women and girls
and remain undetected. After the witch has had his way with a
woman he will scratch her four times on the breast with a thorn
(or, today, a steel needle). This will put her in his power and make
it easier for him the next time he visits, by making her drowsy. A
Seminole woman is terrified when she awakens in the morning
and finds the four telltale scratches on her breast.

Willie said that when he lived at his old place (one mile west of
Wewoka) he had as neighbors a widow with three grown girls.
These four began finding the scratches on their bodies and applied
to him for help. Willie gave them a supply of *ahá lvbv́kca*
(*Gnaphalium obtusifolium*) and cedar leaves and told them to
burn this mixture on top of the stove before retiring. They did so,
and the medicine enabled them to resist the witch's medicine and
sleep lightly. When the *stikini* came the next time they heard him
trying to get in and raised a cry. Willie came running and found
two men standing on the porch of the women's house. One was
the corpulent deacon of a local church, and the other his helper.
When asked what they were doing on this porch at 3:00 A.M. the
deacon hemmed and hawed and finally said that he had come to
deliver some important local news. "Any news you have for us can
wait until morning," they were told, and Willie threatened to
shoot the pair if they were ever found prowling the premises again.
After this encounter the woman and her daughters never found
scratches on their bodies again.

The most effective way to kill a witch is by using a special arrow
fletched with owl feathers and with small grooves cut near the
point, presumably to contain herb medicines. These arrows have
no stone or metal point, merely the sharpened end of the shaft. To
use such an arrow the witch hunter must remove all of his clothes
except for his shoes, circle the house counterclockwise once, and
then shoot the *stikini*. Willie made and gave me such an arrow on
August 13, 1980, and described how he himself had used one to
kill a witch: "One time my wife and I heard a *stikini* around our
cabin. I made a *stikini* arrow, took off my clothes, and went out to
wait for it. Surely enough, it came around that night and I shot it.

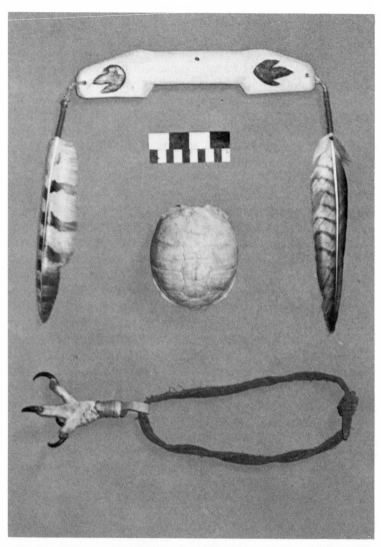

PLATE 23. Ceremonial and magical paraphernalia. *Top*: wand of the type formerly carried in the left hand by the leader of the *Opvnka hajo* or Stomp Dance to accentuate his arm movements. *Middle*: terrapin shell of the type used in preventive magic against tornadoes. *Bottom*: owl-foot necklace worn by a man to ward off witchcraft when he is in a crowd. All items made by Willie Lena, 1981–82.

The next morning Lucille and I looked for the arrow, but we never found it. I guess the human-owl carried it off. We were never bothered again."

Sometimes what is believed to be a witch turns out to be merely an owl, as in another story Willie related: "Another time a Seminole woman said she had been bothered by a *stikini*. She said it would come up to her when she went outside to the toilet and try to get in her pants. She was an awful liar! She had me come over to shoot the *stikini* and when I heard the sound of an owl I went out with my bow and arrow. I found it was just three little screech owls (*ifvlv*) that had come to eat slop put out for the hogs!"

5

CEREMONIALISM:
GENERAL CONSIDERATIONS

For traditional Seminoles, those who have not joined a Christian church and learned that such things are the "work of the devil," life revolves around activities at the ceremonial center, commonly referred to in English as the "square ground" or "stomp ground." Here the single pole ball game is played nearly every Sunday afternoon during the spring and summer, and here take place the monthly Stomp Dances and the potluck dinners and ground-clean-up sessions that precede them. Those grounds where the ceremonial is strong enough are also the sites of the yearly Green Corn Ceremonial, the principal event of the traditional cere-monial year, and the great "match" ball games, likewise of com-pelling interest to Seminole and Creek traditionalists. Thus, whenever Seminoles meet in the supermarket or on the street in Wewoka, Sasakwa, Byng, Holdenville, or Seminole, a part of the conversation will be to impart news of which stomp ground is going to dance next Saturday night, or play ball and feast next Sunday.

Originally these square grounds were the political and residen-tial centers of Seminole society as well as religious centers. All of the members of a particular tribal town lived in a settlement clustered around their town's stomp ground. Outmigration, dic-tated by the need to find jobs in the city, and the loss of tribal land

104

PLATE 24. "The way the white man taught the Seminoles to pray." Pen and ink sketch by Willie Lena, 1982.

have at present reduced the *talwa* or "town" to the status of a ceremonial and religious organization, and the square ground to a place of resort rather than a place of residence. Furthermore, to swell ranks sadly depleted by outmigration, conversion to Christianity, and white acculturation, most towns now include adopted members. These persons are recruited from Seminole and Creek towns that have lost their ceremonials and even from non-Muskhogean tribes such as the Shawnees. Ideally, however, a person belongs to only one square ground, that of his or her mother. Even today the core of a ground's membership consists of individuals born into the group.

Politically speaking, there are twelve recognized "bands" in the Seminole tribe at the present time, and each of these is represented on the tribal council. Originally, each of these bands was a tribal town and had its own square ground, but nowadays this has changed. Some of the original bands, or towns, have converted to Christianity en masse and have abandoned their square grounds. Others, such as Eufala, have become so large that they have had to split up. Thus "band" and "town" or "square ground" are no longer coterminous, and have not been for many years.

Nine square grounds or tribal town organizations were mentioned for the Oklahoma Seminoles by my informants Willie Lena

PLATE 25. Oklahoma Seminole camp at Tallahassee square ground. Such camps are built on the north, west, and south sides of the square ground, but never on the east. Beneath the brush arbor we see a water barrel, a bench and chairs, and a table. At the right is a shelf with condiments. A set of ballsticks hangs on one of the middle posts. A campfire, with a metal grill set on concrete blocks, supports the cooking pots to the right of the brush arbor, and in the background is the pole for the single pole ball game, with wooden fish emblem at its summit. Pen and ink sketch by Willie Lena, 1982.

and Tom McGeisey. Of these, three are dormant, one having been so since 1926, another since 1950, and a third since 1979. One is brand-new, having "put down its fire" (established itself) in the summer of 1980. These square grounds are:

1. Ochesee (*Ocisi*, "hickory leaf"). According to Swanton "Ochesee was the name of the Muskogee or true Creek Indians in the Hitchiti language."[1] But Willie Lena derives the name from *oci*, "hickory," and *issi*, "leaf." To reach this ground one travels two miles south, four miles west, and another half a mile south of Wewoka, Oklahoma. This ground has been dormant since 1950. Tom Larney was the last chief, Barney Larney the last *heniha*, and Sam B. Harjo the last medicine man.

2. Okfuskee (*Okfvski* "in a point").[2] To reach this ground one travels six miles south of Wewoka on Highway 56, then half a mile west and three-quarters of a mile south. The ground has been dormant since 1926. Frazier Fish was the last chief. Johnny Camp, also known as Johnny Stamp or Johnny *Haija*, was the last medicine man.

3. Tallahassee (*Talahasi*, "old town," or *Talahasvci*, "little old town"). To reach this ground one travels seven miles south of Wewoka on Highway 56, continuing south on a dirt road when Highway 56 veers to the southwest. This ground was dormant for many years, but was revived in 1976. It has only part of its ceremony. Willie Lena is chief, Kennedy Wise is *heniha*, and George Beaver is medicine man.

4. Gar Creek (*Łało makweka*, literally "fish pond" but known in English as Gar Creek, and not to be confused with No. 7, below), also called Chiaha. To reach this ground one travels five miles north of Wewoka, then five miles west, then three and a half miles north, then another half a mile west. This ground has a full ceremonial cycle, and is one of the strongest Seminole grounds at present. Jack Wolfe is chief. According to Tom McGeisey it is made up largely of Hichiti people, and one old man there still speaks Mikasuki, the only non-Muskogee speaker remaining among the Oklahoma Seminoles. Otis B. Harjo, however, a prominent ground member, said that the membership includes people from Ochesee, Okfuskee, and old Chiaha, dormant Seminole grounds, and also some Creeks.

5. Eufala (*Ufaloji*, "little Eufala"). To reach this ground one travels to Cromwell, Oklahoma, and from there goes four miles north, three miles west, one mile south, half a mile west, and then a quarter of a mile north. It has a full ceremonial cycle. David Bowlegs is chief.

6. *Tiwałi* (*Tiwałi*, "dividing up"). To reach this ground one travels to Sasakwa, Oklahoma, and from there goes seven miles west, half a mile south, and then half a mile southeast. This ground has a full ceremonial cycle. Robert Wolfe is chief, John Field is medicine man.

7. Fishpond (*Łałokala* "fish" "piece-broken-off" but commonly called Fishpond in English). To reach this ground one travels to Cromwell, Oklahoma, and from there goes four miles north. This ground has a full ceremonial cycle.

8. *Ufáloji* (*Ufáloji*, "little Eufala" but not to be confused with No. 5, which is called "Eufala" in English). To reach this ground one travels two miles south, then two miles west, then another half a mile south of Seminole, Oklahoma. This ground is new, having been founded in 1980. As yet it has only part of its ceremony. Lee Mitchell is chief, Sam Francis is medicine man.

9. Mikasuki (*Mikasuki*, named after the tribe). This ground is located

one mile east and half a mile south of the junction of Highway 270 and Highway 9A, east of Seminole, Oklahoma, on the farm of Bill Ripley, the chief. This ground has been inactive since 1979, because of internal divisions among the membership. The ground is made up largely of Mikasuki descendants. Willie Lena's late wife, Lucille, was a member of this ground, and their children are members here.

John R. Swanton lists the following Seminole square grounds known during the period of his field work (ca. 1912): (1) Ochesee Seminole, (2) Okfuskee Seminole, (3) Tallahasutci, (4) Hitchiti Seminole, (5) Eufala Seminole, (6) Łiwahali Seminole, (7) Chiaha Seminole, and (8) Mikasuki Seminole.[3] He notes that Ochesee Seminole and Hitchiti Seminole had given up their ceremonials. Of the grounds listed by Swanton, numbers 1, 2, 3, 5, and 8 match those named by Willie Lena and Tom McGeisey. Number 4 on my list, Gar Creek or Chiaha, because it is noted as being composed largely of persons of Nitchiti descent, may be a consolidation of the old Chiaha Seminole ground of Swanton's day and his Hitchiti Seminole. My number 6, *Tiwałi*, is almost certainly the same as his *Łiwahali*. *Ufaloji*, a new ground, appeared in 1980. Ochesee Seminole, listed as "given up" by Swanton, was apparently revived sometime after the period of his field work, but was then abandoned once more in 1950. Like *Ufaloji*, Fishpond appears to be a post-1912 addition to the roster of Seminole square grounds, though the name is an old one. Hawkins found a Creek town of this name in Alabama in 1789–99.[4] The phenomenon of a large tribal town (or, today, a square ground) splitting into a number of "daughter" towns as noted above is an ancient one. The phenomenon of a square ground abandoning its ceremonial for a number of years and then reviving its tradition under the same name, however, seems to be a post-Removal phenomenon for the Oklahoma Seminoles and Creeks. The usual reason for such abandonment is the death of a number of key functionaries within the space of a few years, making the usual gradual replacement of ground officials impossible. It then often happens that as the younger people of the ground attain adulthood they decide to revive the ceremonial or "bring back the fire." That this practice has occurred frequently among both the Seminoles and the Creeks was quite evident from remarks made by my informants in the two tribes. Some went so far as to state that no Seminole square ground, and only one among the Creeks (Cedar River Tulsa and its antecedents) has maintained an unbroken tradition as far back as memory reaches.

In order to revive a ground that has abandoned its ceremonial cycle, a definite procedure must be followed. First a "practice ground" is established near the site of the old ground. An organization is formed, and ordinary Stomp Dances and single pole ball games are held during the ceremonial season for a period of four years. During this period, it is hoped, the membership in the square ground is growing continually as descendants of members of the old ground return and join the organization. Next, the group moves back to the old ground from the practice ground and dances and plays ball there. When the ground's activities are considered strong enough, a match ball game is held near the old ground. When this has taken place, the ground may stage a Green Corn Ceremony, at which time it is considered to be "complete" again. To follow any procedure other than that indicated above is to court divine retribution in the form of accidents or illness.

Remembering the discussion of Seminole origins in chapter 1, it is not surprising to find a Creek and a Seminole square ground claiming the same name. It was this duplication of names that caused Swanton to attach the suffix "Seminole" to the Seminole squares named Ochesee, Okfuskee, Hitchiti, Eufala, Łiwahali, Chiaha, and Mikasuki, and he might have done the same for Tallahassee, which also has a counterpart among the Creeks. The Seminoles themselves use the "Seminole" suffix only when necessary to avoid confusion, and will on occasion argue bitterly with members of the like-named Creek square grounds concerning primacy of their own "fires." Willie Lena, for example, stoutly maintains that the "Creek Tallahassee" square ground, near Vivian, Oklahoma, has usurped its name and is not composed even in part of descendants of the original Tallahassee tribal town, located in what is now Tallahassee, Florida. In fact, it was not until June, 1980, that he was finally persuaded to attend a Green Corn Ceremony at this Creek square ground.

The ancient Southeastern pattern of dividing tribal towns–square grounds into Red or "war" and White or "peace" categories no longer carries much weight with today's Seminoles. Of the present Seminole square grounds, Ochesee, Okfuskee, Tallahassee, and Fishpond are in the White group, the remainder in the Red division. Any Square ground considered the others of the same color to be "brother fires." Members of these "brother fire" towns can be recruited by a square ground to amplify their own numbers in a match ball game. Likewise, in the Green Corn, a town would send special invitations to other towns of the same division or "fire."

The Seminoles are divided into matrilineal, exogamous, clans. Spoehr[5] collected the following list of clans among the Oklahoma Seminoles in 1938–39:

1. Bear	8. Alligator	15. Turkey	22. Pumpkin
2. Deer	9. Bird	16. *Kapiccvlki*	23. Salt
3. Panther (Tiger)	10. Potato	17. *Aktayahcvlki*	24. Buzzard
4. Snake	11. Wind	18. *Waksvlki*	25. Fox
5. Wolf	12. Grass	19. Otter	26. Eagle
6. Coon	13. Skunk	20. Toad	27. *Tamvlki*
7. Beaver	14. Mole	21. Earth	28. *Nokfilvlki*

Not all clans are found in every Seminole town. At Tallahassee, for example, only Nos. 1,2,3,4,7,8,9,10,11, and 27 are found at the present time. In addition to regulating marriage and descent the clans at one time dealt out punishment for murders committed by their members and likewise avenged an injury to a clansperson by an outsider. Members of the same clan cannot marry, and this prohibition extends to members of like-named clans at other tribal towns–square grounds. Certain clans have special prerogatives. Chiefs, for example, always come from the Bear, Beaver, or Bird clan at Tallahassee ground. Clans also have a vested interest in dances associated with their clan eponym. Members of the Bird clan, for example, prepare the feather wands used in the Feather dance and take the lead in performing it.

Just as the tribal towns–square grounds within the Seminole

tribe are divided into Red and White divisions, the clans within each town are similarly divided on a dual principle, one being *hvtki*, "white," and the other *cilo·ki*, "of a different speech," but usually given as "red" in English. Most of the original functions of these two intra-town divisions have eroded. There is still a feeling, however, that the members of the "white" clans are peaceable people, and hence the chief is always a member of one of these. Formerly, according to Spoehr's informants, there were intra-town match ball games between clans on opposite sides of the divisions.[6]

At the time the Seminoles were moved to Oklahoma, certain clans were linked with others to form phratries, but these have now disappeared. These phratries, like the clans, were exogamous.[7]

Architectural layout of the square ground

The Seminole and Creek square ground is actually a circle surrounding a square. Grounds differ in size, but average about forty yards in diameter. Each square ground differs from the others in the seating of the clans, the location of the ball pole, and other features, but the diagram of Tallahassee ground in figure 3 provides a general example.

The ground itself is enclosed by a low ring of sweepings, leaves and dust resulting from the annual cleaning of the ground, which is called the *tajo* ("mound"). The circular area inside the ring formed by the *tajo* is the *paskofv*, or dancing ground proper. Within this area are arranged, in the form of a square, four open-sided brush arbors (*apiti*, also called *tipaci*, "little bed"). Each of these is built of six upright posts, forked at the top. The three front posts are about seven and a half feet in height, those in back slightly shorter. These are connected by stringers and covered with leafy willow boughs. The finished arbor is about sixteen feet wide and ten feet deep. Under each arbor are two, sometimes three, benches made of heavy logs flattened on top called *ołikʃta-hvtkʃ* ("chair," "white").

At the opening between the south and east arbors there is a

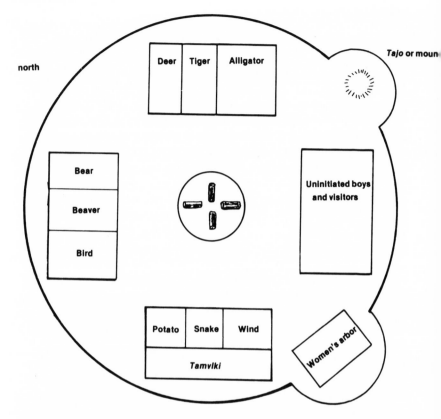

north

Deer | Tiger | Alligator

Tajo or moun-

Bear

Beaver

Bird

Uninitiated boys
and visitors

Potato | Snake | Wind

Tamviki

Women's arbor

FIGURE 3. Layout and seating of clans at Tallahassee square ground, from a sketch by Willie Lena. The ball pole is about 50 yards west of the ground.

slight bulge in the ring formed by the *tajo* of sweepings. Here there is a fifth arbor, placed diagonally, which is used by the women as a resting place in the intermissions between episodes in the Ribbon Dance. At the northeast of the ground, and also embraced in a slight bulge in the ring as viewed from above, is a small, low mound four feet in diameter and three inches in height. This is termed *tajo*, "mound," the same as the ring of sweepings, but should not be confused with it. This feature is rebuilt each year at the time of the Green Corn and serves in a number of significant ceremonial contexts, most important, as the spot from which a designated official "calls" the birds at the beginning of the Feather Dance. Finally, in the very center of the ground is another low mound, four feet in diameter, upon which the sacred fire (*totkv*) is kindled during the Green Corn. This mound, too, is rebuilt each year at Green Corn time.

The various clans are seated as shown in the diagram, figure 3. The Bird, Bear, and Beaver clans are seated in the west or *mikko's* ("chief's") arbor. Potato, Snake, Wind, and *Tamvlki* are on the south. Deer, Tiger (Panther), and Alligator are on the north, and the east arbor is reserved for visitors and uninitiated boys who have not as yet been assigned a seat in the arbor of their mother's clan.

The pole for the single pole ball game, surmounted by its swiveling fish effigy or its cow skull, is located about fifty yards to the west of the ground.

Swanton provides diagrams of the various layouts of the Seminole square grounds which he found in 1912.[8] His diagrams for Tallahasutci (Tallahassee) differ slightly from the one provided by Willie Lena in the seating of the clans and also indicate that some clans present at that time have since died out. Thus the *Tami* and Turkey clans are added in the north arbor, Potato is in the west arbor, and *Aktayatci* and *Kapitca* are in the south arbor.[9] Swanton's diagram indicates that, at that time, the chief was from the Beaver clan and the *mikko apokta* ("chief," "twin") an assistant chief, was of the Bird clan. Swanton terms the north arbor the "warriors' bed," the south arbor the "Aktayatci's bed," and the west arbor the "Chief's or White bed."[10]

Willie Lena noted that there is an architectural feature at each

PLATE 26. The seating of the chief (*mikko*) and assistant chief (*heniha*) in the west arbor of the square ground. The chief is at viewer's right. Pen and ink sketch by Willie Lena, 1982.

square ground that is not apparent to the viewer. It is a large stone buried in the center of the ground directly beneath the mound upon which the sacred fire is built. At Cedar River Tulsa only one stone is used, but at Tallahassee there are four. If the square ground is moved to a new location this stone (or stones) is dug up and moved as well.

He also mentioned that long poles called "dog poles" are placed at the right side of the front of each arbor during the Green Corn Ceremony. Nowadays these persist as mere architectural decoration, but in years past each arbor had a designated official who sat in the seat next to the dog pole and used it to warn off dogs who strayed into the *paskofv*. These dogs might have eaten, and hence would "spoil the medicine" of the fasters.

So sacred are the precincts of the square ground that in time the bark of the posts of the arbors comes to have medicinal value.

When Willie mentioned this to me, I asked if it made any difference what sort of trees have been used (blackjack oak is usually employed), and he said no. The idea is simply that the posts and bark have acquired a healing value from having been associated with the "good medicine" of the square ground and its ceremonies. The illness for which a medicine made from the posts of the square ground is prescribed was described by Willie as "hot lungs and liver." He mentioned a Seminole man, given up by white physicians, who suffered from this ailment. The man's lungs and liver became very small as a result. Bark taken from the posts of one of the arbors at the square ground was soaked in water, and the man drank the infusion and became well again.

Musical instruments

In addition to the human voice, three musical instruments are employed by the Seminoles and Creeks to accompany their music and dance. The most important of these are the women's leg rattles or "shackles" (*locv-saukv* "turtle" "rattle"). These consist of a number of land terrapin (*Terrapene carolina*) shells laced to heavy pieces of leather and worn by the woman on her lower legs. Each terrapin shell has been cleaned, closed by bending shut the underside of the carapace, and drilled in several spots to amplify the sound, which is provided by a number of pieces of gravel inside. An experienced "shell shaker" may have as many as eleven shells on each leg (two rows of four each, plus three tied on above to form a middle row). Since these shackles are very heavy, the women pad their legs by wrapping terrycloth towels around the leg before tying the leg rattle in place. The lacing is on the inside of the leg, and there are no shells at this point. Even so, the shells on the front, outside, and back of a woman's leg rattles are so bulky that she is forced to walk and dance with her legs several inches further apart than normal. "Shaking shells" is definitely an art form, and even in the ungainly stance dictated by the leg rattles, Creek and Seminole women produce remarkable rhythmic effects.

The *locv-saukv* are usually made by a medicine man. The terrapins are killed and their heads, legs, and tails removed, and as

PLATE 27. A shell-shaker girl
wearing terrapin-shell leg rattles.
Pen and ink sketch by Willie
Lena, 1982.

much as possible of the flesh is dug out from inside the shell. The
shells are then placed on a red ants' nest. The ants eat the
remaining terrapin meat. The shells are then further dried in the
sun. Before the shells are closed from the bottom the gravel
"voice" of the rattle is added. As he adds the "voice," the medicine man blows on the gravel four times, then recites the following
sacred formula:

Saukv	*saukv*	*łakko*	*ti*	(repeated twice)
"rattling"	"rattling"	"big"	"one"	
saukv	*saukv*	*tci*	*ti*	(repeated twice)
"rattling"	"rattling"	"little"	"one"	
sa· k!	*sa· k!*			
"causes them to whoop!"	"causes them to whoop!"			

PLATE 28. A shell-shaker girl wearing condensed-milk-can leg rattles. Pen and ink sketch by Willie Lena, 1982.

The individual rattles are then lashed to the heavy leather backing and stout thongs or shoestrings attached for lacing to the wearer's legs. A woman's *locv-saukv* are her personal property and are passed down from mother to daughter or aunt to niece in the matrilineage.

About 1920, a type of leg rattle employing condensed-milk cans in place of the traditional terrapin shells was introduced among the Seminoles from the Natchez-Cherokees of the Medicine Spring square ground near Gore, Oklahoma. This type of leg rattle has become quite popular in the intervening years, especially with younger girls, since it is both lighter to wear and also louder than the terrapin-shell type. The cans are wired together in stacks of three and then fastened to the same type of heavy leather foundation used in the terrapin-shell type of leg rattle. Each of the cans is perforated with a number of nail holes to augment the sound. (plates 28, 29). Conservative Seminoles and Creeks still frown on this innovation. At one ultra-conservative Creek square ground, Hilibi, only terrapin-shell leg rattles are allowed. At other Creek and Seminole grounds both "turtles" and "cans" are used, but in the sacred Ribbon Dance of the Green Corn Ceremony those women and girls wearing "cans" are relegated to the end of the line of dancers. Among the Oklahoma Seminoles and Creeks such leg rattles are used only by women and girls, never by the men.

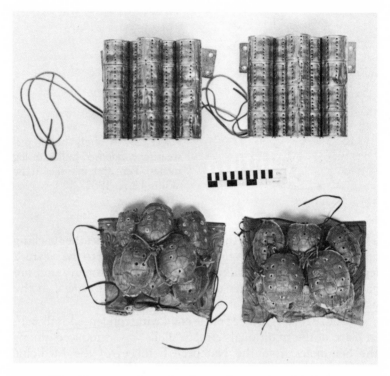

PLATE 29. *Above:* condensed-milk-can leg rattles. Made by Alfred Switch, a Shawnee Indian of Shawnee, Oklahoma, but identical to those used by the Creeks and Seminoles. *Below:* terrapin-shell leg rattles. Made by Willie Lena.

I have seen two or three women wearing a few sleigh bells on a strap instead of either the terrapin-shell or condensed-milk-can leg rattles.

For certain religious and social dancers male singers employ a rattle made from a coconut shell (*tala saukv,* "coconut" "rattle"). Like the women's leg rattles, these are sacred instruments and are customarily made by a medicine man. When making such a rattle the man starts early in the morning, eating no breakfast. He works until noon, then stops for the day. The following morning he

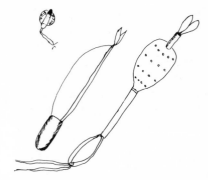

PLATE 30. An *atassa* or war club knife of the type carried by the leading matrons in the Ribbon Dance, and a coconut-shell rattle. Both are decorated with white crane feathers and painted with white clay paint just before their use in the Ribbon Dance. Pen and ink sketch by Willie Lena, 1982.

proceeds in the same manner, perhaps finishing by noon. The coconut shell is first drilled at the end opposite the "eye" and the milk is drained out. This hole is then enlarged to a diameter of about an inch, and through this opening the "meat" is carefully scraped out. The outside is also scraped and polished, using a piece of broken glass. Small holes, less than a fourth of a inch in diameter are now drilled in the coconut shell in a regular pattern to allow the noise inside to escape, precisely as in the women's leg rattles. A hole about a half-inch in diameter is now drilled at the top or "eye" end of the coconut shell and a wooden handle about a foot long is inserted so as to run from the large hole in the bottom of the shell up through the hole at the top. The handle is tapered at its upper end to fit snugly in the holes at the top and bottom of the coconut shell. About an inch and a quarter of wood from the handle is allowed to project from the top hole. Sometimes a tassel of fluffy feathers is attached to this projection. About thirty or forty small pebbles are now placed inside the shell to give the rattle its "voice." Before adding this gravel the medicine man blows on it four times and recites the same sacred formula mentioned in connection with the women's leg rattles. The shell is then attached firmly to the handle by means of a buckskin thong. This thong is wrapped and tied to the handle just below the coconut shell, then brought up over the coconut shell on the outside, wrapped once or twice around the projection at the top, and then brought down on the opposite side of the coconut shell and tied in place around the handle below the shell. A buckskin wrist thong may be tied at the lower end of the handle if desired.

Two such rattles constitute a set, one for each of the two assistant singers who sit on either side of the principal singer, who also plays the drum. When Willie Lena makes a pair of coconut rattles of this sort he calls one of them "male" and the other "female." I can discern no difference between the two, though Willie insists that a difference exists in both the shape and the sound of the two. Such coconut-shell rattles are undoubtedly a modern substitute for earlier gourd rattles, but they were already in use among the Creeks and Yuchis in 1907.[11]

Another type of hand rattle, made like the above but using a single terrapin shell instead of a gourd or coconut for the sound box, was formerly in use but is now obsolete. I purchased an example of such a rattle, made as a souvenir, at the gift shop of the Seminole Nation Museum in Wewoka in 1980 (plate 10). It was later identified by Willie Lena as an old Seminole type, but he added: "They don't hardly use that kind any more." This terrapin-shell hand rattle has the usual Southeastern feature of regularly spaced small holes drilled in the carapace to amplify the sound. Swanton mentions such a rattle as an old Creek type.[12]

The drum (*sapvlka*) used by present-day Seminoles and Creeks consists of a small earthenware pickle crock about six inches in diameter and seven inches in height, with a head made of a piece of buckskin tied over its mouth with a piece of heavy cord. The drum is of the "wet" type. It is filled about one-third full of water, and the head is thoroughly soaked and wrung out before being tied in place. By keeping the drumhead tightly in place, and by sloshing water on it at intervals to keep it wet, a fairly good tone can be achieved, though still somewhat inferior to that of a Plains Indian peyote drum, which is also a "wet" drum of approximately the same size.

The drum is beaten with a single hardwood stick that has a ball carved on one end. The drumsticks I have seen in use among the Seminoles and Creeks are made from some hard wood, such as

Osage orange (*Maclure pomifera*). They are from ten to twelve inches in length and undecorated except for the ball at the end. Most sticks I have seen in use are straight, though Willie carved and gave me one which is slightly curved. He indicated that some ritual singers prefer the curved type, and said that he has even sold his curved drumsticks to Kiowa and Comanche peyotists for use as peyote drumsticks.

An older form of drum, still in use at some square grounds in Swanton's day (ca. 1912) and still remembered by Willie Lena, employed a long cypress "knee" as the drum kettle.[13] A still older form, mentioned by Swanton, used a pottery vessel for this purpose.[14]

The only Seminole musical instrument not used in connection with the human voice is the flute (*fſpa*). This was an end flute made of either cedar wood or native cane, and it had five stops.[15] I did not learn of anyone among the Oklahoma Seminoles who makes or plays this type of flute at the present time. Woodrow Haney, an Oklahoma Seminole craftsman of Seminole, Oklahoma, does make and play a type of Indian flute, but it has six stops and is much larger than the traditional Seminole form. Almost certainly Mr. Haney's flutes derive from a Prairie-Plains prototype (plate 77).

Ceremonial cycle

The ceremonial cycle at a Seminole or Creek square ground begins in the spring, generally in April or May, with an all-night Stomp Dance. There is a sacrifice of meat to the sacred fire on this occasion. Afterward, the men of the ground wash their heads and arms in *hoyvnijv* and drink a small amount of the medicine and then "go to water" (go to a nearby stream to bathe). Stomp Dances are held each month in May and June. Each of these is followed by the men washing themselves and drinking *hoyvnijv* and going to water. These Stomp Dances are a preliminary leading up to the high point of the year, the Green Corn Ceremony, held in June or July. Another Stomp Dance occurs in August, and early in September there is a match ball game. The final event of the year is the Soup Dance. This is essentially just another all-night Stomp, but soup, cooked in a single large cauldron, is served to the dancers toward morning, together with loaves of Indian corn bread. The soup must be from wild game, such as squirrels, or in default of this, from "home raised" chickens (not supermarket poultry). The Creeks serve these foods right in the dance ground, but the Seminoles in one of the adjacent camps. In either case, preparation of the food is a ritual act, and two respected matrons are appointed for the task. Another distinctive feature of the Soup Dance is that it ends, in the morning, with a performance of the Morning or Drunken Dance, not otherwise performed.

The Soup Dance appears to be a much simplified version of the old Horned Owl Dance (*Stikini opvnka*), a lengthy ceremony sharing many features with the Shawnee Bread Dance, such as selecting the cooks by placing a decorated hoop over their heads, a ceremonial hunt by the men while the women are preparing the corn bread, and, later, a distribution of roast venison to the women and bread to the men. The Horned Owl Dance has been obsolete for at least a century.[16] Willie Lena had learned its name but could supply no details regarding its performance.

As noted earlier, some Seminole square grounds do not have a complete ceremonial cycle, lacking the Green Corn and the match ball game. At others, though a Green Corn takes place, it is incomplete, lacking the women's Ribbon Dance or the Feather Dance, or both. In the following chapter is a generalized description of a complete Seminole Green Corn, based upon the observation of a number of such ceremonies by myself at both Seminole and Creek square grounds, corrected, amplified, and illustrated by Willie Lena.

CEREMONIALISM:
THE GREEN CORN
CEREMONY

The Green Corn Ceremony (*vcʃ-opvnka*, "corn dance"; *posketv*, "fasting") of the Oklahoma Seminoles has several purposes: first, to renew and purify the sacred fire, and hence insure the continued health and prosperity of the members of the square ground and their families; second, to provide the purification required before the men can eat the now-ripening green corn (hence the English name for the ceremony), although women may eat the new corn at any time; third, to bestow Indian names upon and assign clan seats to young men not previously initiated, likewise men being adopted into the town; and fourth, to recognize the tutelary spirits of certain animal species, such as birds, snakes, and bison, and hence maintain their continued good will.

At present, the ceremony takes place over a four-day period sometime in late June or July. To accommodate to the white man's work week, this period begins on Thursday afternoon and ends on Sunday morning, allowing the participants to rest up a bit before returning to work on Monday morning. The first day, Thursday, is "camping day." Actually, many of the families belonging to the square ground will have been "camped in" all week, preparing their individual campsites, cooking, and socializing. There are no formal daytime activities on Thursday, though an informal single pole ball game may be gotten up in the late afternoon, and a group

123

of men may gather at the square ground to play dominoes. Each car or pickup truch entering the camping area is the subject of close scrutiny, because Green Corn time brings relatives and friends from out of state who are not seen at any other time of the year. About 5:30 P.M. all visitors and square ground members who are not camped in are invited to eat at one or another of the camps surrounding the ground, and there is much greeting of old friends and joking. Following the evening meal there will very likely be another single pole ball game.

As darkness gathers, some of the largest fallen tree limbs, cow manure, and other trash which has accumulated on the dance ground is removed, but only the minimum required to use the ground. No fire is built. The chief now directs a speaker to circle the camp and tell the people to prepare for an evening of dancing. The speaker makes his rounds at half-hour intervals, at 7:00, 7:30, 8:00 and 8:30. By shortly before 9:00, the "shell-shaker girls" have donned their leg rattles and are seated in folding chairs just outside the square, and the men and boys have taken seats in one or another of the arbors.

This first evening consists mainly of one Stomp Dance (*opvnka hajo*) episode after another. It is quite informal and young boys and other novices who would ordinarily be passed over by the officials who select leaders are given a chance to try "taking a lead." The chief sits in his place at the front of the west arbor and receives gifts of tobacco and cash donated by members as they arrive, noting each item in a small record book. The tobacco is stored in a gunny sack that also contains the musical instruments and other ritual objects of the ground. This sack hangs above the chief's seat, suspended by a stout wire from the front stringer of the arbor. The tobacco is available to any member of the ground during the next three days. As midnight approaches the chief beckons his speaker and through this man announces that the dancing must now end for the night. "Tomorrow will be a strenuous day. We must rise at dawn, so it is now time for us all to get some rest." An experienced dance leader now leads a performance of the Long Dance (*opvnka capko*), continuing into a final round of Stomp Dance, and then everyone goes to bed.

PLATE 31. The ritual of "killing the green wood," about 9:30 A.M. on the second day of the Green Corn Ceremony. Pen and ink sketch by Willie Lena, 1982.

The second day of the Green Corn begins at 5:30 A.M. All male members of the ground report to the chief's arbor and begin to repair the arbors and rake trash from the ground. First the entire area is raked, proceeding in a counterclockwise direction starting from the chief's arbor at the west. Each arbor is then carefully examined, and rotten timbers are removed. The work crew now moves to the nearby woods to cut replacements. Pickup trucks are also sent to secure willow boughs to cover the arbors. These are added last. All of the repair work is done in the same counter-clockwise order, the chief's arbor first, then the arbor on the south, and so on.

When all of the repairs are completed, one man is designated to sweep off each arbor. He begins with the front posts, then the front bench, the the back posts and the back bench all the way around, beginning at the chief's arbor and proceeding counter-clockwise. His broom is made of *wilanv* leaves (*Chenopodium ambrosioides* L., Mexican tea or wormseed), a plant that has a pungent, woody odor. Last of all, he places a small twig from his leaf broom in the forks of each of the front posts of the four main arbors, twelve in all. This is called "killing the green wood" and protects the worshippers from any potential harm which might have entered the ground with the repair materials. If it has been dry during the preceding days, water is sprinkled on the ground before the arbors in the path that will be followed by the women in their dance, which will occur shortly.

While the other male members of the ground are engaged in this repair work, the chief and the medicine man are seated on the back bench of the chief's arbor. Here the chief paints the two *atassa* or *katassi*, the ceremonial knife-shaped clubs that are carried by the two head matrons in the Ribbon Dance. He uses a lump of whitish clay which has been moistened and placed on a large leaf. Using the same clay, he paints the two coconut-shell rattles to be used by the singers who accompany the dance. The clay remaining after the painting he wraps in the leaf and places in the middle fork at the front of the arbor. When he has finished painting these sacred articles he attaches small white crane feathers to the pointed ends of the *atassa* and to the projections at the top of the rattles. Shortly before he has finished he dispatches two "deacons" (*intapalvlki*) to visit every camp and tell the women of the square ground to prepare themselves for the Ribbon Dance.

By the time all of these preparations have been completed, it is noon or shortly after, and time for the principal event of the day to begin, the women's Ribbon or Sun Dance (*Itca opvnka*). Now the women of the ground, decked out in their finest attire, assemble in the women's arbor at the southeast corner of the square ground. Some are dressed in a style approximating the traditional dress of Florida Seminole women and known to the Oklahoma Seminoles and Creeks as "Florida style." This outfit has a long, full skirt with rows of Seminole patchwork, a tight-fitting bodice on the upper body, and over it a long, wide, cape-like garment of gauzy material. Other Seminole women and girls wear the same general costume worn by the neighboring Creeks. This consists of a wide, single-color skirt with two or three rows of ribbon trim near the

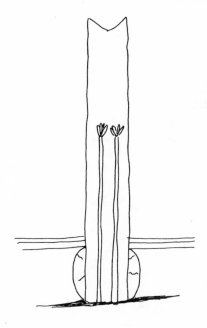

PLATE 32. Staffs carried by the "deacons" (*impuhata cukoafasta*) of the Ribbon Dance. Pen and ink sketch by Willie Lena, 1982.

hem, over it a long apron, generally white or of a pastel color much lighter than the skirt, a yarn sash with large tassels at the waist, and a loose, sleeveless blouse.

With either costume a large silver or german silver comb is worn in the hair at the back of the head, and from it varicolored ribbons are suspended to hang nearly to the ground. Sometimes additional ribbons are attached to the shoulders of the upper garment in front and in back. It is from these supernumerary ribbons that the women's dance derives its most common English name. Many bead necklaces are worn, also earrings, and some women carry wild-turkey-tail fans. Every woman and girl, if she owns a pair, wears either terrapin-shell or condensed-milk-can leg rattles tied around her calves. The long skirts must be cut wide enough to allow space for these leg rattles. Some women paint a single red dot on either cheek being the only design I have observed.

Although this is not their day, nor their dance, and they will be

PLATE 33. Leading matron in the Sun or Ribbon Dance, second day of Green Corn Ceremony. Note the *atassa* carried in her right hand. Watercolor by Willie Lena, 1965.

spectators for the most part, the men and boys also dress in their best for the Ribbon Dance. For most Oklahoma Seminole men and boys today, the ceremonial costume consists of a pair of fancy cowboy boots, a pair of dark trousers, a homemade "Indian" shirt, and around the waist a yarn sash with yarn tassels that fall to the wearer's knees when the sash is in place. Over the shirt, trousers, and sash some men wear a red "hunting coat" with fancy rick-rack or braid trim, or a vest decorated with Seminole patchwork. A few wear "Florida style" patchwork jackets with blousy sleeves. At the neck, some men may wear a bright silk scarf with a sachet of *kaptucka* (*Teucreium canadense* L.) perfume tied in it at the back of the neck. One or two older men may wear a crescent-shaped silver gorget, a family heirloom. On the head is a western-style hat, either felt or straw, with a beaded hatband, and at the right side, near the front, a white crane feather with the vane shaved so that it trembles or vibrates in the slightest breeze. Some of the men wear a white horsehair roach with a single eagle or hawk tail-feather in its center, fastened to the back of the hat so that the center feather droops elegantly down in back. Others wear an upright feather fixed in a spring tube so that it constantly sways back and forth. Thus attired, the men and boys assume their clan seats in the various arbors.

As the women and girls are taking their seats in the women's arbor, a red velvet robe with gold binding is spread over two chairs placed before the front bench of the south arbor, near the east end. This is where the two male singers for the Ribbon Dance will sit. When these two men have taken their places, the chief, seated in the west arbor, sends a messenger to them carrying the newly painted and adorned coconut-shell rattles and two long white crane feathers for them to wear in the front of their hats as a panache.

The chief now summons the two deacons (*impuhata cúko-afasta*, "deacons," "square-ground taking-care-of") to the west arbor and gives them their staffs of office, wooden wands about a yard in length, with white crane feathers attached to the top. Thus equipped, the deacons proceed to the women's arbor and usher the Ribbon dancers onto the dance ground. The women are conducted in a counterclockwise circuit until the two (at some grounds four) leading matrons stand before the two singers in the south arbor, facing east. The others form a long file behind them—first, the adult women wearing terrapin shells, next, adult women with "cans," then, adult women without leg rattles, and finally, small girls at the end of the line or "tail" (*haji*). One of the deacons now walks in a counterclockwise circuit and marks certain positions in front of the north and west arbors by scratching a line in the earth with his staff. These are the stopping points for the head matron.

The musicians now take up their rattles and begin to sing. On the first song the women merely tread in place, using a simple toe-heel left, toe-heel right. The sound produced by fifty or seventy-five women and girls, most wearing leg rattles, and all treading in unison, is awesome. On the second song the chief matron dances out ahead of the file behind her and moves to the point before the north arbor previously marked by the deacon. The other women, led by the second chief matron, now follow in her path and dance up to join her. She then dances ahead of them again to the point previously marked in front of the west arbor, and waits there until the others have caught up. Finally, she dances to the starting point, the women behind following as before. As the women approach the starting point they begin a vigorous skipping step, and the noise of their leg rattles is almost deafening. The men and boys give encouragement as the women dance past, shouting "*Locv!, Locv!*" ("turtles!, turtles!") to indicate that there is not enough noise from the women's leg rattles, and "*Haji!, Haji!*" ("tail! tail!") as the small girls at the end of the line go by, indicating that they should dance faster to catch up. When the women reach a point before the musicians they turn, beginning with the chief matron, ninety degrees to the right to face the singers, jumping in place until the song ends. This constitutes one "set" of the Ribbon Dance. A second set follows immediately, but at the end of it the women are so exhausted that they are ushered out to their arbor by the two deacons for a rest and a drink of water. The deacons then usher them in again for the final two sets. Following the fourth set, the women take another short breather. They are then joined by the men and boys for an episode of the Long Dance which immediately goes into one set of Stomp. A collection is generally taken at this time to "pay" the singers and the two (or four) chief matrons for their services in the Ribbon Dance. This ends the ritual daytime activities of the second day. The men and boys, who have fasted since dawn, are now fed.

At some grounds there is a match ball game for boys between seven and fourteen years of age during the early afternoon. In the late afternoon there is a single pole ball game in which all may participate. At the conclusion of this game, people go to the various camps for the evening meal. Members of the host ground are careful to see that all visitors are invited for supper.

As on the previous evening, there is a session of Stomp Dancing from about 9:00 P.M. until shortly before midnight, when the chief again tells the people to retire and rest.

On the morning of the third day the male members of the ground are called to the square ground at dawn. A work party with shovels is sent to secure moist, black earth to build the mound upon which the sacred "new fire" will be built. The ashes of the old fire are carefully removed and the area is scraped clean and level. Now two men, one in the north and one in the west arbor, sight from the right side of the center post at the back of the arbor along the right side of the center post at the front of the arbor, to the center posts of the arbor on the opposite side of the square. A third man, with a wooden peg, is directed to stick it into the ground where the two lines of sight intersect. Here, at the very center of the square ground, the mound for the fire is built. According to Willie Lena, it should be four feet in diameter and about two and a half inches in height.

Next, with the assistance of the same two "sighters," four regular sections of oak log, each approximately a foot and eight inches in length and four inches in diameter are placed in position on the mound by the ground's medicine man. These are the four logs for the sacred fire. First the north log is placed, then the south, then the west, and finally the east log. The medicine man places the logs slowly and deliberately, praying all the while. The

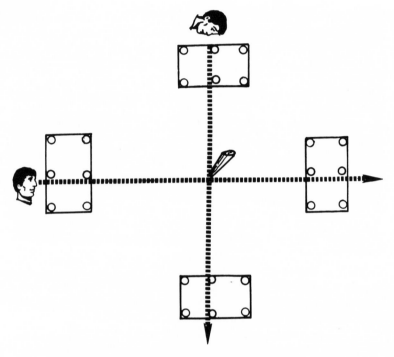

FIGURE 4. Method employed in locating the sacred fire.

cross formed by the logs, resting on the circular mound, is emblematic of the sun, and the sacred fire is, in fact, considered to be the earthly embodiment of the sun. Next the medicine man is handed four perfect ears of the new corn crop by the chief, and he places these next to the logs in the order indicated in figure 5. He blows and prays over each ear for about five minutes before putting it in place, moving his mouth from one end of the ear to the other as he does so. When he has finished, tinder is placed where the four logs meet, and it is ignited with flint and steel. As it blazes up, more tinder and larger dry sticks are added until the fire is blazing nicely and has consumed the four ears of corn, which are thus sacrificed to the fire and the sun. The sacred fire will continue to

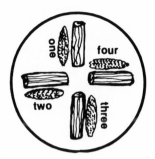

FIGURE 5. *Left*: Order followed in placing the four logs for the sacred fire. *Right*: order followed in placing the ears of sacrificial corn on the sacred fire.

PLATE 34. Medicine man praying over the four perfect ears of new corn before placing them on the fire as a sacrifice, third day of Green Corn Ceremony. Pen and ink sketch by Willie Lena, 1982.

PLATE 35. *Above*: the Green Corn medicines and the implements used in their preparation and storage. *Below*: the assistant medicine man pounding the *hoyvnijv* root. Pen and ink sketch by Willie Lena, 1982.

burn until the end of the ceremony. About 9:30 A.M. four young men, using shovels, carry coals from the new fire to the cooking fires in the various camps, which have been extinguished.

Now the Green Corn medicines are prepared. At Oklahoma Seminole grounds today these are the *pasa* (*Eryngium yuccifolium* Michx., Button snake root) and *hoyvnijv* (*Salix humilis* Marsh.,

PLATE 36. Medicine man "bubbling" the *hoyvnijv* medicine, the third day of the Green Corn Ceremony. Watercolor by Willie Lena, 1965.

Small pussy willow). Two young men are sent to secure these plants, and each returns with a supply. The entire plant of the *pasa* is used, but only small roots of the *hoyvnijv*. Neither medicine requires heating. The *pasa* is merely placed in a large earthenware crock and worked slightly with the hands as water is poured over it. Later it is "bubbled" by the medicine man using his bubbling tube. The *hoyvnijv* roots are first bruised by pounding them on a log, using a wooden mallet, then placed in a washtub with water and "bubbled" (Plate 35). All of this work is done in the east arbor (at some grounds outside the *paskofv*, east of the ground). The medicine man, as he bubbles or blows into the medicines, prays that they will be efficacious. They are ready for use by 9:45 A.M., but are allowed to steep until perhaps 10:30. Meanwhile, a collection is taken up by the chief to pay the medicine man for his services. Before the medicine taking begins, an assistant to the medicine man dips up a quantity of the *hoyvnijv* in a dipper and

PLATE 37. *Above:* the Green
Corn paint, moistened white
clay on a grape leaf plate. *Below:*
offering medicine to the sacred
fire, about 10:30 A.M. on the
third day of the Green Corn
Ceremony. Pen and ink sketch
by Willie Lena, 1982.

circles the ground, sprinkling medicine to the right and left as he
follows his counterclockwise course. He spirals inward gradually
and what remains he pours on the sacred fire as an offering. The
men intone "*Matoooo!*" (Thanks!) as he does this.

Medicine taking and scratching of the women and children take
place next. A tub of *hoyvnijv* is taken to the east edge of the
paskofv and placed just inside the trash mound circling the
ground. Women, girls, and small uninitiated boys come here with
various containers. First they drink and wash their heads, arms,
and legs in the holy liquid a number of times. They are then
scratched if they choose, after which they wash and rinse their
mouths four times, facing east, and retire to their camps.

The scratching ceremony today is done with an ordinary steel needle, not the older implement involving several thorns or pins set in a wooden frame or bent buzzard's quill. Four scratches are made on each upper arm, four on each lower arm, and four on the back of each calf. A woman may select an elder male relative to scratch her and her children. Small children, even babes in arms, are sometimes scratched, however lightly, because the rite is considered beneficial to the health. Red licorice candy is given to small boys and girls after their scratching to produce a positive association, but even with this inducement some of the small children cannot hold back a whimper as the needle bites and the blood wells up. After they have been scratched and rinsed in water the women and children, who have been fasting since midnight, can break their fast.

It is now the men's turn to take medicine. For this part of the ceremony the medicine man and his assistant sit in the east arbor, facing west, the two containers of medicine in front of them. The members of the ground, in pairs, approach from the west and, when they reach the place where the two are sitting, kneel before them. Each communicant has a dipperful of *hoyvnijv* poured over his head. He is then handed a dipperful of *pasa*. Holding the dipper in his left hand and using the first two fingers of the right, he dips out a small amount and, with a flipping notion, sprinkles a small amount to the north, west, south, and east, an offering to the deities of each of the four cardinal points, Then, still using the same two fingers, he applies a small amount to the tongue four times in succession. He then drinks the remainder of the dipperful. He returns the dipper to the medicine man or assistant, and it is returned filled with *hoyvnijv*. Each communicant swallows an enormous draught, and perhaps a second, then rises and walks past the east arbor to the eastern limits of the ground and vomits. Men from the chief's or west arbor take medicine first; and when they have finished, men from the south arbor; and then men from the north arbor. There are no men or boys in the east arbor except for the two men dispensing the medicine. The *pasa* is administered only to initiated men, and to them only during the first episode of medicine taking, not during the last three, when only *hoyvnijv* is employed.

The scratching ceremony for men follows. The medicine man does most of this work for the men. He conducts his operation from his seat just to the left of the front center post of the west arbor, sticking his extra needles into this center post when they are not in use. The procedure in this scratching is the same as that for the women and children, except that the scratches are deeper, and some men elect to be scratched in an "X" across the chest in addition to the arms and legs.

The second session of medicine taking follows. It is the same as the first except that only the *hoyvnijv* is used, and it is limited to the initiated men. Again, it is administered in the east arbor. No cars or camps are allowed on the east side of the square ground on the third day of the Green Corn, because this area must be kept free for evil influences to depart in that direction.

Following the second session of taking medicine, names are bestowed on new members of the ground, either boys taking medicine for the first time who are sons of women of this ground, or adult males who are being adopted. Each one is called before the chief's arbor, where the chief gives him a piece of plug chewing tobacco measuring about one and a half by two by three-quarters inches. The chief then announces the person's name in English, and then the new Muskogee name twice, drawing it out the second time. The recipient of the new name now whoops twice, waving the tobacco over the heads of the chief and *heniha*. He may then, as a prayer for long life, give the plug to some old man seated in the chief's arbor. This individual will bite off a piece of the tobacco and return the remainder to the newly named person who now takes a seat in his mother's clan arbor (or in the case of adopted members of alien tribes, a seat in an arbor designated by the chief). The name given generally has some reference to the clan of the initiate. The chief records both the English name and the Muskogee name of the initiate in his record book for future reference. From this time forward, at that square ground, the individual will be known only by the Muskogee name.

The naming ceremony is followed by the first two episodes of the Feather Dance (*Tcítahaya*). A necessary preliminary to the Feather Dance is the rite known as the "calling of birds" (Plate

PLATE 38. The "feather whooper" (*tafu impehkv*) performing the ritual "calling of the birds" from atop the sacred mound just before the Feather Dance, about 11:30 A.M., third day of the Green Corn. Pen and ink sketch by Willie Lena, 1982.

38). A young man of the Bird clan, known as the *táfv impehkv* ("feather" "whooper"), carrying a short (two feet in length) wand with four white crane feathers attached to its tip, walks once around the fire in a counterclockwise direction and thence to the *tajo* or small mound at the northeast corner of the square ground. Standing atop it and facing east, he lifts the wand heavenward and cries "*Weeee!*" four times. This is to advise the various species of birds that a dance is about to be performed in their honor.

The Feather Dance is led by members of the Bird clan, who are also in charge of preparing the feathered wands used in it. These wands are generally made of native "river" cane, but can also be made of straight tree branches if a good stand of cane is not readily available. They measure about two meters in length. A thread or string is tied from the top to a point about fourteen inches farther down, and crane feathers, both white and blue (bluish-gray), are tied to this string in a rough, but not exact, alternation (Plates 39,

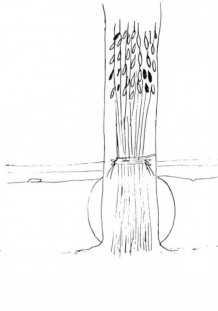

PLATE 39. *Above*: Feather Dance
wands tied to the center post of
the west arbor, third day of the
Green Corn Ceremony: *Below*:
construction detail of Feather
Dance wand. Pen and ink sketch
by Willie Lena, 1980.

40). The wands are prepared on the back bench of the chief's
arbor. When not in use, between episodes of the dance, they are
gathered into a bundle that is tied with a thong or cord to the front
post of the chief's arbor. (Plate 39).

The Feather Dance involves as many dancers as there are
feather wands, plus the three musicians. The principal singer,
usually the medicine man of the ground, carries the crock drum,
and his two assistants carry coconut shell rattles. The feather
dance is performed four times during the Green Corn, each of the
four episodes involving four circuits of the square ground. At some
grounds three episodes are danced on the third day of the ceremony, then a fourth the following morning. At most grounds, all
four episodes take place on the third day.

The dance begins with each of the dancers taking a wand from the bunch at the front of the chief's arbor and moving to form a cluster around the three musicians, who face toward the east. They wear no special costume except for the shaved crane feather stuck in the hat or cap mentioned earlier in connection with the Ribbon Dance. Most of the men, in fact, are probably wearing second-best clothing, since they are in the midst of taking medicine, which involves kneeling in the mud before the tub of *hoyvnijv* and pouring some of the medicine over their heads, and also vomiting up the medicine they have imbibed.

In the dance they hold the lower end of the feathered wand at waist level and dance in place, patting the left foot on the ground before them, drawing it back, and then patting the right foot and drawing it back, and so on. As they execute this step they also manipulate the wand, moving it back and forth at the top. The dancers sing in unison with the musicians. The head singer calls out the words "*apiu, apiu*", and all the dancers whoop. He then begins to sing. Once he has sung the key phrase and the song is recognized, all who know it join in. In spite of the shabby dress of the dancers, the Feather Dance is strangely compelling and beautiful. The swaying of the feathered wands in time with the music creates the odd illusion of a flock of small birds hovering just above the dancers' heads. The songs are quite melodic and attractive as well. Each episode has four parts, and each part employs only one song, which is sung and danced to at four stations. The first station is in front of the west arbor, the second in front of the south arbor, the third in front of the east arbor, the fourth in front of the north arbor. These locations vary from one ground to another, however, and at some grounds there is a station at the *tajo* or mound. At some grounds the dancers and singers march slowly from one station to another, intoning the cry "Hi-i-i" as long as they can hold their breath, then ending with a whoop. At others the dancers run pell mell from one station to the next. During the fourth episode the dancers do not stop at the last three stations but merely march slowly around the ground, dancing and singing.

Willie Lena says that there are only four songs for the Feather Dance, but I am certain that I have heard at least twelve different

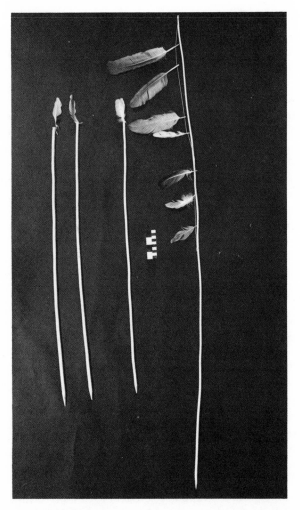

PLATE 40. Green Corn Ceremony staffs and wands. *Left to right*: staffs carried by the two "deacons" (*impuhata cukoafasta*) who escort the women in and out of the square ground in the Ribbon Dance; wand carried by the "feather whooper" (*tafu impehkv*) in the "calling of the birds" ritual that precedes the Feather Dance; and a Feather Dance wand. All items made by Willie Lena, 1980.

melodies, and Willie himself has provided different songs to make up the four on various occasions. Perhaps he means that only four songs are used for each episode. He gives the songs as follows:

1. A song composed by the blue crane (*wakułakko*).
2. A song composed by a type of snake (*aki^{n}ta*).
3. A song composed by a turkey vulture or "buzzard" (*yasuli*).
4. A song referring to all the birds circling before they fly south in the autumn. (Hence the custom of not halting at the various stations when this song is sung)

I asked Willie what a snake song was doing in a dance dedicated to birds, and he said he did not know. Swanton was told by a Tuckabahchee Creek informant that one of the songs of the Feather Dance had been learned from a summer crane.[1]

Following the first two episodes of the Feather Dance, the wands are again tied to the front post of the west arbor. Medicine is now taken for the third time. There is now a lull in the proceedings, the initiates passing the time in conversation or preparing crane feathers as hat ornaments by shaving the vane. Anyone who wishes to relieve himself is allowed to leave the square ground to do so, but must go in the company of another medicine taker, presumably to avoid any "cheating" by breaking his fast in secret and thus spoiling the medicine. Those who leave are also asked to bring back firewood on their return. This is placed on a large pile southeast of the square ground.

Two more episodes of the Feather Dance follow, preceded by the *táfv impehkv* calling the birds, and then comes the fourth session of medicine taking. The entire group now "goes to water." Led by the chief, who slowly beats the drum, the fasters form into a long file that circles the fire four times and then leaves the ground between the north and west arbors. They march in single file to a nearby creek or pond, where they wash thoroughly and then march back to the ground in the same order. To enliven the occasion, a designated man at the rear of the line will whoop, and be answered by those near him. Another whooper at the head of the line does the same, and is answered by those near him. This continues throughout the return march. This whooping contest is called, for reasons not clear to me, "stalking the deer." When all have returned to the ground and taken their seats, the chief, through his speaker or "tongue," gives a long prayer, and the group is dismissed.

Often the fasters have organized a lottery to bet on the time of dismissal, and now the lucky winner collects his prize money. Depending upon the number of men and boys taking medicine, the hour may be as early as 4:00 P.M. or as late as 5:30. The dancers are weary, sweaty, and ravenous, having fasted since the previous evening. A sumptuous repast awaits them at the camps, where the women have prepared a royal feast. There are great dishes of *apvski, sofki*, fried pork, blue dumplings, macaroni and hamburger in tomato sauce, and boiled potatoes, and great platters of fried bread, Indian bread (bannock), and biscuits, and iced tea and coffee in ample pitchers. For dessert there are pies of various kinds and sheet cakes, and bowls of fruit cocktail. When one "table" of diners has finished, the dishes are quickly removed and the table cleaned and set for another. Some of the fasters now make a quick trip to town for a shower and a change of clothing.

About 6:00 or 7:00 in the evening, depending upon how late the medicine taking continued, everyone dresses in his or her ceremonial best for the Buffalo Dance (*Yvnvsv opvnka*). This is the most colorful and dramatic feature of the Green Corn. The women dress in the same finery worn the previous day in the Ribbon Dance, but minus the ribbons. The men likewise wear the same "dress up" outfit as yesterday (western style hat with shaved crane feather and hat roach, Indian shirt with yarn sash at the waist, and perhaps a red "hunting coat," dark trousers and cowboy boots), but in addition each carries a single ballstick or a fancy carved and feather-decorated "buffalo cane." In either case, this stick or cane represents the forelegs of the bison. In the dance they lean forward on this cane to mimic bison. Willie Lena makes beautiful buffalo canes, carving a small bison hoof at the end so that the dancer using the cane leaves a path of tiny hoofprints in his wake.

Two men selected by the chief for their dancing ability lead the dance. In former times they were naked except for a breechcloth

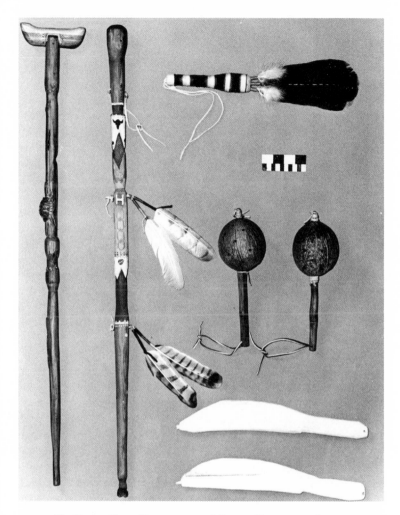

PLATE 41. Green Corn Ceremony and Stomp Dance ritual equipment. *Left*: cane of the type carried by the two officials who select leaders for the Stomp Dance; *Second from left*: Buffalo Dance cane. Such canes are carried by some male dancers in the Buffalo Dance instead of a ballstick. Both cane and ballstick represent the forelegs of a bison. Note the tiny bison hoof carved at the bottom of the cane. *Right, above*: wild-turkey-tail fan of the type formerly carried in the Horned Owl Dance. The handle is decorated with a wrapping of varicolored yarn. *Right, center*: set of coconut-shell rattles. *Right, below*: set of *atassa* or war club knives of the type carried by the two leading matrons in the Sun or Ribbon Dance. All items made by Willie Lena, 1965–80.

and wore headdresses made of bison scalps with horns.[2] Today
they dress like other male dancers, except they they wear a face
painting consisting of three or four horizontal lines of red paint on
either cheek. They are followed by a pair of women wearing leg
rattles, then a second pair of male dancers known as *yvnvsv
impehkv* ("buffalo," "whoopers"), then another pair of women
with leg rattles, another pair of men, and so on. On musical cue
the leading dancers cry out "*Whe, whe, yo, yo,*" bend low, shake
their heads, and turn to the right or left, imitating bison bulls. As
they do this, the whoopers lead the male dancers in a series of
piercing yells. This is repeated at intervals as the dance continues.

The Buffalo Dance begins at the *tajo* or mound at the northeast
corner of the ground. The singer stands on it and beats a rapid
flurry on the drum. He then begins the characteristic song of the
dance to a steady beat and the dancers, two by two, begin circling
the mound in a counterclockwise progression. Their step, both
men and women, is a double pat of the left foot followed by a
double pat of the right. Often the tremendous noise of the
women's leg rattles accentuating this duple beat and the whooping
of the dancers almost drowns out the singer. When all of the
dancers are formed into a great, milling spiral around the mound,
the singer, moving ahead of the dancers and walking showly
backwards, reverses the line of direction and uncoils the spiral into
a straight line, leading the dancers into the square ground and
around the fire in a counterclockwise spiral until another great
pinwheel of stamping, whooping "buffalo" is massed there. He
then unwinds the coil again and leads them out to the pole
used in the single pole ball game. This movement is called
nanopkv apiitv ("pasture" "going-to"). Here he coils them into a
counterclockwise spiral again, and the dance ends in a rapid
milling around the pole.

The Creek-Seminole Buffalo Dance is, in my opinion, one of
the most colorful and exciting American Indian music and dance
events in North America. The insistent duple beat of the shell
shakers punctuated by the "bellowing" of the "buffalo bulls" and
the juggernaut-like progression of the dancers, raising great clouds
of dust, is incomparable.

PLATE 42. An Oklahoma Seminole man dancing the Buffalo Dance.
Watercolor by Willie Lena, 1982.

PLATE 43. An Oklahoma Seminole man attired for the Buffalo Dance. Note the characteristic red face painting customarily worn by the two leading male dancers. Watercolor by Willie Lena, 1965.

PLATE 44. Oklahoma Seminole man's Buffalo Dance or "Red stick" coat. Maker unknown. Purchased in Shawnee, Oklahoma, 1971.

When the last Buffalo Dance song ends, the dancers maintain their positions around the ball pole. The male dancers pass their ballsticks or buffalo canes to friends who are not dancing. The pairs of men and women now form into a single file, one man, one woman, and so on, for a performance of the Long Dance (*opvnka capko*). The leader of this dance, which will be described in the next chapter, leads the dancers into the square ground and around

PLATE 45. Oklahoma Seminole male finery and protective medicines. *Top*: beaded sash with yarn ends and tassels. Made by Lucinda Johnson, Creek and Seminole, of Shawnee, Oklahoma, 1974. *Second from top*: loom-woven yarn sash. Made by Kennedy Wise, Seminole of Holdenville, Oklahoma, 1980. *Bottom, left to right*: owl-foot necklace worn by a man to ward off witchcraft when he is in a crowd; set of german silver gorgets with neck chain. Made by Woodrow Haney, Seminole, of Seminole, Oklahoma, 1977; protective medicine. *Hʃlʃs hvtki* (*Solanum nigrum* L.), tied in a buckskin disk and equipped with a buckskin neck cord. This and the owl-foot necklace were made by Willie Lena, 1981.

PLATE 46. Oklahoma Seminole men's hat ornaments. *Top*: loom-beaded hatband with gourd-stitch slide at the side. *Bottom, left to right*: a "trembler" hat ornament with spring base designed to make the ornament rock back and forth with the slightest movement of the wearer's head, Creek or Seminole, maker unknown, purchased in Tulsa, Oklahoma, 1971; a shaved crane-feather hat ornament, emblematic of participation in the Green Corn, made by Willie Lena, 1971; a "spinner" hat ornament, designed so that the feather gyrates wildly in the slightest breeze, made by Willie Lena, 1971.

151

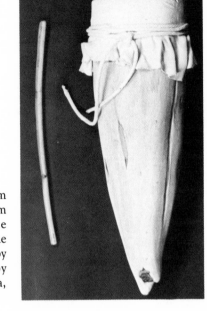

PLATE 47. Cypress-knee drum and drumstick. This type of drum became obsolete among the Creeks and Seminoles about the turn of the century. Drumstick by Willie Lena, 1968, drum by James Howard and Willie Lena, 1981.

the fire in a counterclockwise circuit. When he finishes the Long Dance songs he immediately leads one round of Stomp dance (*opvnka hajo*), and the dancing ends. The dancers and spectators now disperse to the various camps to partake of a second magnificent evening meal. This ends the formal "daytime" activities of the third day of the Green Corn.

A final night of Stomp Dances, with other social dances intermingled, begins at 9:00 or 10:00 P.M. and does not end until the following morning well after sunup (about 7:30 A.M.), which is the fourth and final day of the Green Corn. No matter how drowsy they become, members of the local square ground are not allowed to sleep at any time during the night. The Stomp Dancing ends with a final performance of the Long Dance. The male members of the ground now "take medicine" for the last time, after which they "go to water." When they return they are dismissed by the chief in a final prayer and address.

A single pole ball game usually takes place about 8:00 o'clock the morning of the fourth day. Players and spectators are called to breakfast about 8:30 or 9:00 A.M. After breakfast the group begins to break camp, and the Green Corn is over for another year.

COMMENTARY

The above is, I believe, the most complete and accurate account of an Oklahoma Seminole Green Corn to appear in print. There are minor differences from one ground to another. At Gar Creek, for example, the sacrifice of the four perfect ears of new corn takes place at 12:30 P.M., and each of the four ears is stored in the willow brush covering of one of the four arbors before being put in the fire. At the same time, a beef tongue is sacrificed to the fire. Likewise at Gar Creek there is a fifth and final session of medicine taking at 12:00 midnight on the third day. It is my impression, and Willie's contention, that there are no major differences between Oklahoma Seminole and Creek Green Corn practices. There are many differences, however, between the Oklahoma form and that described for the Florida Seminoles.[3] In Florida the ceremony lasts seven instead of four days, and has retained more of its ancient juridical and political functions, as exemplified by the "big noon meeting" on Court Day, the fifth day of the ceremony. The Feather Dance, an annual feature in Oklahoma, can be omitted three out of four years in Florida, the Buffalo Dance appears to be a much less formal affair, and the women's Ribbon Dance is not mentioned at all. The most salient difference, however, is the fact that the display of a medicine bundle, a necessary accompaniment to a Florida Green Corn, is totally absent in Oklahoma.

When I asked Willie about this lack of medicine bundles as a Green Corn feature, he said that although the Oklahoma Seminoles no longer employ bundles in this way, he believed that they had done so in his grandfather's time, that is, as late as the 1920s. Willie stated, in fact, that his grandfather had kept such a medicine bundle, and he himself was quite familiar with its contents.

The usual Oklahoma Seminole name for these portable shrines is *sukca tvpiks* ("bag," "flat"). His grandfather's bundle consisted

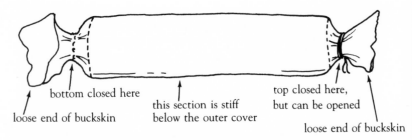

bottom closed here

loose end of buckskin

this section is stiff
below the outer cover

top closed here,
but can be opened

loose end of buckskin

FIGURE 6. An Oklahoma Seminole sacred bundle.

of a piece of heavy buffalo rawhide rolled into a cylinder which in turn was wrapped in a buckskin covering and tied shut at either end. The tie was loosened at one end when it was necessary to remove the contents. Willie sketched the bundle (figure 6). In every such bundle, among the Oklahoma Seminoles, certain items were invariably included. There were:

1. Four pieces of *hoyvnijv* (*Salix humilis*).
2. A supply of ground charcoal to be used as face paint by warriors.
3. A supply of *fuki cati* ("face-paint," "red") probably vermilion powder, also used as face paint by warriors.
4. A number of pieces of *citto hflfsaw*, also known as *citto yvpfsawaka* ("snake," "medicine"; "snake," "antlers"), fragments of the horns of the Giant horned snake, as described in Chapter 4.
5. A supply of *mabilanoji* (*Polytaenia nuttalli* DC., Prairie parsley), the Seminole war or wound medicine.

Copies of several old treaties between the Seminoles and the United States government were also stored in his grandfather's bundle, but Willie was uncertain whether this was a standard feature. From Willie's description of the bundle, it would appear to be of the type known as a "war bundle" or "war bag" to midwestern tribes such as the Sauks, Potawatomis, and Shawnees, though it lacks the warclub or tomahawk usually found in these bundles. I asked Willie if any stones, such as the various types mentioned by Capron for the Florida bundles were known to him.[4] He mentioned that "thunder stones" (probably small meteorites) were regarded as powerful personal medicines by the

PLATE 48. An Oklahoma Seminole medicine man carrying his medicine bundle. Pen and ink sketch by Willie Lena, 1982.

Oklahoma people, but that they were not, so far as he knew, a part of the contents of his grandfather's sacred bundle or any other Oklahoma bundle that he knew of.

Another type of medicine bundle is simply an elongated buckskin pouch with a shoulder strap attached. It is used by the medicine man to carry the various herbs that he uses in curing, and other items such as his sucking horn and flint knife. This type of bundle appears in two of Willie's sketches, one of the medicine man praying over the four ears of corn that are to be sacrificed to the sacred fire during the Green Corn (plate 34), and one a portrait of an old-time Seminole doctor (plate 48). A related type was merely carried in the hand by the doctor when he was gathering herbal medicines. Willie made models for me of both of these doctor's bundles in 1981. He also gave me an ancient "little brown bag" of the type used by white physicians in the late nineteenth century, saying that it had been used by a Creek medicine man of Tulsa square ground named Paskofa Washington in the early years of this century. Paskofa had passed it on to Netche Gray, the famous Creek singer and ritualist, and when Netche died, it had been passed on to Willie.

Although the Oklahoma Seminoles have not used sacred bundles in connection with their Green Corn Ceremony for many years, some Creek square grounds have done so. Ira Bird Creek, a Creek Indian of Shawnee, Oklahoma, said that he has attended Creek Green Corns where the chief, in his concluding prayer and address to the members of the ground, said repeatedly "Our bundle is here. Now our bundle is pleased with our efforts. Now when we have finished we will take away our bundle." One square ground specifically mentioned by Ira as having a bundle is Muddy Water or *Wiogufki*, an Upper Creek ground located four miles west of Hanna, Oklahoma. The contents of this bundle included a red painted warclub, which was carried in this town's Buffalo Dance. Ira's description of this dance sounded more like the Shawnee *Hileni wekawe* or War Dance than like the usual Creek-Seminole Buffalo Dance as we have described it in this chapter.[5] Certain other Creek towns also had the same dance and an associated bundle, Ira said, but the dance has now lapsed because no singers remain who know the songs. The above data demonstrate, I believe, that the close association of sacred bundles with the Green Corn Ceremony among the Florida Seminoles is an old Muskhogean complex, not a phenomenon post-dating the Seminole wars and the Removal.

When I asked various Oklahoma Creek and Seminole town chiefs, who prefer to remain nameless, why the sacred bundles, which were once so important to their worship, had been given up, they invariably replied with words to the effect that it is the Green Corn Ceremony itself that contains the purifying and healing power, consequently the bundles are not considered necessary.

CEREMONIALISM:
THE NIGHTTIME DANCES

Except for the dances performed during the Green Corn Ceremony and the players' dance around the goal preceding and
following the match ball game, most Oklahoma Seminole dancing
takes place at night. A night of dancing occurs each of the first
three nights of the Green Corn, likewise on the night preceding a
match ball game. An all-night dance also opens the ceremonial
season each spring and closes it in the fall, and such dances occur
at monthly intervals after the opening dance and before the Green
Corn. In English, these all-night dances are called Stomp Dances.

The term Stomp Dance is used in two senses by Woodland
Indians in Oklahoma. In the first sense it refers to the entire
sequence of nighttime dances performed at a square ground. Thus
a square ground is often referred to, in English, as a "Stomp
ground." In the second, more limited, sense the term refers to a
particular dance form, *the* Stomp Dance, which is the most
popular and often-performed dance at these gatherings. In the
Muskogee tongue it is called *Opvnka hajo* ("dance," "crazy,
berserk, devil-may-care") or *Satkita opvnka* ("common,"
"dance"). All of the Northeastern and Southeastern tribes now
resident in Oklahoma except for the Choctaws have the specific
form of dance known as the Stomp, but the Seminoles and Creeks
are acknowledged by all to be its most expert practitioners. To say

that it is their favorite dance is a gross understatement—they dote on it, embrace it, are endlessly fascinated by it, and elevate it above all others. Good "stomp leaders" have a status comparable to that of rock stars or baseball heroes in the major culture and are known throughout the tribe and even throughout the state in those tribes that share the dance.

I will therefore begin my account of the nighttime dances with a description of this dance and its characteristic antiphonal music, which is produced by the dancers themselves. At some nighttime dances, in fact, it is the *only* form danced, the members of the ground becoming so engrossed in its performance that they apparently forget to include performances of the other nighttime dances of the tribe. To begin a night of Stomp Dancing the chief directs that two young men build a fire in the center of the ground. This is not done ceremonially except at Green Corn time. He also directs his speaker to summon the people to the ground, which the speaker does at half-hour intervals, beginning at 7:00 P. M., then again at 7:30, 8:00, and 8:30. By shortly before 9:00 o'clock, all is in readiness. Two more officials, each carrying a cane and a flashlight as a symbol of his office, are appointed to select the leaders throughout the night. They do this one dance ahead each time, so that the leader chosen can prepare himself and collect his assistants and shell-shaker girls.

To begin an episode or "lead" of the *Opvnka hajo* the man selected, followed by his male assistants, generally three in number, enters the *paskofv* from one corner and begins to walk around the fire in a counterclockwise direction. He is not dancing, just walking. Other experienced male dancers who can "answer" Stomp Dance songs now separate themselves from the crowd of spectators outside the square or rise from their benches in the arbors inside it and fall in at the end of the file. When a few men have joined and "broken the ice" women and girls also join and soon a long file of dancers, men and women interspersed, are walking slowly around the fire. Inexperienced dancers and small fry join at the end of the line. It is considered bad form to crowd in at the head of the line after it has formed, and particularly poor etiquette to take a place between the leader and his first, second, or third follower. After glancing over his shoulder to determine that sufficient dancers have joined in to make a good showing (at least fifteen or twenty) the leader begins his introduction. This is a low, throaty shout "Yu-woooooo!" to which the men and boys in the line following answer in unison with a cry "Yu-woooo; Hi!" The leader then shouts another introductory vocable, and is answered, and still another. When he comes to the vocable "Hehie," he begins the cadenced shuffling trot or "stomping" which is the basic step of the dance, followed by the other dancers.

Before his introductory songs are completed, another important functionary emerges from the crowd and takes her place directly behind the leader, pushing in between him and the man following. This is the shell-shaker girl, who provides most of the rhythmic accompaniment for the dance. Often she is the wife or teenage daughter of the leader, though not invariably. On the outside of her calves she wears the traditional "shells" or leg rattles from which the shell-shaker girl takes her name, described in the previous chapter. By a skillful combination of toe and heel action she produces the characteristic duple beat of the dance, which might be rendered "Ch-ch, ch-ch, ch-ch," and which can easily be heard above the singing of the dancers. If more than one shell-shaker girl joins the dance, as is usually the case, the additional females space themselves behind the second, third, and fourth men in the line, the sexes alternating.

Once the shell shakers have joined the dance, the leader has nearly finished his introductory songs or shouts. Now he begins with what might be termed the Stomp songs proper. Formerly, according to some older informants, these songs followed one another in a prescribed sequence, but this is no longer the case. Most leaders simply string together a sequence of their favorite songs, ones known to be familiar to their seconds, who must be able to answer them with the appropriate musical phrase.

The usual pattern of these songs is a short phrase, rather low in pitch, with an equally low-pitched but somewhat shorter answering phrase. This is repeated two or three times. Then the same phrase, or a different one, is sung at a higher pitch, and is echoed by a higher pitched answer. There is then a slightly lower pitched lead phrase and answer. These last two phrases and their answers may be repeated, after which the leader returns to his original low pitched phrase, and so on. Several such short antiphonal songs make up a "lead" or episode of the dance. Some leaders signal the end of each short song with a cry of "Whii!" Others touch the front of their hat brim. Most simply pause slightly and go immediately into the next song.

Often the pattern of the dance is unvaried—a mere shuffling trot in a counterclockwise direction, flat foot left followed by flat right in quick succession. Once the dance is well underway, however, some leaders introduce variations in both step and figure. For example, on the second or third song the leader usually turns ninety degrees to the left, facing the fire, and side steps to the right, at the same time holding his arms out over the fire, and waves his hands and arms up and down as if performing a gesture of supplication (which, indeed, this movement probably was at an earlier time). Apparently all of the male dancers are supposed to follow him in this, though only a few at the head of the line actually do so. Again a leader, when he has really "warmed up," may remove his hat and wave it from side to side over his head, rock back on his heels, and tread in place or even back up for a short interval. If he is in a gay mood he may wind the entire line of dancers into a tight serpentine coil, then reverse and uncoil again, or even lead the dancers out of the *paskofv* to the ball pole and end the dance there, though this variation is more common with Cherokee than with Seminole and Creek leaders.

To end the dance, the leader sometimes uses a set of short songs or shouts much like the introduction, gradually speeding up the tempo to indicate that the conclusion is near. Finally, having built up the speed to a furious climax, he raises his right arm high above his head and with a sharp cry "Whiii!" concludes the performance. Sometimes, anticipating the ending, he has wound the whole group into a tight spiral of moving bodies and dust. With the end of the episode the dancers drift to their seats for a breather before the next leader and his assistants take the center of the square for another ten or fifteen minutes of action.

No less important than the leader is his shell-shaker girl. A good leader, it is said, is nothing without a good shell shaker. Her ability to match the rhythm of her shells to the tempo of the leader's songs is almost uncanny. She can produce a sound similar to a drum roll when it is required, then quickly change to a fast duple beat. To punctuate the end of each short song she may hop adroitly to produce a sharp triplet. Though always a "girl," some of these women are in their fifties and sixties. They nevertheless manage to dance through the night with only a short break now and then.

No special costume is required for the Stomp Dance for either sex. A leader sometimes wears a hat roach at the back of his western style hat, a felt or patchwork vest over his skirt, and perhaps a yarn sash with large tassels at the ends which hang to well below his knees on either side. Levis and cowboy boots complete his costume. Women usually wear a sleeveless blouse and a fairly short, very full skirt to accommodate the leg rattles. A shell-shaker girl may wear a yarn sash as well, but with tasseled ends on the right side only. Tennis shoes or other "flats" are the preferred footwear.

Today the Stomp Dance, using the term now in its more extended sense, is quite secularized, but to dismiss the nighttime dances as mere "drunken frolics," as has been done by local whites and the native Christian element, is a gross misrepresentation. Even today, certain ritual acts accompany the first and last dances of the season—at the first, an offering of meat to the sacred fire (Plate 49), and at the last, at some grounds, the preparation of a ritual kettle of soup. At some grounds medicine (*hoyvnija*) is taken at the last dance as well. At all dances the sacred center fire is the focal point of the dances. Drinking has been a problem at the dances in the past, but at all Seminole and Creek dances I have attended, the inebriates, if their condition is at all apparent, are quickly hustled out of the gate and warned to stay away or be jailed. Not too many years ago more draconian measures were employed. A Ponca friend told me of showing up at a Seminole dance in a drunken condition and spending the remainder of the night chained to a large tree.

The two officers who select the dance leaders also serve to maintain order. Each dance leader, after being selected, is an-

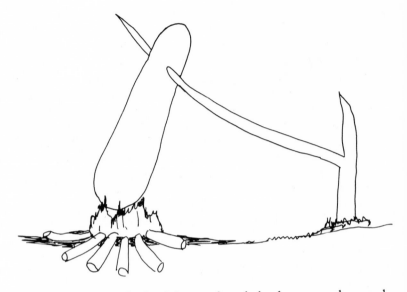

PLATE 49. "Feeding the fire," the sacrifice of a beef tongue to the sacred fire that is kindled on the occasion of the first Stomp Dance of the season, and at some grounds during the Green Corn. Pen and ink sketch by Willie Lena, 1982.

nounced by one or the other of these men, using the rapid, staccato delivery of formal Muskogee oratory: "We have a good leader for you. Now get out there and help him!" Then, after his "lead," the man is thanked by the entire group intoning "*Mato-o-o*" ("thank you") in unison.

In the 1920s the Stomp Dance, as I have described it above, spread beyond the limits of that part of Oklahoma settled by the eastern tribes and was adopted by such prairie groups as the Quapaws, Poncas, Otoes and Pawnees. It remained popular for a number of years as a late-night, post powwow feature, and good leaders and shell shakers developed among these borrowing tribes. The popularity of the Stomp Dance has waned in most of these groups in recent years, though the Quapaws and Otoes still have Stomp Dance leading and shell-shaking contests in connection

PLATE 50. A Stomp Dance episode, Seminole Nation Days, Seminole, Oklahoma, 1980. Photograph by James Howard.

with their annual powwows, with large cash prizes offered. Seminoles and Creeks resent this popularization and commercialization of the Stomp Dance. To them, although the dance may not be religious in the same sense as the Feather Dance, Ribbon Dance, and Buffalo Dance of the Green Corn, it still has definite ceremonial overtones. Thus, at a Seminole or Creek square ground, visitors may be excused if they arrive late and leave sometime before dawn. Members of the local ground, however, are expected to dance enthusiastically throughout the night. At the Stomp Dance that follows the third day of the Green Corn, male members of the host ground constantly watch one another for signs of sleepiness, and awaken, not too gently, any member who has yielded to fatigue and dozed off in his seat. More than any other dance, then, the Stomp Dance or *Opvnka hajo* might be termed the national dance of the Seminoles and Creeks.

PLATE 51. James Milam, Seminole chief, dressed for the dance. Seminole Nation Days, Seminole, Oklahoma, 1980. Photograph by James Howard.

Most Stomp Dance songs are merely strings of vocables or "burden" syllables. Some, though, do have meaningful texts. These range from the warlike to the amorous, and from the tragedy of the Trail of Tears to the obscene.[1] Two examples of humorous song texts are these, provided by Willie Lena:

LEADER:	ANSWER:	
Wahiawahiie (vocables)	*Hiawahiie* (vocables)	
Pʃncacahoka "a turkey gobbler"	"	"
Hopoiipaya·tie "I am looking for"	"	"
Fvnika calʃskan "Put it on my shoulder"	"	"
Ankaska neekʃn "shot" "one"	"	"
Tvpockv hankan "musket" "shotgun"	"	"
Ilijayati "killing"	"	"
Sulʃomtʃn "a turkey vulture"	"	"
Capozi caha·ni "Grandmother" "scolding me"	"	"

In summary, the text tells of a young boy being sent to hunt wild turkeys with an old single-shot shotgun. He sees and kills what he thinks is a fine turkey gobbler, but when he carries it home, his grandmother tells him that he has brought home a turkey *vulture*, and scolds him for his stupidity.

Another humorous song, employing the same tune as the former, Willie called a "spring song":

LEADER:	ANSWER:
Wahiawahiie (vocables)	*Hiawahiie* (vocables)
Fvtcakozi "a little dog"	" "
Cvpiyʃcv "I play with it"	" "
Fuslanoji "a little yellow bird"	" "
Yvhoko·f "starts to sing"	" "
Tvzikoskowi "a big striped squash"	" "
Lokce jen "I planted and it is already ripe"	" "

A very popular "word song" at the present time is said to have been borrowed from the Yuchis by the Creeks and Seminoles, who then added Muskogee words:

LEADER:	ANSWER:
Hvmakimata "That man used to say this"	*Hvmakatca* "Say it again"

This is repeated several times, and then on a higher pitch:

Calipatites "After I die (this dance will continue)"	*Hvmakatca* "Say it again"

This song, emphasizing the continuity of the Stomp Dance through the generations, has great symbolic value for present-day Seminoles and Creeks.

OTHER DANCES

At an all-night dance, other dances may be introduced between the Stomp Dance episodes from time to time, to add variety.

Generally this is done only when a large number of experienced leaders are present. Seminole dances I have observed, or which were described to me by Willie Lena, that belong in this category are the following:

Bean Dance (Tvlako opvnka)

The Creek-Seminole Bean Dance has one leader, who is also the principal singer. Men and women form a long line, the leader at the head. Immediately behind the leader, who is always a man, is a woman, then a man, then another woman, and so on. Each person holds hands with the individual just in front and just behind. The leader carries a coconut-shell rattle in his right hand. To begin the dance he holds the rattle over his head and vibrates it, then brings it down to waist level and begins to shake it in a regular loud-soft rhythm, at the same time starting to sing. When he has sung the introductory phrase, the entire file behind him answers with the refrain. The step of this dance is simply a slow walk. At first the dance is merely a counterclockwise progression around the fire, but as the dance progresses the leader takes the group in and out of spirals "like bean vines growing."

This dance is a cognate of the Shawnee Moving Dance, also known as the Corn or Bean Dance;[2] the Iroquois Corn or Bean Dance; the Delaware Bean Dance; and the Caddo Bell Dance. The Seminole and Creek Bean Dance songs are somewhat similar to those of these other tribes.

Buzzard Dance (Suli opvnka)

This dance, long obsolete, was in honor of the turkey buzzard (vulture). Willie Lena mentioned that the dancers moved their arms in imitation of the vulture's flight (Plate 52). At one point the women hopped in place. One song, he said, went like this: "*Talatanawe, talatanawe.*" Another had the words: "*Haliwohale, haliwohale*" At the end of the song the singer pretended to vomit, like a vulture, at the same time intoning: "*Yaaaah!*"

PLATE 52. The Buzzard Dance.
Pen and ink sketch by Willie
Lena, 1982.

Cow Dance (Wak opvnka)

This dance is also obsolete. Willie recalled seeing it performed at a
Creek dance ground in 1926. As he remembered, the dancers
formed into a double file of pairs, two men, then two women, etc,
and moved about the fire in a counterclockwise progression. At a
certain point in the song they jumped in a characteristic fashion.

Doublehead Dance (Ka-hokkoli opvnka)

This dance is still performed. There are three figures. The dance
requires two leaders, each of whom carries a coconut-shell rattle.

Two ranks of dancers form on the east side of the fire; one of
men, the rank closest to the fire, the other of women. Both ranks
face the fire. The dance begins with the two ranks dancing toward
the fire. When the men's rank is almost at the fire, both ranks
reverse and dance away from it, still keeping in their ranks. This
movement is repeated four times.

The second figure has two files, each composed of men and
women alternating, one moving clockwise and the other counterclockwise. Each file is led by a man who carries a coconut-shell

rattle and sings. Only one of the leaders sings at a time. It is from this feature that the name "doublehead" derives. The two files circle and pass each other four times.

In the third figure the dancers form a double file, with men and women alternating. Two men, facing forward, head the file. They are followed by two women, then two men, etc. The file dances counterclockwise around the fire, finally winding into a tight coil at one corner of the ground to end the dance.

The dance is described by Swanton in much the same manner.[3] A dance called "Doublehead" is, or once was, known to the Alabamas, Koasatis, Tunicas, Biloxis, Choctaws, and Chickasaws. The Choctaw and Chickasaw Doublehead, however, is entirely different from the Creek and Seminole dance, and this may be true of the others as well. The Doublehead Dance apparently was not known outside the Southeastern culture area.

Duck Dance (Fuco opvnka)

This dance is still performed. There is one principal singer for the Duck Dance, who accompanies himself with a coconut-shell rattle. He stands east of the fire. The male dancers, formed in a double file, each man paired with another, stand to his south at the beginning of the dance, facing north. The women, also in a double file of pairs, are to his north, facing south. As he begins to sing, both groups tread in place, using a toe-heel left, toe-heel right step. When the singer intones the musical cue "*Yakole ha!*" and raises his rattle over his head, the two double files move forward, and the pairs at the head of each dance opposite each other briefly and then pass, quacking like ducks as they do so. On the next cue the first pair passes the second pair of the opposite sex, and so on. This passing and quacking continues until all of the pairs of men and women have danced before and passed each other.

Now the male and female double files begin to circle the fire in opposite directions, the men moving counterclockwise. As they pass, west of the fire, the men form a bridge with their arms and the women "duck" under it, still dancing. The two double files meet again before the singer east of the fire and the men take up a certain chant in counterpoint to his song as they reach this point. The singer now begins another song, and the entire sequence of passing and quacking by separate pairs and the circling west of the fire and passing under the bridge of arms is repeated. Four such episodes complete the dance. Swanton describes the dance in much the same way.[4] The Choctaw Duck Dance is a cognate of the Seminole and Creek form.

Four Corner Dance (Kvnawa opvnka)

This dance is still performed on occasion. Men and women form a long file, holding hands. The leader, a man carrying a coconut-shell rattle, sings and takes the group in a counterclockwise direction, using a simple walking step. When he reaches the east side of the square ground he gradually winds the group into a tight spiral, like a watchspring. His song is: "*Wehe yahaiyo-o*" and the answer, sung in unison by those following him, is "*wehe yahaiyo, wehe yahaiyo.*" This is repeated over and over. When the group is tightly coiled the leader sings "*oho oho,*" reverses and uncoils the spiral using the first song again. When the line is straightened out he leads the group to the north side of the ground, where he coils and uncoils the group as before, and then does the same at the west and south sides of the ground—hence the name "Four Corner Dance." The dance ends at the south side.

The dance is performed in honor of the four Giant Horned Snakes that reside at the four corners of the world, and the coiling and uncoiling of the line of dancers represents the coiling and uncoiling of snakes. The song for this dance is unusually haunting and beautiful, and has been adopted as an ordinary Stomp Dance song by the Cherokees, Oklahoma Seneca-Cayugas, Quapaws, and other groups in northeastern Oklahoma, though not by the Seminoles and Creeks.

Willie Lena says that when the leader has the entire group wound into a coil he may flirt with the shell-shaker girl immediately behind him by singing: "*ʃkucifani cimopapipɛn nocoyaketi*" ("my elbow" "lay your head upon it").

Fox Dance (Culv opvnka)

This is a dance for women alone. All of the dancers wear leg rattles. Two male singers, one with a drum and one with a coconut-shell rattle, stand east of the center fire. The women, in single file, enter the ground from the southeast corner, following one of their number who is designated their leader, as in the Ribbon Dance. They dance around the square in a counterclockwise direction, and when they have reached a point in front of the chief's arbor on the west, the main singer nudges his assistant. The assistant raises his rattle over his head and this is the signal for the women to put their hands on their hips, turn ninety degrees to the left, facing the fire, and hop on both feet. They complete their circuit of the ground using this hopping step. There are four songs for the Fox Dance, one for each circuit.

The Fox Dance is now obsolete among the Oklahoma Seminoles, though Willie Lena speaks of reviving it with his sister as head dancer. He knows three of the four songs pertaining to the dance. The Fox Dance is still performed, I am told, by the ultra-conservative Creeks at Hilibi square ground.

Swanton supplies information regarding the dance not mentioned by my informants:

> Before the fox dance was held two men went all around the grounds to drive the dogs away, for, if any dogs should come in or any men except the two musicians, it would be unlucky. The two musicians, a drummer and a rattler, sat near the fire and did all of the singing. One of the women acted as leader of the dancers and they went around the fire in sinistral circuit. The dance began slowly and increased in rapidity until it became very fast at the end. The two "dogwhippers" were provided with long sticks with needles, gar teeth, or crawfish claws at the ends, and, if a woman was slow or lazy in dancing, they reached these out and scratched her ankles. Sometimes old women performed this function. . . .[5]

Friendship or Love Dance (A·nokʃcka)

This dance is still performed. The men form a single file east of the fire, the women another just west of the men. Both files face

north. There is one principal singer, a man, who carries a coconut-shell rattle. He sings one song to begin the dance, the dancers
simply treading in place. On the second song the two files meld,
the women inserting themselves between the men, and all join
hands. The leader, the principal singer, now takes the group in a
counterclockwise but somewhat serpentine circuit of the ground,
and sometimes leads them out of the *paskofv*, around the ball pole
and soda pop stand, then back into the dance ground again,
winding the group into a counterclockwise spiral to end the dance.
The dancers answer, in unison, the song phrases of the leader.

According to Willie Lena this dance is "almost the same" as the
Cherokee Friendship Dance. However, it lacks the sexual
familiarity described for the Friendship Dance as performed by the
Eastern Cherokees.[6]

Garfish Dance (Isapa opvnka)

This dance is still performed. There is one singer, who accompanies himself with a drum. The men start the dance, formed in a
single file. They begin dancing in a counterclockwise progression,
using a toe-heel left, toe-heel right, step. Soon a file of women
joins them, the head of the women's file directly behind the last
person in the men's file. The first song of the dance has the leader
intoning: "*We, hayone,*" to which the men answer: "*We-e,
hayone.*" This is repeated several times. Then the singer cries:
"*Yahule ho!*" At this signal the last man in the men's file turns and
grabs the first woman around the waist and swings her around in
place one time, as in the quadrille. After he has "swung his
partner" she moves up one place, between him and the next-to-
last man. The dance now continues as before until the next cry of
"*Yahule ho!*" when the last two men swing the first two women.
The dance proceeds in this manner, the women moving up one
place after each "swing," until finally the leader of the women's
file has been swung around by the leader of the men's file. At this
point all of the dancers join hands and circle the fire four times.
The dance usually ends with one round of Stomp Dance (*Opvnka
hajo*).

Some singers introduce other song texts as the dance progresses, referring to "old garfish," "good to eat," or other appropriate items. In 1981, at Cedar River Tulsa square ground I saw the dance performed in a different manner by the Creeks there. The singer and dance leader, Ollie Tiger, accompanied himself with a coconut-shell rattle. The dancers joined hands at the beginning of the dance and he led them in an eccentric pattern around the ground, winding them into tight spirals, then unwinding them again, as in the Friendship Dance. The songs, however, were clearly Garfish songs, though the cry "*Yahule ho!*" was omitted and there was no swinging of partners. This dance, and its accompanying songs, are both similar to the Chickasaw Garfish or "Hard Fish" Dance, though not identical in either choreography or music.

Guinea Dance (Kowʃk opvnka)

This dance is still performed, though rarely. Either one or two singers provide the music. One carries a coconut-shell rattle. Men and women, in couples, form a double file facing north on the east side of the fire. The couples hold hands in the "skater's embrace." The step is a toe-heel left, toe-heel right, around the fire in a counterclockwise progression.

Horse Dance (Coɫakko opvnka)

This dance has been obsolete for many years. Willie Lena knew only that the dancers imitated horses and that they even kicked one another in the manner of horses, which eventually led to its being banned. Fortunately, Swanton was able to secure a good description of the dance from his informants:

> The music was furnished by two drummers near the fire—or some-times by only one. They drummed and sang. The men danced in two bands and in single file. The two came from opposite sides of the fire, one from the south, we will say, circling sinistrally outside, and the other, from the north, circling dextrally inside. As the two lines passed, the men would kick out at each other like horses. Meantime

the women were standing on the outside, each holding a handkerchief by one end, and the second time around each man seized the end of a handkerchief and danced around, the woman following him dancing, until they had danced four times in all. Then all went back to their places and the same thing was repeated three times more, four in all. The Mikasuki horse dance was practically the same except that there was no drummer and but one rattler. There were two songs.[7]

Long Dance (Opvnka capko)

The Long Dance is the most highly respected dance of the Seminoles and Creeks. It is always performed immediately after the women's Ribbon Dance on the second day of the Green Corn, likewise immediately after the Buffalo Dance on the third day of the same ceremony. It is often performed immediately after the Mother Dance at the beginning of the all-night dance that follows the third day of the Green Corn. It is also performed as the penultimate dance of every all-night Stomp Dance. The Long Dance itself is always followed by at least one episode of the Stomp Dance (Opvnka hajo), led by the same person who led the Long Dance.

The Long Dance requires one singer, who is also the lead dancer. In addition, there is one chief whooper. The dancers form a long file to begin the dance, the leader-singer at the head, then a shell-shaker girl, then the chief whooper, then another shell shaker, and men and women continue in alternation to the end of the file.

A characteristic feature of the music of this dance is the prolonged undulating call by the leader at the beginning of each song, immediately followed by four barking antiphonal whoops, initiated by the chief whooper and answered by the men behind him. The dancers merely walk quietly during this portion of the song, dancing hard only when the song settles into the antiphonal call-response pattern. During the first part of the song the leader turns half left in his dancing and extends his right arm, and during the second part he turns half right and extends his left arm. At the end of each short song the dancers revert to the quiet walking progression.

A performance of the Long Dance is always impressive, with its dignified, deliberate progression, its whoops, and its continual starts and stops. The attitude of the dancers is one of intense concentration. The round of Stomp Dance which follows it, on the other hand, is usually the occasion for considerable horseplay by the male dancers, who often punctuate their antics by rendering the famous turkey-gobble war whoop.

At some square grounds the Long Dance that follows the Ribbon Dance is begun at the ball pole used in the single pole ball game. The Long Dance episode that follows the Buffalo Dance usually begins here as well, since this is where the Buffalo Dance has just ended. At other grounds the Buffalo Dance begins and ends at the *tajo* or mound at the northeast corner of the ground, hence the Long Dance begins here. The Long Dance episode that ends the all-night Stomp Dance, however, begins near the center fire.

Morning Dance (Hvthiyvtki opvnka) or Drunken Dance (Hajo opvnka)

This dance, at the present time, is performed only as the last dance episode at the Soup Dance, the last all-night dance of the year at a Seminole or Creek square ground. The first name of the dance derives from the time of the dance's performance, after sunrise following a night of Stomp Dance episodes. The second name, Drunken Dance, refers not so much to the actual inebriation of the dancers as to the high pitch of excitement of the performers.[8]

One man sings for the dance, accompanying himself on a drum. The dance is very loosely structured. The male dancers, for example, may dance in pairs or trios, with their arms draped over their neighbors' shoulders. As Willie put it "They act as if they were drunk as hell." The shell-shaker girls often remove their leg rattles before this dance and whoop and answer the songs like the men. Chinubbi McIntosh reports that sometimes four men dressed as women act as clowns during the dance, staggering about and making advances to the male dancers. The songs of this dance are very beautiful and some have suggestive texts. One represents a man asking a woman the direction to her home. For this reason the *sapiya*, the powerful love medicine of the Seminoles and Creeks, is described as singing Drunken Dance songs. Other songs are humorous, detailing the weakness of the male or female sex, or ridiculing well-known personalities.

Variants of the Drunken Dance are known to a number of tribes besides the Creeks and Seminoles, but there are slight differences in the performance. The Seminoles and Creeks, for example, lack the custom of the women "capturing the drum," a standard feature of the Shawnee and Delaware Drunken Dance.[9] The Choctaw Drunken Dance is different in both music and choreography.

Mother Dance (Opvnka itcki)

This dance is often used to begin a night of Stomp Dancing. Participation is limited to the male members of the particular square ground where the dance is given. Though called the Mother "dance," it is not so much a dance as a singing in unison by a male choir, just as the women sing before the ballsticks on the night before a match ball game.

The performance takes place at the *tajo* at the northeast corner of the ground. The principal singer, carrying a coconut-shell rattle, stands atop the mound, facing west. The other men, including one who has been selected as chief whooper, stand in an irregular cluster before him, facing east. Four whoops, led by the chief whooper, begin the performance. The singer then begins to shake his rattle and sing. As he intones the first phrase of each of the songs they are taken up by the others, singing in unison. Following each song the chief whooper cries "*Yoooo ho!*" and the others answer "*Whi!*" The singer then begins the second song, and so on. There are four songs in all. On the last, the head singer descends from the *tajo* and leads the group in a walking step around it. He immediately follows this with one round of Stomp Dance (*Opvnka hajo*) around the mound to end the rite. He uses his coconut-shell rattle as rhythmic accompaniment for this Stomp episode, since there are no women in the group and hence no shell shakers.

According to Willie Lena, this dance is dedicated to all of the mothers of the town, past, present, and future. It is through the women that a Seminole or Creek town perpetuates itself, and this dance is the men's way of acknowledging their ties to the ground according to the matrilineal principle.

Old People's Dance (Atcolvlki opvnka)

The *Atcolvlki opvnka* ("old-people," "dance") is now obsolete. It was danced in the autumn. Only men danced. They wore masks made of bark, watermelon rinds, and the like, grotesque hats of grass, and old, mismatched clothing. Willie Lena has been interested in this dance for a number of years and has questioned elderly people concerning its various features. On the basis of his research he made me a sketch of the dress of the dancers (Plate 53), and also a miniature replica of one of the bark masks used in it (Plate 54).

Swanton writes of this dance as follows:

> The old men's dance was danced about the time when pokeweed berries are ripe—i.e., about the middle of October. Young men were usually the performers. They fixed themselves up in imitation of old-time Indians. Each wore a mask made out of a pumpkin, gourd, or melon, holes being cut for the eyes and mouth and the latter provided with teeth made out of grains of corn. A headgear was constructed out of leaf stalks of the sumac, the small ends of which were tied together and the body opened out and fitted over the head. Long earrings were fastened to the mask and a shawl thrown over the head behind. They stained the outside of the mask with the berries of the pokeweed (osá in Creek). Finally the performer fastened tortoise-shell rattles on his legs, drew a blanket round himself, and performed all sorts of antics to make people laugh. He carried a bow and arrows improvised for the occasion, pretended to see game, and did other things supposed to be amusing. The children were scared half to death with his performances. . . .[10]

The possibility of some distant connection between the Creek-Seminole Old People's Dance and its cognates in other Southeastern tribes and the very similar masked dances imitating little old

PLATE 53. Costume worn in the Old People's Dance, as reconstructed by Willie Lena in a pen and ink sketch, 1982. Note the mock "medicine bundle" in the dancer's left hand.

PLATE 54. Miniature reproduction of an Old People's Dance mask made by Willie Lena in 1979. The miniature measures about two by three and a half inches.

men that were common in Mesoamerica in the early historic period is tantalizing. One of these, *Los Viejitos*, is still performed in the state of Michoacán. The "wild game" association of the Creek and Seminole dance is echoed in the custom of the *viejitos* carrying a cane with an animal head at the top, the symbol of Huehueteotl, the Old God, a synonymn of Xiuhtecuhtli, the Aztec Fire God, Lord of the Year.

There undoubtedly are, or were, many more animal and other incidental dances known to the Oklahoma Seminoles at one time. In addition to those described above, Swanton lists the Chicken, Catfish, Small frog, Sheep, Screech-owl, Horned-owl, Beaver, Quail, Snow, Skunk, Snake, Crane, Bear, Mosquito, Alligator,

PLATE 55. An Oklahoma Seminole girl dressed for a Pan-Indian powwow. Pencil and crayon sketch by Willie Lena, 1982.

Terrapin, Crow, Hair, Chigoe, Wolf, Leaf, *Hinvta*, *Akilv*, *Kinia*, Pumpkin, Bed, War, Scalp, Blackbird, Bone, Tick, *Okvjibvja*, and Rabbit dances.[11] Claude Medford Jr. identifies the reasons for the gradual disappearance of these incidental dances in the following paragraph:

> As changing times and beliefs caused the power of the animal and bird spirits to be lessened, the simpler stomp dances became more popular, and fewer and fewer of the shell shakers learned the complicated rhythms and dance movements necessary in the animal dances. Each Green Corn season sees more and more of these animal dances dropped from the Ceremonial, and many towns and stomp grounds have few or none of them, as the songs have been forgotten.[12]

8

SPORTS AND GAMES

The Oklahoma Seminoles are devoted to sports of all kinds, both their own traditional games and those adopted from the major culture. This interest in athletics is no recent development, but rather a continuation of a cultural pattern with its roots deep in antiquity. So important were sports in the traditional Creek and Seminole way of life that certain games are deeply imbedded in the tribal religion. Thus the ball pole and surrounding playing field of the single pole ball game have been inevitable architectural features of every ceremonial center or square ground since earliest times. Likewise, the "match" or inter-town stickball game ranks with the Green Corn Ceremony as the high point of the ceremonial season. The strong association of sports with religion occurs throughout the Southeast and undoubtedly derives, ultimately, from Mesoamerica.

The single pole ball game

The single pole or men-against-women ball game is the most frequently played aboriginal game with today's Seminoles and Creeks. It is often played during the afternoon preceding one of the all-night Stomp Dances at a ceremonial ground, and again the following morning. Persons of all ages and both sexes play com-

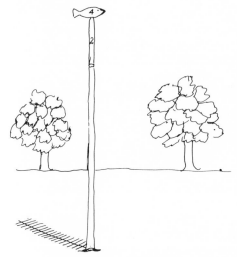

PLATE 56. Ball pole used in the single pole or men-against-women ball game. Pen and ink sketch by Willie Lena, 1982. The numerals on the fish effigy at the summit of the pole and on the top of the pole just below it indicate the points to be gained by hitting these objects. At the base of the pole, to the left, Willie has indicated the manner of keeping score.

mingled, male against female. The area of play is always close to the square ground, usually about fifty yards to the north of it. In the center of this circular playing field is the single tall pole from which the game takes its name. The pole is surmounted by the target, which may be either a cow skull or a carved and painted wooden effigy of a fish. If a fish effigy is used it is made with a swivel at the top of the pole and on the underside of the fish, which causes the fish to pivot when hit directly by the ball. Formerly the bark was removed from the top of the pole to a point about ten feet from its summit. At present it is customary to simply nail a tin can from which the top and bottom have been removed around the pole ten feet from the top to form an encircling band. The object of the game is to hit either the cow skull or fish effigy at the top of the pole, or, failing that, to hit the pole itself above the band. Men and boys must handle the ball with a pair of ballsticks, but women and girls can carry and throw the ball with their hands.

A hit on the object at the top of the pole scores four points, a hit on the pole itself, above the band, scores two. Thirty points constitute a game. Score is kept by marking horizontal slashes along either side of a line scratched in the earth out from the east side of the base of the pole. Marks on the south side of the vertical line indicate points scored by the men, those on the other, points scored by the women. An older man tosses the ball into the air for the scrimmage which starts the game, and does so again after each score. This same man also keeps score, using a long pointed stick to furrow the ground. The game is always played in an atmosphere of high good humor, with much good natured scuffling, tearing of clothing, and shouting. Invariably the scorekeeper, being a male, is accused of cheating by the women, yet the women usually win. The manner in which the men and boys catch the ball, which is no more than an inch and three-quarters in diameter, in the loops of their ballsticks is almost incredible, and is a skill developed from childhood.

Willie Lena said that the main purpose of the single pole game, aside from its social functions, is to train the male players in catching and throwing the ball, skills that can be transferred to the match or inter-town stickball game. Other Seminoles have indicated that the game is of recent origin, merely a way of sharpening the skills of the men and boys for the less frequent match games. Careful research would negate this interpretation, however, and reveals that the single pole ball game is quite important in its own right and has a very respectable antiquity. The earliest European accounts of Southeastern Indians mention the game, and there are strong indications that it was played in prehistoric times in the Mississippian archeological period, perhaps as early as the twelfth or the thirteenth century.[1]

The match or inter-town stickball game

The match or inter-town stickball game is a much more formal affair than the single pole game. Only able-bodied men and boys participate. The ball is maneuvered with ballsticks over a field 150 yards in length. The object of the game is to pass the ball through one or the other of two goals located at opposite ends of the field. The goals are made of two wooden uprights spaced about a yard and a half apart, with a crosspiece connecting them about six feet above the ground. The ball must go through the goal from the front, that is, the playing-field side of the goal. A curious feature of the Southeastern match ball game is that the players on the opposing teams, when they march onto the field and take up their positions, face *away* from the goal through which they will presently attempt to drive the ball. They regard this as *their* goal, not the goal of their opponents, precisely the opposite of the custom in white men's sports.

The match ball game was termed the "little brother of war" by the Creeks and Seminoles, and for good reason. Not only was the game extremely rough, often resulting in cripplings and deaths, but the formalities preceding it are, according to Willie Lena, in most respects identical with those that preceded the departure of a Creek or Seminole war party in earlier days. Even today, although inter-town grudge games are rare, and teams are purposely selected in such a way that half of a town's players will be on one team and half on the other, the game is still as dangerous as ice hockey or football, and broken bones and bloody heads are common. The element of danger and the swift changes of position tend to heighten the excitement for players and spectators alike. This, and the fact that the game is accompanied by a great deal of formality and ritual, make it one of the most spectacular events in Creek and Seminole culture.

THE PRELIMINARIES ACCOMPANYING A MATCH GAME
DESCRIBED BY WILLIE LENA

Perhaps the young men of one Creek or Seminole town find that members of another town are too boastful. They decide to challenge this town to a match ball game. A small ballstick is prepared, just like a regular ballstick but only about six inches long, and a small white crane feather is attached to the handle. A person designated by the challenging town's *mikko* is sent to the other town. When he arrives he doesn't stop to talk to anyone, but goes directly to their square ground. He enters the ground at the *tajo* (the small mound located at the northeast corner) and goes counterclockwise until he is in front of the chief's bed at the west. He turns to face the bed and hangs the little ballstick just to the

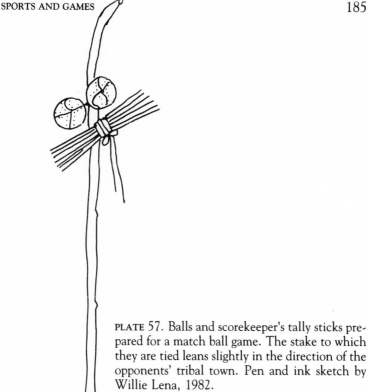

PLATE 57. Balls and scorekeeper's tally sticks pre-pared for a match ball game. The stake to which they are tied leans slightly in the direction of the opponents' tribal town. Pen and ink sketch by Willie Lena, 1982.

right of the *mikko*'s seat, on the front stringer of the arbor, between the *mikko* and the *heniha* of the challenged town. This stick has the name of the challenging town attached to it. The messenger then continues around the square in a counterclock-wise direction and leaves by the same route that he entered.

When the messenger has left, the men of the challenged town council meet to see if they should accept. Maybe they are short of players. In this case it is permissible to secure players from brother fire towns, or to bring back some of their own members who have married into other towns. In this case the opposing town must

PLATE 58. The women's ball dancing on the evening before a match ball game. Note the set of ballsticks suspended at the far right on the horizontal stringer of the brush arbor, to the right of the upright post. These sticks belong to a player whose wife is pregnant, and hence are segregated. Pen and ink sketch by Willie Lena, 1982.

agree to any players brought in. The decision about who is to be allowed to play occurs when the "lineup" takes place. It is held at a tribal town or place intermediate between the two towns that are going to play. Each side has selected its captain by this time. The teams and their captains line up facing each other at this intermediate point. They growl and act fierce in an attempt to "psych out" their opponents. At the lineup some players are likely to be eliminated as ineligible. This happens when it is discovered that they are not really members of the town they are representing, nor even of a brother fire town, but are instead "ringers," champion players that have been brought in by one or the other side to give an unfair advantage. There is a lot of argument at the lineup before things are finally settled. At the lineup the captains of the opposing teams may wrestle. The outcome is supposed to indicate which town will win in the upcoming game.

Both teams now return to their own square grounds to begin their preparations. Every night for a week or more they take medicine and dance. The twenty-four hours just before the game

PLATE 59. The captain of a match game team "shaking hands with the fire" (leading the man's ball play dance) on the evening before a match ball game. He thinks to himself "I will be here next year. I won't be hurt in the game." Note the ballsticks in his right hand with his rolled-up breechcloth, roach headdress, and "tigertail" attached, and the balls and scorekeeper's tally sticks attached to the stick in his left hand. Pen and ink sketch by Willie Lena, 1982.

PLATE 60. Layout of the match ball game field. The field is about 150 yards in length. The line midway between the two goals is where the "lineup," war speeches, and tossup take place. Pen and ink sketch by Willie Lena, 1982.

they fast. The night before the game the women dance. The players' ballsticks are hung up on the front stringer of the arbor where the musicians are seated. The principal singer employs a small water drum tied over a cypress knee or an earthenware crock. His two assistants sit on either side of him and shake coconut shell rattles. The women stand in ranks facing them and respond to their songs. The purpose of the dance is to strengthen the "medicine" of the home team and to weaken that of their opponents. If the opposing town is east of their town, the ballsticks are hung on the east arbor of the square ground, and the dance takes place in front of it. Players whose wives are pregnant hang their sticks apart from the rest, at the end of the cross piece where a few green branches are left. The women stand and dance facing the direction of the opposing town.

Early on the morning of the game each team "goes to water" at a nearby stream or lake, each at a separate place. Afterwards, assisted by their medicine men, the players paint and don their ball-game regalia. The costume of a Creek or Seminole ballplayer consists of:

1. A small, circular horsehair roach with one or two feathers attached in the center (*sikalega*), which is tied to a scalp lock braided just back of the top of the head.

2. A necklace of red cloth cut into a fringe (ʃnocʃt-cati), worn to disguise the blood which often runs down the neck and chest of players once the game is underway.

3. Ligatures (*wvnakv*) of wet bison rawhide tied on the arm muscles, which, according to Willie, "make the muscles hard."

4. A breechcloth (*takhaga*) narrower at the ends than in the center, often decorated with "medicine" designs.

5. A finger-woven yarn sash (*sohwvnakv*) with large yarn tassels.

6. Sometimes an ornament called a "tiger-tail" (*kotcv haci*). The tiger tail is made of a strip of otter fur that has been wrapped around a wooden base made something like a small ballstick. It has a red yarn pompon at its upper end and thongs at the bottom for attachment to the player's waist. The tiger tail is worn under the player's sash in back, projecting out and up from the base of his spine at a thirty-

degree angle. In addition to its decorative function, the tiger tail is a powerful "medicine," giving the wearer the strength and agility of a puma or "tiger." So strong is the sympathetic connection between a player and his tiger tail that it supposedly reflects his mood. Thus when the player gets angry during the game the hairs of the otter fur in his tiger tail stand out straight, like the fur of an infuriated feline.

7. A pair of ballsticks (*tokónhɟ*). The sticks used in a match game are usually heavier than those used in the single pole ball game. They are usually made of hickory, whereas sticks for the single pole game are often of pecan. Formerly some players would make their ballsticks even more lethal by driving two horseshoe nails through the wood at the top of the loop so that about a quarter-inch of steel projected out from the front. This was, of course, illegal but difficult to detect.

A medicine made from mud taken from a yellow jacket wasp's nest and *hoyvnijv*, both mixed with water, may be rubbed on ballsticks, arms, legs, and tiger tails by the players. This gives the player and his equipment the "sting" of a wasp. Willie commented "A small player with this medicine can make a larger man run by simply touching him with his doctored sticks. The man runs like he has been bitten by yellow jackets. It makes him look like a coward!"

Players also paint for the game. One traditional painting consists of a line drawn from just below the eye outward along the cheekbone, thence down to the angle of the jaw, then down the neck, over the collarbone, and down onto the chest. Another consists of a horizontal bar below each eye and another on the chin. Both of these paintings were generally done in red paint (vermilion), but if this was not available, powdered charcoal could be used. Both paints, according to Willie, were also used by Seminole warriors in former times.

At the same time they are painting and attiring themselves for the game, some players ask the medicine man to scratch them on the arm and leg muscles. This is to improve muscle tone and prevent stiffness. The medicine man may also perform the following rite to endow the player with the power of a bison. The medicine man chews a small piece of *hoyvnijv* and then recites the following sacred formula:

Yvnvsa illi vmvlati
"buffalo" "legs" "make my relation" } entire formula
Yvnvsv illi vmvlati   repeated twice
"buffalo" "legs" "make my relation"

He then rubs the athlete's legs with a bit of the medicine, and snaps his finger on the leg muscles, saying: "*tʃm, tʃm*" ("big," "big").

He then recites the formula for the arms:

Yvnvsv svkpv vmvlati
"buffalo" "arms" "make my relation" } entire formula
Yvnvsv svpv vmvlati   repeated twice
"buffalo" "arms" "make my relation"

He then rubs the medicine on the player's arms, snaps his finger on the arm muscles, and says "*tʃm, tʃm.*"

When all of the players are costumed, painted, and "doctored," they march to the place between the two tribal towns where the match game is to take place. Each side carries its own goalposts on this march, and these are not allowed to touch the ground en route.

Willie's account of the match ball game ends here. When I pressed him to continue he replied that I already knew what followed, since I had played in two match games myself, and there have been no changes in the game in recent memory. I commented that the games in which I had played were at Cedar River Tulsa, a Creek ground, but Willie dismissed this with a wave of his hand, saying that Oklahoma Creek and Oklahoma Seminole practices in regard to the game are identical. I will therefore continue my account of the match type stickball game with a narrative of the game held at Cedar River Tulsa square ground, near Holdenville, Oklahoma, on August 31 and September 1, 1980. In one respect my account is inaccurate, in that the game I describe was not between two tribal towns. Such inter-town games are now extremely rare, because of the violence which came to be associated with them in the early years of this century. Now, in

PLATE 61. An Oklahoma Seminole man attired for the match ball game, front view. Watercolor by Willie Lena, 1969.

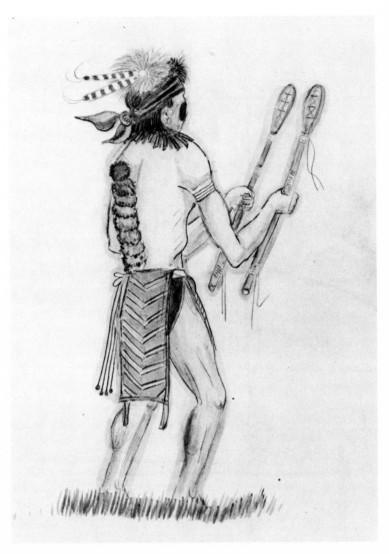

PLATE 62. An Oklahoma Seminole man attired for the match ball game, rear view. Note the tigertail ornament attached to his waist in back. Watercolor by Willie Lena, 1980.

order to prevent inter-town grudges from erupting into general mayhem on the playing field, the town sponsoring a game arbitrarily divides its players into two groups. Visiting players from other tribal towns are similarly divided between the two teams. Thus brother may be pitted against brother, father against son, and an atmosphere of good sportsmanship prevails. Even this toned down match game is extremely dangerous, and every game has its list of injured players. I myself acquired a nasty knot on the head in this particular contest.

MEN'S BALL GAME, CEDAR RIVER TULSA GROUND
AUGUST 31–SEPTEMBER 1, 1980

I arrived at the dance ground at 5:00 P.M. August 31. A bingo game was being organized to raise money for the ground. Various persons contributed groceries to make up fifteen prizes. The game was conducted in the English language. Following the game, about 6:00 P.M. everyone was fed at one or another of the camps surrounding the square ground. There were many visitors—Creeks from other tribal towns, Seminoles, Shawnees, and Archie Sam, the Natchez-Cherokee.

At 11:30 P.M. the ballplayers were asked to bring their equipment and line up in the square ground. Many, but not all, of those who were to play the following day appeared for this lineup. All of these players were from the local ground. Some took part in the lineup but did not bring their equipment. Those who did brought a pair of ballsticks and a rolled-up ballplayer's breechcloth, all tied together with a yarn sash. They all lined up west of the fire, facing the chief's "bed" or arbor, which is at the west. Here Spencer Franks, who is an excellent orator in the Muskogee language delivered a long and vigorous harangue, walking back and forth in front of the players. Willie Lena, who said that its content was similar to the locker room pep talk of coaches in the major culture, identified this oration as a "war speech." Then an older man appeared carrying a short stick to which the two balls to be used in the upcoming game and the twelve counting sticks used in keeping score were tied at one end. This man, carrying the stick, led the

PLATE 63. A Seminole ballplayer's regalia. *Above*: roach headdress with two pendant hawk feathers. *Center, left to right*: tigertail ornament, buckskin arm cinctures, necklace of fringed red trade cloth. *Below*: Breechcloth. All items secured from Willie Lena, 1969.

players in the Ballgame Dance around the sacred fire in the center of the square. The dance was a counterclockwise circling of the fire, the dancers in a single file behind the leader, providing antiphonal response to his songs. The songs reminded me of Long Dance songs, with much whooping. One boy near the head of the line was designated as the whooper. At the conclusion of the dance the ballplayers took their equipment to the south part of the west arbor. The willow-bough covering of this part of the arbor had been removed, and the ballsticks were tied in a row on the

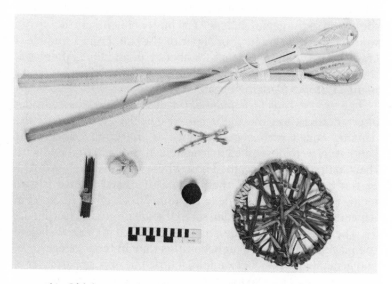

PLATE 64. Oklahoma Seminole gaming equipment. *Above*: pair of ballsticks for use in a match ball game. *Center*: pair of miniature ballsticks. Now made and used as ornaments and souvenirs. Sticks of this type formerly figured in the ceremony whereby one tribal town challenged another to a match game. *Below, left to right*: a set of tally sticks used by scorekeeper in the match ball game; a set of two balls for use in a match ball game; a ball used in single pole ball game; a hoop with bark netting used in the rolling hoop archery game. All items made by Willie Lena in 1969 except for the single pole game ball, which was made by Robert Lee Sumpka, Creek and Seminole, of Blackgum, Oklahoma, in 1969.

front horizontal stringer, where they remained throughout the rest of the night.

Now Ollie Tiger, medicine man at Cedar River Tulsa, and two assistant singers positioned themselves on the log bench just below the ballsticks, facing west. Ollie, in the center, had a water drum, and his assistants each carried a coconut-shell rattle. The women were now called to sing for the ballsticks. They stood in three ranks facing the singers and the suspended ballsticks, and, more important, facing the ball field, located directly behind the east arbor. The male singers would start a song and the women would take it up and repeat it. Some of the songs have words referring to the action of the game, such as "You [my opponent] cry like an old woman when you are hit," or "I pursue the ball, I run, I stumble, I crawl." This singing went on for about half an hour. Afterward, the singers returned the drum and rattles to the chief's arbor, and a night of Stomp Dancing began.

The two deacons (ʃntapalalvlki) called one good dance leader after another, and the night passed quickly. At 7:00 A.M, the dancing ended with a performance of the Long Dance. The ballplayers were now asked to assemble in the square ground with their equipment once again. Those whose gear was hanging on the east arbor retrieved it. Others joined them and formed in two facing ranks on the west side of the fire. Which rank one stood in depended upon where his clan sat in the square ground (see Figure 7). The sticks and other equipment were placed in two rows before the players, who were matched at this time in terms of age, size, and general ability—for example, a little boy opposite another of the same size. The two assistant singers from the previous night, carrying their coconut-shell rattles, now walked the length of the two ranks from south to north and then back again, treading carefully between the displayed sticks to ensure that the two sides were equal in personnel. When this had been done, the visiting

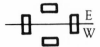

FIGURE 7. Method of dividing the players for a match ball game.

ballplayers were called to join the lineup, tribal town by tribal town, to stand at the ends of the two ranks. Each town's players were divided equally between the east and west teams. As each tribal town entered, on the run, they gave the spine-chilling turkey gobble war whoop of the Southeastern tribes. The visiting towns that provided players on this occasion were Hickory ground, Arbihka, and Okfuskee. Now there were two long, facing ranks, each man with his ballsticks, breechcloth, and sash tied up as a package and lying on the ground before him. Now, Spencer Franks once again gave a stirring war speech, pacing up and down between the two opposing teams. As had been done the night before, the speech was followed by a performance of the Ball Game Dance around the fire.

Each team now went off into the woods to dress and prepare themselves. I went with the west group to an open place in the woods about 400 yards northwest of the dance ground. Some of the players did not dress at all. Others, more traditional, wore red cloth fringe necklaces, breechcloths over athletic trunks, and yarn sashes. Two men wore hair ornaments. One had an owl feather, another a downy eagle feather and a regular eagle tail feather. I saw no tiger tails or painting. A few of the members of my team were "scratched" by the team's medicine man.

When all were ready, the team marched to the playing field and performed the Ball Game Dance around the west goal, ending by facing the goal posts and whooping. They then marched through the goal, moving eastward, and formed a long rank facing east. Our opponents, the east team, did the same at their goal and marched out to form a rank facing us at center field. Once again Spencer Franks gave a war speech, pacing between the two teams. When he had finished, there was a great whoop and clashing together of ballsticks by the players.

Spencer Franks put the ball into play by throwing it high in the air at midfield. The two teams quickly divided into three sections, one at either end and one at midfield. The objective of the west team was to put the ball through the west goal, that of the east to put it through the east goal. After each score the ball was changed. Ollie Tiger kept score by sticking pointed wooden pegs in the

PLATE 65. Scorekeepers in the match ball game. Willie Lena's note on the back of this sketch reads "They are great liars." Pen and ink sketch by Willie Lena, 1982.

ground at a point just north of the playing ground at midfield. Small boys took part in the game but were assigned a particular area, the south side of the midfield. No adult or even a bigger boy contested the ball when it was in this space. Once it was carried or thrown out of this section, however, it was once again in the public domain.

The match ball game is famous for its violent nature, and for good reason. In this particular game two players were put out of commission temporarily, but fortunately there were no permanent injuries. It is the custom for a player, whenever he is hit, to immediately give voice to the famous turkey gobble war whoop to indicate his invincibility. Pretty girls with dippers and buckets of water entered the field from time to time to water down the players, and medicine men were spotted here and there on the field to render assistance to injured players.

Great excitement built up whenever the ball was carried near one of the goals. Then a great mob of pushing and struggling young men would form around the ball, each trying to get his sticks on it.

PLATE 66. Women performing the ritual of "calling the ball" to their team's goal in the match ball game. Pen and ink sketch by Willie Lena, 1982.

The clashing together of their ballsticks was clearly audible half a mile away. To add to the noise and excitement, two designated women from the side whose goal this was would position themselves behind it at these times. One carried a water drum, the other a rattle. As the ball neared the goal they would make a great racket with these instruments, attempting to magically "call the ball" through the goal. This custom is called *pokko inuikvlgi* ("ball calling").

The game was for twelve points, and the west team attained this score just after the noon hour on September 1. Following the game, the players, coaches (*pokkfcvlgi-alfkcv*), and town chiefs assembled under a shady tree north of the playing field. Here the local chief, Barney Leader, through his "tongue" or speaker, thanked the visiting towns for coming to Cedar River Tulsa for their annual match game. Each visiting chief in turn, through his speaker, expressed his gratitude for the hospitality.

The members of the winning team now danced the Ball Game Dance once more around the west goal posts. All ballplayers now marched to the square ground and washed themselves in a large pot of *mikko hoyvnijv*. Two players at a time presented themselves to Ollie Tiger and his assistant, who handed them a large dipperful of the medicine. When all had washed, the players were dismissed. At one o'clock everyone was served lunch, cafeteria style, at Susanna Reed's camp, and the crowd gradually dispersed.

After the game, Willie Lena supplied a few additional details. He said that only one official is allowed to touch the balls (*pokko*) used in the game. Each side brings two balls to the game, a total of four. A ball belonging to the challenged side is thrown up first to begin the contest. This is followed by a ball belonging to their opponents after the first score, then the first team provides a ball again, and so on in alternation.

Practicing with owls and snakes

Willie also described an ancient method of training a boy who wanted to play in a match ball game. This involves the boy pitting his speed and skill against two of the swiftest and wiliest members of the animal world, the owl and the blue racer snake. The boy puts on his ballplayer's costume, takes his ballsticks, and goes out on the ballfield alone, at dusk. Here he calls the owls by imitating their cry. The owls, infuriated when they find the solitary boy instead of members of their own kind, fly in to attack him. If he can avoid their tearing talons with his quick movements and successfully fend them off with his ballsticks, he is considered ready for the rigors of the match ball game. A boy testing himself in this manner always reports the results of the contest to an older male relative, grandfather, uncle, or father, and they decide whether or not he has acquitted himself well.

A variant of this test involves the boy going out, in ball-game array, to a field where blue racers are called. These snakes, according to Willie, always come in pairs, one attacking from the right, the other from the left. If the player is quick enough to fend off one snake, the other generally leaves as well. Again, the results are reported to a grandfather, uncle, or father for their verdict.

Making ballsticks and balls

When I stopped by to visit Willie on July 11, 1980, I found him busy making ballsticks in the yard west of his house, where he has an outdoor workshop under two shady trees. Since Willie is famous among both Seminoles and Creeks for his high-quality ballsticks, I was delighted to learn just how he makes them. From white hickory logs about five inches in diameter and five feet in length, Willie cut a number of staves, each about two inches by two inches and four feet in length. Then, near one end, each stave was whittled down to a thickness of three-quarters of an inch, as shown in figure 8. The thinned area was also beveled slightly from

FIGURE 8. A stave cut to make a ballstick.

left to right. The end of the stave (a) was then put in a vise on Willie's work table and bent to form a loop. The loop end was then trimmed down and clamped with a screw vise, and the loop was smoothed out with wood rasps of various degrees of coarseness. If the loop was lopsided—for example, if one side was straight but the other curved—this defect was remedied using a small vise. No heat or steam is involved in bending the loop. All that is required is that the wood be green. The stick is allowed to remain quite thick just below the loop. A slight elevation is left on the small end of the wood forming the loop at the end of its final taper, this to prevent the binding from slipping out of place.

Next, holes for the strings were drilled, using a brace and bit. The drill bit Willie uses is a sixth of an inch in diameter. There are various ways of stringing ballsticks. Willie strings his by drilling

FIGURE 9. Method employed in lacing a ballstick.

one hole at the top of the loop near the upper (wide) face of the loop, then three holes on either side of the loop near its lower (narrow) face. Then, using a buckskin thong about a quarter-inch wide, he strings the ballstick. Starting from the hole at the top of the loop he pulls half the length of his thong through the hole. He then twists the two ends together for a short distance below this hole. One end is then carried to the first hole on the right side of the loop and one end to the first on the left, each twisted as he proceeds. Each end is passed through the top hole, then brought out to the center of the loop and carried to the second hole on the opposite side of the loop, as in lacing a pair of shoes. Through this second hole they come back to the center again, cross, and are carried to the third and last lateral hole. From here the two ends are brought to the middle of the loop once more, twisted together to form a single element, and then brought down to form the uppermost of the three bindings of the loop extension that secure it to the handle of the ballstick. Two additional bindings are added to hold the extension in place against the handle. Another wrapping of buckskin is placed halfway down the handle, and sometimes a second just above the end of the handle as well. The purpose of these last two are to prevent the player's sweaty hands from losing their grasp on the sticks during play.

Willie's sticks usually have handles that are square in cross-section, but sticks with rounded handles are probably more common among the Seminoles. Seminole ballsticks have handles of equal length, as do those of the Creeks, Cherokees, and Chickasaws. Choctaw sticks, however, always have the right-hand stick slightly shorter than the left. Willie says that a man's ballsticks

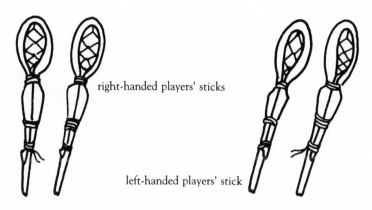

right-handed players' sticks

left-handed players' stick

FIGURE 10. The difference between "right-handed" and "left-handed" ballsticks.

should be long enough to reach the ground comfortably without unnecessary stooping. Children's sticks have handles that are scaled down, some no more than a foot in length.

He explained that some sticks are right- and some left-handed (see figure 10). In right-handed sticks the small extension from the loop is at the left as the player holds his sticks with the wide part of the loop upward. When the left-hand stick is turned over to catch the ball, the small extension will be at the right. A left-handed player's sticks are just the reverse, with the small extension at the player's right. The Cherokees make the right-hand stick with the small extension to the left, but the left-hand stick has the extension to the right. Thus when Cherokee sticks are cupped the small extension of both sticks will be on the right. The Creeks and Seminoles do this occasionally, but not often. Willie said that it is difficult for a right-handed player to throw the ball with force using left-handed sticks.

Florida Seminole ballsticks are distinguished by their extra-large loops. Oklahoma Seminoles find this characteristic amusing.

I asked Willie about the bending upward of the loop seen in some sticks. He knew of this custom, which is particularly evident in Choctaw ballsticks. He said that it is sometimes done in match game ballsticks to make them more effective as clubs.

FIGURE 11. The upward tilt in a ballstick loop.

Hickory, he said, is the best wood for match game sticks, because it can take a lot of abuse without splitting. For use in the single pole ball game, sticks made of a lighter wood, such as pecan, are preferred.

The traditional material for a match game ball covering is the skin from the hind leg of a snapping turtle. Special hunts were organized to secure turtles for this purpose. Willie's sketch (plate 67) shows a young man who has just found a turtle he plans to use

PLATE 67. A youth who has just found a turtle for use in making a match ball game ball. Skin from the hind leg of the turtle is used to cover the ball, and an inch-worm is placed in its center. Pen and ink sketch by Willie Lena, 1982.

for this purpose. The ball is sewed together like a baseball. It was traditionally stuffed with Spanish moss, but today cotton or rags are usually substituted. For the match game balls an inchworm was secured by the team's medicine man and placed in the very center of the ball. This supposedly made it difficult for the opposing team to get their sticks on the ball, because the inchworm, cooperating with the medicine man who had placed him there, would move the ball just a little bit each time a player from the other team reached for it.

Archery and archery games

Willie Lena is an accomplished archer and makes bows and arrows for his own use and to sell and give to his particular friends. He commented that the Seminoles used two types of bow. Both resemble the English longbow in their general configuration, but one has the bowstring lashed to the bow a few inches from either end (figure 12). This gave the bow more power, according to Willie. He said that his grandfather told him that when shooting at a deer he should hold his bow near the horizontal to give the arrow a flat trajectory.

FIGURE 12. An Oklahoma Seminole bow that has been lashed for more power, from a sketch by Willie Lena.

For shooting at rabbits, squirrels, and birds, blunt arrows called "rabbit arrows" were used. These had one end carved into a knob, and would kill the small creature by stunning it without tearing the fur or plumage or the flesh (figure 13). Arrows for larger game were equipped with steel points. Poisoned arrows were used only on bobcats and other animals that were not to be eaten. They were poisoned with snake venom.

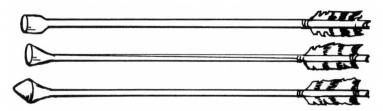

FIGURE 13. Types of Oklahoma Seminole blunt or "rabbit" arrows, from a sketch by Willie Lena.

To train small boys a special arrow called a "snake arrow" was prepared. Willie's grandfather made him such an arrow when he was a small boy. The shaft of the snake arrow was striped. To decorate it in this way the bark of the shoot from which the arrow is made is wrapped around the shaft in a spiral manner. Then the arrow is held over a small fire in order to smoke and scorch those portions of the shaft not protected by the bark wrapping. When the bark is removed the arrowshaft has a handsome decoration resembling a barber's pole (figure 14). A small boy was given such an arrow and told to hunt with it. The rule was that he must hit an animal with the snake arrow within four days. He was told that unless he succeeded, a snake would come and bite him, which provided strong motivation for success. If he took game within the allotted period it was said that he would always be a good hunter in his future life, and the snake arrow was kept as a hunting charm.

FIGURE 14. A Seminole "snake" arrow as described by Willie Lena.

Another type of "medicine arrow" involved a special type of fletching. Willie remarked, "There is a kind of hawk we call the swift hawk. It is reddish in color. When it hunts it swoops down and hits its prey in a power dive. It has a sort of moustache, four

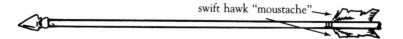

swift hawk "moustache"

FIGURE 15. A Seminole medicine arrow with "swift hawk" fletching.

little feathers where the beak joins the head. If you can get hold of one of these little feathers, add it to the fletching of your arrow like this (figure 15). This will give your arrow more power to take game. It will hit whatever you shoot at just like the swift hawk hits its prey.

"Swift hawks are signs of good luck. At Tallahassee ground we saw a swift hawk swoop down at the fish on the top of our ball pole. This was a good sign. Later we saw a whole group of them diving around the pole. This showed we were going to have a good square ground."

The special arrow used to kill a witch, the *stikini* arrow, has already been described in chapter 5. It is fletched with owl feathers and has small grooves cut near the point, presumably to contain herb medicines. The *stikini* arrow has no stone or metal point, merely the sharpened end of the shaft.

A number of different archery games were played by the old-time Seminoles. One game involved shooting an arrow a long distance and managing to have it land on top of a pile of brush. The arrow had to land with its entire length on top of the brush, not sticking into the brush pile.

The Seminoles also had "cornstalk shoots." These were not like those of the Cherokees, where the archers shoot at bundles of stalks placed horizontally on the ground. The Seminoles always shot at standing cornstalks. One contest involved knocking down the standing cornstalk with a blunt "rabbit arrow." The other, using a hunting arrow, required that the player stick his arrow in the erect cornstalk. In both games the winner confiscated the arrows of the losers, and sometimes even the bows.

The archery contest at which Willie excelled was flight shooting. "Once I made a real strong bow and was able to shoot an arrow as much as three hundred yards, but I was never able to make one that would shoot an arrow four hundred yards."

The Seminole version of the widespread hoop and pole game involved one man rolling a small wooden hoop with a netting of bark strips past another man who shot at this moving target with arrows. Willie made and gave me a hoop of the type employed in this game in July, 1978 (plate 64). This game was excellent training for hunters.

The most dangerous archery game was Eartip shooting (*hvcko tʃtcʃtv akopvnkv*). More than any other, with the possible exception of the match ball game, this sport typifies the fearless, "don't give a damn," attitude of the old-time Seminoles, the same attitude that made the Seminole Scouts the equal of any unit in the United States Army during the Indian Wars. The game involved one family inviting another family or families to their home, and there was considerable betting on the outcome, wagers of chickens, hogs, even horses.

The archer, with his bow and a single steel-tipped arrow, would position himself about twenty yards from the log cabin of the host family. Another man, his living target, would stand at the corner of the cabin and stick his head out so that only a little of his ear showed. The object of the game was to nick the exposed ear with the arrow. If the archer missed the two men changed places, the game continuing in this manner until one or the other scored. The "target man" dared not flinch or he lost the bet. Sometimes bad accidents happened in this game. Willie remarked that his grandfather had been hit in the neck when an arrow hit the edge of the cabin and ricocheted.

The cow bone game

A more peaceful pastime was the Cow bone game (*waka hvlalo akopvnka*). Willie described it as being played with one of the bones from the joints in a cow's leg. From his drawing, figure 16, the bone referred to is evidently the astragalus. The game was played by pushing the bone back and forth between two people seated opposite one another on the ground a few feet apart.

FIGURE 16. Cow astragalus used in the Seminole
cow bone game.

Usually the bone falls on one of its two flat sides at the end of the
push. Sometimes, however, it lands on its other side, which
counts two points. Very rarely it will land standing up on its end,
in which case the pusher wins the game. Curiously enough, the
only reference I have found to a game anything like the Seminole
cow bone game anywhere else in North America is among the
Papagos of Arizona.[2]

9

SUPERNATURALS

In addition to the Giant Horned Snake, already described in Chapter 5, the Oklahoma Seminoles are familiar with a number of other supernaturals. All or most of them are known to the Creeks, and many have counterparts elsewhere in the Southeast.

The Little People

Like the Creeks, Choctaws, and Chickasaws, the Seminoles frequently speak of a race of diminutive human beings. These Little People are invisible most of the time, but occasionally let themselves be seen by young children and by medicine men. They are described by Seminoles as looking like Indians and speaking Muskogee. Sometimes they are described as wearing "old time" Indian garb, made of buckskin. They frequently take in small children who have wandered away from home. They feed and care for these children and often teach them the use of herb remedies. Seminole parents, therefore, are not unduly concerned when a small child turns up missing, since the child is thought to be with the Little People, and will reappear unharmed in a day or two. The Muskogee name for these Little People is *fsti lvpucki*.

On July 17, 1980, I went to visit Willie Lena in Wewoka, and he asked me to drive him out to see Tony Holata, who was reported to

be ill. We drove to Tony's house, and while we were there Wesley
Green stopped by and invited us for dinner. At Wesley's house the
talk turned to the ʃsti Ivpucki, and Wesley commented that his
grandson had recently visited the Little People. The little boy,
who was present (aged about five years), nodded in agreement. He
is reported to have described them as being "ugly." His grandparents, Wesley and Cora Green, said that the boy often plays
with these Little People.

Willie then told several stories of encounters with the Little
People by children. One child, he said, saw the Little People and
they were packing all of their goods in tiny wagons as if they were
about to move. "Our house is going to be destroyed," they told the
child. Surely enough, a tornado came and tore up the grove of
trees in which they lived. Another time the Little People told a
child the same thing, and about eight months later a highway cut
through the clump of trees where they lived. Willie described the
Little People as ugly, but otherwise just like old-time Indians.
They have women and children and live in trees. Willie had never
heard that the bones of Little People were a medicine.

About this time, Wesley's grandson, who had gone out of the
house, came back in with a large bunch of weeds in his hand.
Wesley asked him "Did the Little People tell you this was a
medicine?" The child answered "No." Later, I observed Cora
throw the bunch of weeds out.

Tall Man

Tall Man or ʃsti capcaki is described as resembling a human being
but of immense stature, ten feet or more in height, and covered
with gray hair. He customarily carries a great wooden club made
from a branch broken from a tree (Plate 68). Tall Man is reported
to have a penetrating odor, like the smell of a stagnant muddy
pond.

Willie said that his father had seen Tall Man on one occasion
when he (Willie) was very small.

When Daddy saw it he told Mamma and said that it looked like he

PLATE 68. An encounter with Tall Man (*ʃsti capcaki*), a Seminole supernatural. Pen and ink sketch by Willie Lena, 1982.

had made his club from a limb of one of the trees on our place. Mamma said "If that is so, that tree he broke the limb from will soon be dead!" We all doubted this, but surely enough, the tree died. Where the branches had been there were big holes. It is in holes like this that Seminole women bury stillborn babies. I used to hear a baby crying at one of these trees near our house. There were little bones in there.

Long Ears

Long Ears or *Hvcko capko* is described as an animal with gray hair, standing about three feet tall. It resembles a horse, with a horse's tail, but has a head more like that of a wolf, and enormous long ears. It is extremely ugly, and like Tall Man it smells like stagnant

PLATE 69. Long Ears (*hvcko cap-ko*), a Seminole supernatural an-imal, front view (*above*) and side view. In both sketches Long ears is shown standing on the top of a rocky hill, his favorite locale. Pen and ink sketches by Willie Lena, 1982.

muddy water. Willie commented that the creatures frequent rocky areas, where they are often observed watching people as they pass. One man, he said, recently saw two of them near New Tulsa.

Swanton says "It is about the size of a mule, has immense ears, and a very hideous appearance generally. It has a disagreeable odor and causes a dangerous disease, but fortunately it is rarely seen. There are two varieties of this animal, one of a brown color nearly black, the other of a slate color."[1]

Willie sketched front and side views of Long Ears (Plate 69).

FIGURE 17. *Nokos oma*, a
Seminole supernatural
animal, as sketched by
Willie Lena.

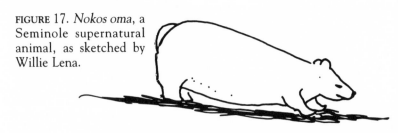

Nokos oma

Nokos oma ("like a bear") was described by Willie as standing
about two feet tall. It moves slowly and smells "worse than a
skunk." He sketched a side view of the creature (fig. 17). Swanton
describes the animal thusly: "It is about the size of an ordinary
black bear, but it always carries its head near the earth. It has
immense tusks which cross each other and when seen it is going
along a trail with the gait of a pacer. More often, however, only
the noise made by the males is heard, and this sounds something
like 'kȧp kȧp kȧp kȧp'."[2]

This account of the animal sounds suspiciously like an account
of a wild boar, fossilized in the telling over many generations.

Fire Dogs

The Fire Dogs or *Totki fa* were described by Willie as about a foot
in height. Male and female always travel together. They have

FIGURE 18. *Totki fa*, or
Fire Dog, a Seminole su-
pernatural animal, as
sketched by Willie Lena.

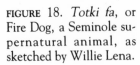

sharp ears. Perhaps these are what Swanton calls *Hátcko fáski* or "sharp ears."[3] He writes that they "seem to go in pairs and never travel east or west but always north or south. They are observed especially near the sources of small streams. They have sharp noses, bushy tails, and globular feet."

Wak oma

Wak oma means "like a cow," but according to Willie this is a type of bird. Its name, he says, refers to its similarity to a cowbird. He described it as the most dangerous of birds, commenting that it will even attack and kill a wolf. Its call sounds something like *tak, tak*.

Swanton, however, described *wak oma* as an animal "usually pied in color and resembling a big steer. Several travel together and they move in single file and alternately. One moves on for a certain distance and stops and moves on again. The one behind moves up to the place which the first had occupied, stops, and moves on again in the same manner."[4]

Lokha

Lokha was described by Willie as a spirit animal that lives in a person. It goes out through the person's mouth at night and changes into the shape of a chicken. In this form it practices witchcraft, stealing and eating people's hearts. The *Lokha* sounds exactly like a chicken. A person with an indwelling *Lokha* can be detected by the way he or she breathes. Of the *Lokha* Swanton writes only "There is an animal called *Lokha* which sometimes appears in the shape of a cat, sometimes as a chicken."[5]

Two "bad omens" involving chickens that were mentioned by Willie may relate to the *Lokha*: "When a chicken goes out in the hot sun and stretches its wings out and lies down, this is called 'having a fever'. It is a bad sign and means that someone in the house will have a fever within four days. When a hen crows like a rooster it is a sign of death. Such a hen is immediately killed and its body is destroyed, not eaten."

Chief deer

The chief deer (*Ijo mikoji* "deer" "little-chief") is a tiny race of cervids about two or three inches tall. Sometimes one hears them rustling the fallen leaves in the forest. If you are lucky enough to see the male of this species you will have the gift of learning sacred formulas easily. When the chief deer come out, the does always come first, then the bucks. Swanton writes of the chief deer thus: "There was said to be a little deer about two feet high and either speckled like a fawn or white, but it differed from a fawn in having very lofty horns."[6]

Human snakes

Creatures with attributes of both humans and snakes, and able to assume either form, are described in the following Seminole folktale collected by Eva Howard at Gar Creek in 1981.

SEMINOLE FOLKTALE, COLLECTED BY EVA HOWARD

There was a Seminole man who was rather undistinguished, even ugly, in appearance. Because he was so unattractive he was not popular with the young women, and was a bachelor. One night he went to a Stomp dance and at this dance he noticed a particularly beautiful Indian girl among the dancers. Surprisingly, she smiled at him and soon the two of them were having a good time dancing together and visiting.

Toward morning the girl announced that she must return home, since her parents, who were away, would be displeased if they returned to find her absent. Wishing to learn more of the girl, the young man asked if he might see her to her door, but the girl made various excuses, telling him it was only a short way. He insisted, however, and she finally agreed to let him accompany her. To his amazement, instead of taking any of the several paths leading from the dance ground, the girl plunged into the woods on her homeward journey, passing through dense thickets and wading creeks. Finally they arrived at an immense tree which had large above-ground roots. At the base of the tree, between two roots, there was a large hole in the ground. "This is where I live," the girl said, and descended into the hole.

This baffled the young man, since he had never met anyone who lived in a cave. He called after her but there was no reply. Determined to see what sort of house was beneath the tree he lowered himself into the hole. It was pitch dark so he struck a match. The light revealed a tangled mass of giant snakes. They resembled blind snakes, but had bodies as large as tree trunks. Terrified, the young man scrambled out of the snakes' den and ran wildly until he was safe at home.

He shortly became ill, and when the medicine man came to treat him he told of his experience. No treatment could save him, and he died babbling of his encounter with the snake woman. Other Seminoles were inclined to dismiss the tale as the result of his fever, but since he had mentioned a number of specific landmarks in the area where he had followed the snake woman to her den, a group of his friends decided to retrace his path to either prove or disprove his story. Carefully following the route described by the young man on his deathbed they arrived at the tree and saw for themselves the giant snakes in the den beneath it. The medicine man, who had accompanied them, said "These are not ordinary snakes, but a source of great evil. They must be destroyed."

The Seminoles returned to their village and under the direction of the medicine man prepared a medicine bundle strong enough to counteract the evil power of the human snakes. Rags and clothing used by menstruating women and soaked in their blood were burned and the resulting ashes were carefully gathered and tied in a deerskin. A menstruating woman was directed to carry this bundle to the den of the human snakes and lower it among the tangled mass of serpents. As she did so the human snakes writhed and hissed in agony, some of them assuming a human or semi-human form in their death throes. When all were dead, the den was carefully filled with earth and stones. This incident supposedly took place near present Perkins, Oklahoma.

10

THE SEMINOLE WORLD

At the time the first Florida Seminoles were removed to Indian Territory, their culture was already a mixture of aboriginal elements and traits derived from contacts with the Spanish, English, and Americans. This white acculturation has proceeded in the years since, and complexes derived from Prairie and Plains groups in Oklahoma have been added to the amalgam. The average Seminole, unless of an unusually reflective turn of mind, does not bother to try to sort out which parts of his or her culture are of non-Indian derivation and which are not; or, of the aboriginal elements, which are Seminole and which come from tribes to the north and west. If it works, if it satisfies, they use it—and origins be damned!

Although they have borrowed heavily from the non-Indian world, particularly in the realm of technology, outward appearances can be deceptive. When one visits Seminole homes and listens in on conversations it becomes quite apparent that in spite of their neo-Oklahoman-style housing, pickup trucks, and television sets, today's Oklahoma Seminoles have nevertheless managed to preserve the core of their traditional value system. Some of them, it is true, seem to have lost themselves between two cultures, and here we find the pathetic alcoholics and ne'er-do-wells. But most of them have reached a more-or-less comfortable accommodation to the two lifestyles. Thus the working week may be spent filling a niche in the economic world of the major culture as a welder, construction worker, oilfield roughneck, rancher, secretary, nurse, teacher, or artist, but on weekends there is the "ceremonial return" to the Indian world, its values, activities, and attitudes. Now the rancher becomes the *mikko* or *heniha* of one of the square grounds, and the secretary or nurse becomes a matron at her tribal town, donning terrapin-shell leg rattles for the *opvnka hajo*. Some Seminoles achieve the "ceremonial return" via participation in the Pan-Indian Gourd Dance or War Dance.

Much of the workaday life of today's Oklahoma Seminole man, woman, boy, or girl is in no way different from that of their non-Indian neighbors—going to work at the plant or office, shopping at the supermarket, playing softball or watching television. Other aspects are different. The distinctively "Indian" content of any person's life-style will depend largely upon the degree of white acculturation present in that person's family and upon that person's age. The material in the remaining pages of this chapter, though not exhaustive, will give some idea of the distinctively "Indian" aspects of the Oklahoma Seminole world. Since most of this information was secured from Willie Lena and other older traditionalists, it definitely reflects the "traditional" end of the acculturation scale. In some cases it represents "memory culture" accounts that Willie gained from relatives and ancestors now deceased.

Growing up a Seminole

The Seminole baby enters a world in which he or she is immediately an important member. Older siblings, aunts, and uncles all take time to handle and play with the child. When not carried in its mother's arms the child is placed in either a cradle of willow bows or a baby swing. Willie still makes cradlles of the traditional type for relatives and friends and is probably the only person to do so at present. The cradle he makes consists of a rectangular frame constructed of dowels about an inch in diameter. The rectangle measures about two and a half feet in length by fourteen inches in

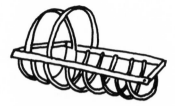 

FIGURE 19. *Left*: Oklahoma Seminole frame for baby cradle. *Right*:
Oklahoma Seminole baby cradle.

width. The end pieces of the rectangle are attached to the side
pieces by whittling down their ends to fit into holes about half an
inch in diameter, drilled to receive them. Eight more holes are
drilled vertically along either side of the rectangle to receive
pencil-size (about a quarter-inch) willow wands bent in a "U"
shape to form bows about ten inches in depth. These form the
bottom of the cradle. Two more such bows are attached to the top
of the cradle at the head end. To finish the cradle a cloth pad is
placed in the bottom and a sun shade fastened over the two bows at
the top (see figure 19). The baby swing is simply a small hammock
made from a folded blanket and a length of clothesline rope. The
rope for the swing is usually fastened to eye bolts in the wall of one
corner of the living room. Any member of the family, when he or
she passes, gives the swing a slight push to rock the baby.

When traveling outside the home, early-day Seminole mothers
frequently placed their babies on their backs at the level of the
neck and held in place with their shawls, but this practice is seen
infrequently at present. Willie mentioned that Seminole mothers
and babies formerly wore matching cloth caps with earflaps, but I
have never seen these in old photographs or in museum collections.

As soon as children begin to toddle around the house, older
siblings are taught to watch that they do not get into trouble.
Soon, small boys are following older brothers and uncles and girls
are following older sisters and aunts, watching and learning.

Although there is not as great an elaboration of specifically "child oriented" cultural forms among the Seminoles as in the major culture (such as Mother Goose rhymes) there are a few items of this sort. Willie mentioned that in the evening when the small children were supposed to go to sleep, a parent or other older relative would join the children in reciting the following "lullabye":

Locvji	*naiyo*	*kulko*	*sowata*
"little turtle"	"is drowsy"	"many lights"	"very close"
hanokʃli	*ɬvtak*	*wupus*	*josvt*
"nodding"	"snoring"	"sleeping"	"(waking) broken off"

which might be freely rendered in English:

"Little turtle is drowsy,
the stars appear close enough to touch
He nods, he snores, he sleeps soundly."

All of the children would begin reciting this in unison, but gradually, one by one, the little voices would trail off into slumber.

Another child's verse was recited as they marched off from home for a day of fishing:

Ɬaɬo	*Ɬaɬo*	*hawayeho*	*ha!, ha!*
"fish"	"fish"	"jumping"	"be on guard!"

From time to time, some older member of the family would gather a number of the children around and tell them entertaining stories that explained the world and at the same time imparted behavioral norms. Willie provided two examples of these.

HOW THE ANIMALS AND BIRDS ACQUIRED THEIR DISTINCTIVE MARKINGS

One time, in the days when animals and people could converse, the chief called a council of all the creatures. They assembled in the council house, each fancifully painted according to his own taste. The vulture had his entire head painted red. The bluejay had painted his body entirely blue, with black stripes. The rac-

222

coon had painted a black mask on his face and black stripes on his tail. The opossum had his great furry tail arched proudly over his head.

When all had taken their seats, the chief announced the purpose of the council. A miraculous child had appeared and would claim one of the creatures as its father. This father would be blessed by having such a child to raise, so all were anxious for it to claim them as father. As the miraculous boy walked around some of them whispered to it "Call me Daddy!" The chief made another announcement to the effect that whoever was not chosen as the child's father must not get angry or they would suffer the consequences.

Meanwhile the white crane, on its way to the council, was fishing along the way. Four times it saw fish and dived to catch them. The four fish it strung by the gills on a stick. When the crane reached the council house the miraculous boy saw the fish and realized that the crane was a good provider. "That's my Daddy!" he said, and went to him. At this the other creatures became angry, because they had painted themselves so beautifully but had not been chosen. Now the chief announced the consequences. Because of their anger their fanciful paints would remain their characteristic markings until the end of the world. The opossum was punished by having his proud, arching, furry tail rendered hairless and dragging.

The beautiful white crane, alone among the creatures in not ever being jealous or angry, became the symbol of peace. For this reason his feathers are worn today by Indians when they take part in the Green Corn Ceremony.

RABBIT AND WILDCAT HUNT TURKEYS

One time Rabbit and Wildcat went hunting turkeys together. They went to a place where there was a lot of turkeys and Wildcat, who was pure white in those days, played dead. Rabbit organized a dance for the turkeys, attempting to lure them within reach of Wildcat. Rabbit sang pretty songs and soon the turkeys were dancing, just like the Shawnee women do in their Turkey dance.

As he sang, Rabbit gave instructions to Wildcat in the words of his songs: "Don't take the little one. Get the big one with a red head and necklaces around its neck!"

One turkey listened to the words of the song and said "Wait a minute! It sounds like you are trying to catch us!" but Rabbit answered "No, those are just the words of my song." So Rabbit sang on and the turkeys danced. When the big red-headed turkey got near Wildcat, Wildcat jumped up and grabbed it. But the turkey was so big it flew off through the brush carrying Wildcat with it. He got scratched by thorns and that is why he is marked like we see him today.

A year later he saw his friend Rabbit and said "Look what happened to me! I used to be white!"

After reaching the age of eight or ten, children of opposite sex customarily tended to keep to themselves, and there was a gradual decrease in the extent to which the two sexes associated with one another. At this time boys and girls began to learn the tasks of adults from older family members of the same sex. Within the family it was the father's job to take care of the training of the boys; the mother's, to look after the girls. Children were taught basic good manners, such as not to interfere in adult discussions and to leave their parents' presence when visitors came to call.

On the whole, the traditional upbringing of children was rather strict. The mother might punish small children by an occasional use of the switch, but the father never attempted any form of physical punishment. This was left in the hands of the mother's brother (capáwa), and took the form of "dry scratching" the forearms and legs of the child with a needle. The children's attitude toward their mother's brother was one of respect. As a male representative of their mother's clan, which was also their own, the mother's brother was vitally concerned with the welfare of his nieces and nephews. Later, as they became older, he would attempt to find suitable wives and husbands for them. As Spoehr notes: "The mother's brother should not be construed as taking the place of the father. On the contrary, in a way he strengthened the position of the father, for the imposition of punishment was shifted out of the sphere of the elementary family. The parents had

PLATE 70. An Oklahoma Seminole elm-bark house. According to Willie Lena, the Seminoles sometimes lived in structures of this type when they first came to the Indian Territory. Sheets of elm bark were fastened to a framework of bent poles. The use of this type of dwelling by the Seminoles is not confirmed by other sources, though documented for the neighboring Sauks and Shawnees. Pen and ink sketch by Willie Lena, 1982.

a much easier time of it as a consequence; when their children were misbehaving they called in the mother's brother, who lectured the youngsters on obeying their parents, punished them, and hence saw to it that the parents' teachings, as well as his own, were followed.[1]

When a Seminole girl menstruated for the first time, and during her monthly periods thereafter until menopause, she was isolated from the rest of the family, for her menstrual blood was a contaminating influence and weakened the men of the household. In former times, if it was summer, a little camp was built about 150 yards from the family dwelling. The girl stayed there in isolation for four days. She was provided with everything she needed to get by, such as cooking pots and a plate and cup to eat from. She was also provided with a change of clothing. At the end of her period she would bathe in the nearby creek. No one, particularly not men or boys, must bathe downstream from her.

If a young man, from motives of bravado or disregard of tribal rules, bathed downstream from where a menstruating woman had bathed and this became known, the youth was apprehended, hung up by his wrists, and given twenty-five lashes by the lighthorsemen. Such a youth was termed a "worthless Indian."

In winter the woman or girl stayed in a small cabin located a shorter distance from the family dwelling. Above all, women in this condition must stay away from ceremonies, lest they spoil the medicine. If a woman or girl dances, as in the Ribbon dance at the Green Corn ceremony, during her period, she will continue to bleed, perhaps to the point of death. Willie mentioned a woman of his acquaintance who was foolish enough to try this. An Indian doctor finally managed to save her, but only after a long and difficult period of treatment. She never ventured to try it again.

Today's Seminole women isolate themselves from the rest of the family during their period, eating apart from the men, but do not stay in a separate dwelling.

Hunting

The traditional role of a Seminole man was that of a hunter. Deer were the principal quarry, but bears, rabbits, opossums, and squirrels were taken as well. Today, hunting is still a favorite avocation for Seminole men, and wild game is still an important supplement to the family food supply. When Willie Lena was growing up, wild game was even more important. In those days ammunition for

FIGURE 20. Creek style throwing stick.

rifles and shotguns was very expensive, so children were taught to take game in other, less costly ways, with the bow and arrow and the throwing stick. Throwing sticks were used by most Southeastern tribes to kill small game, such as squirrels and rabbits. In July, 1979, Willie made and gave to me examples of both Creek-and Seminole-style throwing sticks. The Creek stick is straight with an enlarged end (figure 20). It is called *kitcvboci* or *svfvlka*. The Seminole style has a projection on one side of the end, which gives it an erratic, back and forth movement as it slides through the grass. It is called *fokofoko*, which is onomatopoetic, representing the sound of the stick when thrown along the ground (figure 21).

FIGURE 21. Seminole style throwing stick.

Willie's grandfather was a great hunter, and entertained Willie with tales of "how it used to be" when Willie was a small boy. Willie recalls his grandfather's tales of how Seminole used to take passenger pigeons by knocking them out of the trees where they roosted at night. These birds were so numerous and so easy to kill that sometimes it was possible to get fifty birds from a single tree.

The most exciting hunt without firearms, however, was that for wild pigs. These animals, the wild descendants of the swine introduced into the Southeast by the Spanish, are among the most dangerous creatures in the southern forests. They are totally fearless when aroused, and their ripping tusks are lethal. The Seminoles, nevertheless, hunted these beasts with clubs. A stout tree with a branching limb at just the right angle was located and then cut and trimmed to make a club about three and a half feet in length.

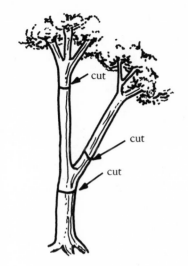

FIGURE 22. Method of cutting a club for hunting wild pigs.

The hunter would stalk the wild pigs while they slept, then quickly rush up and attempt to land a death-dealing blow just behind the animal's foreleg. The hunter would then run away as fast as possible and climb a previously selected tree. Sometimes the infuriated pig would pursue, but if the blow had been properly administered, it would soon die.

To hunt bears, the Seminoles sought the animals out in their dens. Some of the hunters carried torches with which they blinded the animals while others shot them with rifles or bows and arrows. In April, 1981, Willie made me a Seminole hunting torch of the traditional type. It is constructed from a straight hackberry branch about four feet long, with a fork about seven inches long at its upper end. A bunch of dried grass stems (*Andropogon gerardii* Vitmann, big bluestem; *Albizzia juliprissin Durazzini*, mimosa; and *Menispermum canadense L.*, moonseed) about 20 inches long and three and a half inches wide is wedged in the forked end. Strips of green bark are lashed around the center of the bunch of grass and also the tip of the forked end of the handle, to hold the inflammable material in place.

PLATE 71. Hunting the wild pig. After dealing the sleeping swine a terrible blow with the mallet-like club, the hunter runs and climbs a tall tree until the wounded animal has spent himself and dies. Pen and ink sketch by Willie Lena, 1982.

Seminole hunters used magical techniques and charms to improve their chances of success. In chapter 5 I have discussed the *sapiya* and the medicine derived from the horns of the Giant Horned Snake. Paint that has been stored with either of these substances magically attracts game to the hunter. Another hunting amulet is a sprig of red hickory leaves worn in the hunter's headband at the front (plate 72). The hunter selects this sprig by observing the tree and noting that sprig which seems to vibrate constantly, even when there is little wind. Willie commented that Seminole men still use this hunting charm at the present time, sticking the sprig in their cap or hatband.

The Seminoles have great respect for the animals they hunt, the same respect found in most societies where hunting is important. The hunter, it seems, recognizes that the uncertainty of his own condition is closely akin to the uncertain condition of the animals he must hunt to survive. Thus the Seminole hunter's quarry is an adversary who must be outwitted, but never an enemy—a creature whose motives and desires are believed to be much the same as those of the man who pursues him. The Seminole attitude toward game animals is well exemplified in the following hunting story recounted by Willie.

PLATE 72. An Oklahoma Seminole hunter. Note the sprig of red hickory leaves in his headband, a hunting charm, also the pouch of *aha lvpvcka* and cedar leaves hung from his neck, a protective charm. Pen and ink sketch by Willie Lena, 1982.

A STRANGE OCCURRENCE

One time my grandpa's dad [Willie's great grandfather] went hunting deer with a bow and arrow. He came up on a large white buck. He took careful aim and scored a hit. The buck cried out like a human and thrashed around with his legs. My great-grandfather heard something whiz by his head and hit the tree behind him. The deer gave a great jump and ran away. My great-grandfather examined the tree and found a projectile which resembled the end of a deer's antler.

The next time he went hunting he took a muzzle loader. He went to the same place and saw the same large white deer. He took careful aim and fired. He scored a direct hit. Again the buck groaned like a human and threw out its legs, and again great-grandfather heard a missile fly past him and hit a tree. The buck took a great jump and fell dead. Great-grandpa again found a missile of deer antler imbedded in the tree. Had it hit him it would have killed him. When he examined the dead buck he found that at two places the tips of the antlers were missing, as if they had broken off. We say that sometimes deer shoot back at hunters this way.

Wolves are particularly respected by Seminoles because they, too, are great hunters. Willie remarked:

"We Seminoles have great respect for wolves. We call them 'Indian dogs.' Wolves can tell you about the weather. When they give short barks it means bad weather. When they give a long howl it means good weather. We say that a wolf has four voices, the two ears, his nose, and his mouth. Each opening has a different sound and one wolf can make himself sound like four.

"One time I saw a wolf that was being chased by dogs. He came quite near to where I was, and looked awfully tired. I talked to him, 'Don't go that way, toward that farm, go the other way towards the woods.' The wolf understood me. He turned and headed for the woods.

"Once a White neighbor of mine was losing chickens. A wolf was killing them. I saw this man and told him I had seen some of his chickens, dead, and that it was a wolf who was killing them. 'So that's it! I am going to shoot that damned wolf tonight.' he said. I told him 'Don't ever talk like that. Wolves are fortune tellers. They can hear you talking. When you want to kill a wolf, keep quiet about it. Just go and do it, don't announce your plans!' Surely enough, the wolves cleaned out all this man's chickens.''

Warfare

Although they were skilled warriors, the Seminoles did not have a War Dance that they performed before engaging the enemy—at least Willie has never heard of one. Instead he described the preliminaries as resembling those that precede a match ball game. The leader would line up his men and harangue them, pacing back and forth before them as he did so. According to Willie, his speech might go thus: "Don't be afraid! Something sharp will come! But the Powers Above will take care of you. If you are killed there will be no blame on you. The blame will be on your leaders." The warriors were painted in black and red, the war colors, using the same designs as those used in the match ball game.

Each war party was accompanied by a shaman who carried a medicine bundle. In the bundle was a goodly supply of *mabilanoji* (*Poltaenia nuttalli DC.*, Prairie parsley) the traditional war or wound medicine of the Seminoles. Should any member of the party be hit, the medicine man chewed the heads of this plant and then stuffed them into the bullet or arrow wound to stop the bleeding. Willie's grandfather, who was a Seminole scout with the United States Army, reported seeing a bullet "fall out" of a wound several hours after the application of this medicine. The wound then healed with no further treatment.

Brave deeds in battle were commemorated in war names awarded at the Green Corn Ceremony. The suffixes for some of these war names have become family names of present day Seminoles: for example, Harjo (*hajo*, "fearless in battle"), and Fiksiko (*fiksiko*, "heartless").

PLATE 73. An Oklahoma Seminole woman pounding corn to make *sofki*. Watercolor by Willie Lena, 1969.

Gathering and agriculture

While the men won food by hunting, the women raised large gardens of corn, beans, and squash, and also gathered wild plant foods such as berries and nuts. Before the Removal, another wild plant food was very important to the Seminoles. This was coontie (in Muskogee, *kvnta, Zamia* sp.). Since it does not grow in Oklahoma, Willie has never seen this plant, but has heard older Seminoles speak of it. The root was dug, dried, and grated. The grated root was then put in a cloth and water was poured over it to carry off the starch. This starchy water was collected in another vessel placed below the cloth and allowed to settle. When it had settled the water at the top was poured off and the starchy material was saved to be cooked into cakes resembling corn cakes.

Hickory nuts (*oci∫m iti*) were pounded and boiled to secure the grease, which rose to the top. This material was used to flavor hominy and other dishes. Plate 14 shows a Seminole woman preparing nuts for this purpose.

Securing salt for flavoring their food was a problem for the old-time Seminoles, and they had a great craving for this condiment. Now and then they would find a place where deer had licked salt that was coming out of the ground. They called this "deer salt," and so great was their desire that they would go there and lick the ground after they had eaten, to get their salt.

PLATE 74. Pounding hickory nuts to make "hickory nut grease," a favorite flavoring for hominy. Pen and ink sketch by Willie Lena, 1982.

In order to make them grow better, seed corn and seed beans were mixed with *totak'kapi* or redbud blossoms (*Cercis canadensis L.*). Willie said that he and his first wife used to do this regularly when they planted their corn and beans years ago.

Although old-time Seminoles, like other eastern Indians, considered gardening to be the proper sphere of women, there was one plot of corn which was worked entirely by men. This was the acre set aside by each square ground where the "sacrifice corn" for use in the Green Corn ceremony was grown. This acre was prepared

PLATE 75. A source of pottery clay used by the Oklahoma Seminoles from shortly after the Removal until the 1920s. Willie Lena assisted his grandmother in securing pottery clay from this source until shortly before her death. The clay deposit is located a mile south of Wewoka, Oklahoma, just south of the cemetery. Photograph by James Howard, 1980.

entirely with hoes, never a plow, by men who were married into the tribal town, and women were not allowed to touch it.

Pottery making

For many years after the Removal, until the mid 1920s, the Oklahoma Seminoles continued to make and use their own domestic pottery (*vtkvswv*). Willie Lena recalled assisting his grandmother in gathering raw materials from her favorite source of pottery clay, which is one mile south of Wewoka, just south of the cemetery on the slope of a hill behind Willie's sister's house.

His grandmother used to secure her clay in the autumn. The preferred time was when a light rain was falling. The clay was stored, wet, in a gunny sack. It was left in the sack for three or four days. When she was ready to begin, it was Willie's job to work the clay with his hands, removing bubbles and impurities. Mussel shells were gathered from a stream bed, burned, and then pounded as temper.

The pots were constructed using the coiling method. A flat dish was used to start the pot. The coils were rolled between the palms and then added to the base by pinching each coil to the one beneath it as one proceeded. Some coils were about a foot long. The joints were carefully worked out with a small stick, to consolidate the vessel walls. A bone tool was used to scrape the walls of the vessel thin.

After the pot had been shaped it was dried for about a day and a half before firing. For the firing *tawa takko* (*Rhus glabra L.*, smooth sumac) stems were used initially, then blackjack oak. This material was piled around the pot and ignited.

In August, 1980, Willie took Richard Bivins, a ceramics professor at Oklahoma State University, and myself to the place where his grandmother formerly gathered her pottery clay. Bivins pronounced the clay to be of excellent quality and collected a sample for experimentation at Oklahoma State University.

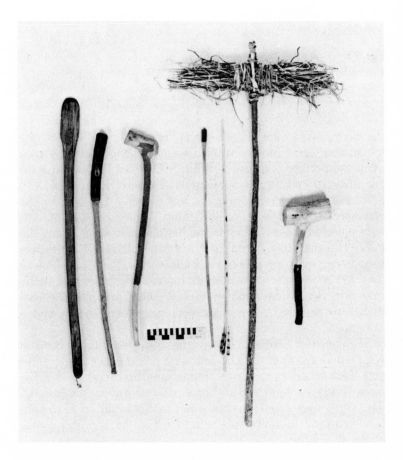

PLATE 76. Men's and women's tools and equipment. *Left to right: sofki* stirring paddle used by "Grandma Fixico" at the turn of the century; Creek style throwing stick; Seminole style throwing stick; blunt arrow used to kill birds and small game; arrow used to kill witches; hunting torch; hammer of the type used with a frow to split shingles. All items except the stirring paddle were made by Willie Lena in the period 1973–81.

Sign Language

Intertribal communication by means of a series of standardized hand signals, the so-called "Indian sign language," is generally associated with Prairie and High Plains groups. I was therefore quite interested to learn from Willie that the Seminoles used this method of communication as well. Some of the signs, in fact, are the same as those used by Plains tribes, yet others are different. A few of the signs demonstrated by Willie were these:

1. "God" — Right hand raised high over head, palm forward, left hand over heart.

2. "Riding a horse" — First two fingers of right hand formed into a "V," inverted and put over left hand which is held vertically (imitating rider's leg astride the horse).

3. "A long way" — right hand arched and pointed in the direction being discussed.

4. "Biscuits" (*tvklikucʃ*)" — cupped hands placed together repeatedly (as in forming biscuits).

5. "Pancakes (*apvtv́kv*)" — flattened palms placed together repeatedly.

6. "I am hungry" — press stomach with both hands.

7. "I am thirsty" — cup hand at mouth

Picture writing

Most Indian tribes in eastern North America used pictographs to record important events. Members of war parties frequently left a record of their passing by stripping a patch of bark from a tree near the trail and, on the bare spot, painting pictographs indicating the tribe and clan of the party, their numbers, and their success against the enemy. Sometimes tribal history was recorded in pictographs painted on a tanned animal hide. Thus the speech of the Creek chief Chekilli to Governor Oglethorpe was recorded by pictographs painted on a bison skin.[2] Willie Lena still uses such pictographs to leave notes for his children when he is away from home. He commented: "I still use picture language to leave notes for my family. If I want to tell them I went fishing with one of the

FIGURE 23. Seminole picture writing "I went fishing with my son."

kids, I draw this (figure 23). If I want to say I went down town to the store I draw this (figure 24).

FIGURE 24. Seminole picture writing "I went down town to the store."

Sometimes Willie combines written English, Muskogee, and pictographs in his communications, as in the note that I found tacked to his door on an occasion when I came to visit (figure 25).

"Broken Days"

To keep track of the passage of time before some important event such as a ceremonial or a match ball game in order to coordinate attendance, the Seminoles distribute small bundles of sticks, usually splinters of native "river" cane. These are called "broken days" in English, from the Muskogee *nittv-kvlkʃ* ("days," "broken"). Seven sticks is the usual number in such a bundle. One stick is thrown away each day, beginning with the day the bundle is delivered, and the last day is the day of the beginning of the ceremony or other event.

FIGURE 26. Seminole *nittv-kvlkʃ*, or "broken days" calendar board.

Willie made and gave to me a variant type of *nittv-kvlkʃ* consisting of a small, flat board about twelve and a half inches long and an eighth of an inch thick, carved in the shape of an arrow. Seven holes were drilled along its length and it was provided with a small peg which was to be moved one hole each day until the week was up. An extra hole near the "feather" end of the device is for hanging the object to the wall. A similar device was noted by D. W. Eakins among the Creeks in the mid-nineteenth century.[3] Willie had heard of similar calendars involving knotted strings used by Seminoles in former times, a method mentioned by Adair for the eighteenth-century Creeks: "They count certain very remarkable things by knots of various colours and make, after the

---

FIGURE 25 (*opposite page*). Seminole picture writing, a message from Willie Lena. Fully translated this means: "I'll be home at 10:30 P.M. *Fus hace*" (Willie's Indian name, meaning "Single eagle feather," which is followed by a drawing of an eagle feather). "Going with Frank to the dance" (indicated by a pictograph of a man dancing). "The key (indicated by a pictograph) is in back (*yopa*) in the usual hiding place."

manner of South-american aborigines."[4] Adair's reference, of course, is to the famous Peruvian quipus.

Miscellaneous beliefs and customs

Willie noted that the Seminole story-telling season was from September to April. When he was a small boy, parties used to go from cabin to cabin, a different home each evening, to tell and listen to stories. "I can remember the line of people going from house to house, all carrying lanterns. When they came to our

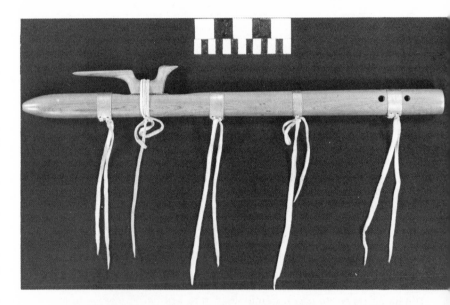

PLATE 77. Oklahoma Seminole flute. This flute was made by Woodrow Haney, a Seminole of Seminole, Oklahoma, in 1980. Mr. Haney's flutes seem to represent the adoption of the Prairie-Plains style flute rather than the continuation of the original Creek-Seminole flute-making tradition.

PLATE 78. A storytelling session. Pen and ink sketch by Willie Lena, 1982.

place it was my job to pass around the snacks. These were persimmon cakes cooked in grease, also peanuts and cups of *sofki*. If people saw a shooting star while they were telling stories, they had to stand up and spit four times before the flash disappeared. Otherwise their teeth would fall out. I guess that's what is wrong with me.

"At 12:00 o'clock on Christmas eve and again at 12:00 on New Year's eve, people would go outside, to some quiet place, and listen for something that passed over in the sky. I have heard this myself. It is a low, blowing sound, something like one of today's jets. If you can hear it, it will be a good year. If you don't, make a loud noise on a drum. Hit it four times, or fire a musket four times. It brings good luck.

"Shortly before New Year's they would go out to a patch of poke salad (*osa*). They would clean all the weeds and dead growth from around four plants. Only the roots were left. On New Year's Day they would go out and inspect the roots. If a man saw tiny leaves on his roots it indicated a good growing season. A man might say 'This will be a good year for corn.'

"When the trees begin to leaf out, the old-time Seminoles used to go out in the woods and pray and contemplate the new season. A man might ask himself 'What are we going to do this year?' (plate 80)

"Sometimes a fox acts like a human, groaning and in pain. This is a sign that someone will die. The death of Lilly Factor, a 'congressman' at New Tulsa square ground, was predicted by my ex-wife in this way . The fox was running around the cabin where

PLATE 79. The fortune-telling ceremony. Pen and ink sketch by Willie Lena, 1982.

we lived and made this sound. She said, 'I'll bet grandpa is gone.' Surely enough, they found out that he had died.

"In the same way, a howling wolf predicts cold weather.

"When Seminoles saw white cranes flying north someone would say 'Well, now it is time to plan for the Green Corn.' They would set a date for a meeting.

"Sometimes the older men would tell fortunes. They would clear a patch of ground of all weeds, grass, and trash, and make it smooth. One man would sit at each of the four directions. The man at the west would draw a circle in the earth with his cane and the four would study the surface of the earth inside the circle to predict the future. Maybe a bug would walk across part of the circle. It all had a meaning." (plate 79)

A Seminole philosophy

On May 31, 1980, while I was interviewing Willie at his home in Wewoka, a visitor came to call. This was Robert Wolfe, a Seminole of Holdenville, Oklahoma, who is a "tongue" or speaker at Tallahassee square ground. Having overheard a part of our discussion as he walked up to the porch, Wolfe asked me if I understood the meaning of the Stomp ground. I was a bit taken aback by the directness of his question, but Willie quckly remarked "I think he wants to tell you something." Robert then proceeded to deliver a lengthy discourse on the subject of the native religion. He had obviously read a great deal about astrology and tied this in with his

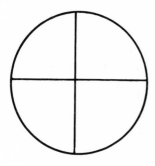

FIGURE 27. A Seminole cosmic symbol, drawn by Robert Wolfe.

PLATE 80. A Seminole philoso-
pher contemplating his people's
welfare. Pen and ink sketch by
Willie Lena, 1982.

Seminole lore. Some interesting points brought out were these:

"The stomp ground here on the earth is a reflection of astrology
[I took this to mean "pattern of the heavens," JH]. It can be
explained in this symbol. [See figure 27]

"The fire is the earthly manifestation of the sun, the source of
all power and life here on the earth. The stomp ground fire used to
be kept pure. It was given to the Indians by the Master of Breath,
God. The Indians don't need a Bible, since they have the
teachings of the ancients passed down at the Stomp ground. The
fire at the Stomp ground must be gentled at the Green Corn.
That's why we pour medicine on it at that time. If it isn't gentled
periodically it will become too powerful and destroy us."

Willie interjected at this point that the fire is not only given medicine at the Green Corn but is also "fed." This feeding takes place at the first Stomp Dance of the season. At Tallahassee, Willie said, the fire is fed liver. It is placed on a stick and hung so as to be consumed by the fire. I saw such "feeding" of the fire at Hickory ground (*Otciapofa*), a Creek square ground near Henryetta, Oklahoma, in 1966. In this case the town chief (*mikko*) put a beef tongue on the fire during the final day of the Green Corn Ceremony.

11

MORTUARY PRACTICES

Even today, traditional Seminoles prefer to bury their dead in family cemeteries, most often with small wooden grave houses erected over the graves. These cemeteries, with their groups of grave houses, can be seen here and there in Seminole County, a reminder of the strength of native tradition.

In the past, stillborn infants were placed in hollow trees, a custom also found among the Shawnees and Kickapoos.

When a death occurs, any Indian medicine that had been brewed for the deceased that remains unused is not merely thrown out anywhere, but carefully poured on a large rock to dissipate its strength.

Funerals at the present time are generally conducted in a funeral home or chapel, and are in no way different from those of the major culture. Often a white minister is asked to conduct the funeral services, both at the funeral home and at the graveside.

A Seminole woman is always buried in new clothing. Favorite old clothes are placed in the casket as well. A man is buried in his best clothes, not necessarily new. A jar of *sofki* is often put in the casket to nourish the deceased on the way to the afterworld. Cigarettes are also put in, especially if the deceased was fond of smoking. Just before it is lowered into the grave, the lid of the casket is unscrewed.

At a Seminole burial, after several shovelfuls of earth have been put on the casket, each member of the funeral party, in turn, comes forward and throws one clod into the grave. This is called "shaking hands for the last time." When the grave is filled and mounded over, additional clothing, such as a hat or overcoat, or a cane, may be placed on the grave.

Following the burial, a feast takes place, provided by the family of the deceased and usually held at the deceased's home. A small amount of each of the dishes served at this feast is saved out and later placed on the grave. Willie commented "White people think this is foolishness. One time a white minister asked an Indian 'When is the dead going to eat this food?' The Indian answered 'The same time the white people's dead rise up and smell the flowers you put on your graves.' "

It is thought that walking on the earth from a grave causes arthritis. For this reason gravediggers and other members of the funeral party are careful to wash themselves in and drink an infusion of *hoyvnijv* (*Salix humilis*) and *kofutcka* (spearmint?). The mourners drink this four times and also wash their faces and hands in it. Even the shovels used in digging the grave are washed in this liquid. Speck notes that among the Creeks, *kofutcka* is the specific for a type of fever believed to be caused by spirits.[1]

The Seminole bury their dead with the feet to the east. At the west, near the head, a small wooden stake is driven into the ground, and a few feet west of it a small fire is kindled. Relatives and friends of the deceased stay there every night for four nights, remaining until midnight. This is to show their love for the dead. It is thought that it takes the deceased four days and nights to reach the afterworld.

The Seminole have no prohibition against speaking of the dead or using their name. Later, at Christmas and on other festive occasions when there is special food, a little bit of each sort is saved out and put on a plate, which is taken to the grave. As Willie explained, "It isn't necessary that there be a large amount, as the dead only 'taste' the food."

In the old days a man's widow did not talk to any man for a period of six months. She could talk to women. She was given

PLATE 81. Oklahoma Seminole grave houses south of Wewoka, Oklahoma. Photograph by James Howard, 1980.

black clothing to wear at the funeral, and continued to wear this for the entire period of mourning, never changing clothes. Neither did she comb her hair. At the end of this period she was released and could bathe, comb her hair, put on new clothes, and go out in public.

Willie showed me a number of Seminole grave houses on his family's land near the clinic on highway 270 south of Wewoka, and urged me to photograph them as a record of Seminole tradition (plate 81). They are all about three and a half feet high, made of a wooden frame to which an asphalt shingle roof has been attached. The sides are made of upright palings with spaces in between so that one can look through. Inside is the mound of the grave. I also noticed wreaths and in one or two a box containing some favorite items of clothing and objects, such as a cane, used by the deceased in life. All of the houses were painted white with grey asphalt shingle roofs. A name plaque was attached to the front of each. All of the houses, like the graves, were oriented east and west. Some tombstones were present among the grave houses, all of which were quite close together. There were no recently erected tombstones.

12

EPILOGUE

In the preceding chapters I have attempted to indicate, largely through the accumulated experiences of one man, and from his perspective, the surprising amount of traditional culture still remaining among today's Oklahoma Seminoles. This culture, with its square ground religion, attitudes, beliefs, and distinctly "Southeastern" world-view, persists in spite of more than four hundred years of exposure to European and American culture on the part of the Seminoles and their Creek forebears, and many conflicts and forced migrations of a most disruptive nature. Willie's testimony, if one reads between the lines, also demonstrates the remarkable resiliency of Seminole culture, which, though often bent, has never broken. It is also quite clear from the material here presented that although much has been lost and much changed, there will undoubtedly continue to be American Indians in Oklahoma who proudly call themselves "Seminole" for many years to come.

On the other hand, one must admit that the detailed knowledge of herbal and other remedies, magical formulae, and ceremonial procedures possessed by Willie and others of his generation will undoubtedly become increasingly attentuated as the years pass. I suspect that the immediate future will see the Seminoles turning more and more to a "Pan-Indian" basis of self-identification. By

249

this I mean that instead of devoting their energies toward the maintenance of strictly Seminole cultural forms, however these are perceived, the younger generation of the tribe will turn toward cultural forms which, though American Indian, are intertribal or non-tribal in nature. This process, in fact, has already begun with the adoption of the Plains Indian (or better "Pan-Indian") pow-wow complex by the Seminoles, complete with such features as the Gourd Dance, "Straight" and "Fancy" style War Dancing, and "powwow princess" contests. At the 1980 Seminole Days celebration, in fact, I even saw a Plains Indian tipi, made and erected by a Seminole family, standing out like the proverbial sore thumb in the midst of more traditional Seminole camps. Such occurrences, in my view, are not merely fashionable foreign importations, but a harbinger of things to come, an increasing tendency of the Seminoles to think of themselves as North American Indians rather than Oklahoma Seminoles. Some individuals have already turned this corner, as evidenced by membership in the American Indian Movement and other Pan-Indian political action groups.

Even arch-conservatives like Willie Lena have been affected by Pan-Indianism to some extent. Here and there among Willie's sketches of traditional Seminole scenes and types, one finds a representation of an idealized Plains Indian "princess" with braids and a long buckskin dress, or a Pan-Indian "fancy" War dancer with huge neck and back bustles. On one side of a small wooden "medicine box" that I purchased from Willie several years ago I even found the ultimate in Pan-Indian kitsch — a hackneyed view of tipis on a hillside overlooking an incredibly blue lake. Willie has apparently learned what is likely to appeal to touristic tastes.

It is obvious, though, that for Willie and most other Seminole traditionalists Pan-Indian gatherings are a crashing bore. Willie will sometimes appear briefly at a Pan-Indian powwow, but mainly to sell some of the miniature drums, ballsticks, and other small items upon which he relies for income, and he always leaves early. Stomp Dances, stickball games, and Green Corns are a different thing entirely. These events, the very food of the Seminole soul, are planned for weeks in advance. For them he appears in his best Indian shirt and hat ornament, arriving early and staying late.

It will remain the task of future scholars to chronicle the increasing loss of distinctly Seminole, or Southeastern, cultural forms by the Oklahoma Seminoles and their gradual replacement by others—either elements derived from western tribes or from the major "white" culture, and to note how these changes are correlated with the self-perception of future generations of the tribe.

NOTES

PREFACE

1. Clay MacCauley, *The Seminole Indians of Florida*, p. 507. The idea that the name is a corruption of *cimarron* has been credited to Herbert E. Bolton, historian of the Spanish borderlands. Frederick W. Hodge and others have held that Seminole is basically a native word.

2. George P. Murdock and Timothy O'Leary, *Ethnographic Bibliography of North America*, 4th ed., vol. 4., Eastern United States, pp. 222–33.

CHAPTER 1   A SYNOPSIS OF SEMINOLE HISTORY

1. Charles Fairbanks, *The Florida Seminole People*, p. 6.

2. Fairbanks, *The Florida Seminole People*, p. 4.

3. Fairbanks, *The Florida Seminole People*, p. 5.

4. William C. Sturtevant, *Creek Into Seminole*, p. 101.

5. Fairbanks, *The Florida Seminole People*, p. 5.

6. Sturtevant, *Creek Into Seminole*, p. 102.

7. Sturtevant, *Creek Into Seminole*, p. 103.

8. John R. Swanton, *Early History of the Creek Indians and their Neighbors*, p. 403.

9. Benjamin Hawkins, *A Sketch of the Creek Country in the Years 1798 and 1799*, pp. 24–25.

10. Howard F. Cline, *Colonial Indians in Florida, 1700–1823* quoted in Sturtevant, *Creek Into Seminole*, p. 105.

11. Charles Fairbanks, *Ethnohistorical Report of the Florida Indians*, p. 134.

12. Sturtevant, *Creek Into Seminole*, pp. 105–106.

13. Fairbanks, *Ethnohistorical Report*, pp. 208, 211.

14. Virginia B. Peters, *The Florida Wars*, pp. 57–58.

15. Sturtevant, *Creek Into Seminole*, p. 107.

16. Peters, *The Florida Wars*, p. 69.

17. Peters, *The Florida Wars*, p. 91.

18. Edwin C. McReynolds, *The Seminoles*, pp. 125–28.

19. McReynolds, *The Seminoles*, p. 145.

20. McReynolds, *The Seminoles*, pp. 145–46; Peters, *The Florida Wars*, p. 95.

21. McReynolds, *The Seminoles*, pp. 193–95.

22. McReynolds, *The Seminoles*, p. 234.

23. Charles H. Coe, *Red Patriots: The Story of the Seminoles*, pp. 191–209; Kenneth W. Porter, "Billy Bowlegs (Holati Micco) in the Seminole Wars."

24. Muriel H. Wright, *A Guide to the Indian Tribes of Oklahoma*, p. 232.

25. McReynolds, *The Seminoles*, p. 258.

26. McReynolds, *The Seminoles*, pp. 275–76.

27. McReynolds, *The Seminoles*, p. 316.

28. Wright, *A Guide to the Indian Tribes*, p. 235.

29. McReynolds, *The Seminoles*, p. 323.

CHAPTER 2   SEMINOLE HERBAL REMEDIES

1. James Mooney, "Cherokee Theory and Practice of Medicine," pp. 44–50; Charles Hudson, *The Southeastern Indians*, pp. 156–59.

2. John R. Swanton, *Social and Religious Beliefs and Usages of the Chickasaw Indians*, pp. 263–72.

3. Frank G. Speck, *Ceremonial Songs of the Creek and Yuchi Indians*, pp. 211–40; John R. Swanton, *Religious Beliefs and Medical Practices of the Creek Indians*, pp. 636–39; J. N. B. Hewitt, *Notes on the Creek Indians*, pp. 154–57.

4. Robert F. Greenlee, "Medicine and Curing Practices of the Modern Florida Seminole," pp. 317–28.

5. Mooney, "Cherokee Theory and Practice of Medicine," pp. 45–46.

6. Swanton, *Religious Beliefs*, p. 659.

7. John Pope, *Tour through the Northern and Western Territories of the United States*, p. 63.

8. Swanton, *Religious Beliefs*, p. 645.

9. Swanton, *Religious Beliefs*, p. 660.

10. Frank G. Speck, "A List of Plant Curatives Obtained from the Houma Indians of Louisiana," p. 63.

11. Virgil J. Vogel, *American Indian Medicine*, p. 344.

12. Dorothy Milligan, *The Indian Way: The Chickasaws*, p. 72.

13. Edward P. Claus, [Edmund Norris] Gathercoal, and [Elmer Hauser] Wirth, *Pharmacognosy*, 3rd ed., rev., pp. 512–13.

14. Albert S. Gatschet, *A Migration Legend of the Creek Indians* 2:11.

15. Benjamin Hawkins, *A Sketch of the Creek Country in the Years 1798 and 1799*, p. 79.

16. Hawkins, *A Sketch of the Creek Country*, pp. 78–79.

17. Swanton, *Religious Beliefs*, p. 656.

18. Swanton, *Religious Beliefs*, p. 656.

19. James Adair, *The History of the American Indian*, p. 103.

20. Swanton, *Religious Beliefs*, p. 656.

21. Swanton, *Religious Beliefs*, p. 656.

22. Caleb Swan, *Position and State of Manners and Arts in the Creek or Muskogee Nation in 1791*, p. 268.

23. Adair, *History of the American Indian*, pp. 102–103.

24. Swanton, *Religious Beliefs*, p. 656.

25. Swanton, *Religious Beliefs*, p. 668.

26. Greenlee, "Medicine and Curing Practices," p. 323.

27. Adair, *History of the American Indian*, p. 103.

28. Adair, *History of the American Indian*, p. 103.

29. Swanton, *Religious Beliefs*, p. 661.

30. Swanton, *Religious Beliefs*, p. 663–64.

31. Swanton, *Religious Beliefs*, p. 660–61.

32. Frank G. Speck, *Choctaw-Creek Medicines* (MS).

33. Milligan, *Indian Way: The Chickasaws*, p. 72.

34. Frank G. Speck, *Catawba Medicines and Curing Practices*, p. 90.

35. Swanton, *Religious Beliefs*, p. 647.

36. Swanton, *Religious Beliefs*, p. 658.

37. Swanton, *Religious Beliefs*, p. 662.

38. Swanton, *Religious Beliefs*, p. 658.

39. Swanton, *Religious Beliefs*, p. 668.

40. James Mooney, *The Sacred Formulas of the Cherokees*, p. 325.

41. Milligan, *Indian Way: The Chickasaws*, pp. 77–78.

42. Hawkins, *A Sketch of the Creek Country*, p. 77.

43. Swanton, *Religious Beliefs*, p. 668.

44. Vogel, *American Indian Medicine*. p. 205.

45. Benjamin Smith Barton, *Collections for an Essay Towards a Materia Medica of the United States, 3rd ed. with additions*, p. 33, app. 56.

46. William Bartram, *Observations on the Creek and Cherokee Indians, 1789*, p. 43.

47. Swanton, *Religious Beliefs*, p. 662.

48. Swanton, *Religious Beliefs*, p. 662.

49. Swanton, *Religious Beliefs*, p. 657.

50. Swanton, *Religious Beliefs*, p. 657.

51. Swanton, *Religious Beliefs*, p. 667.

52. Swanton, *Religious Beliefs*, p. 668.

53. Melvin R. Gilmore, *Uses of Plants by the Indians of the Missouri River Region*, p. 70.

54. Claus, Gathercoal, and Wirth, *Pharmacognosy*, pp. 215–16.

55. Gatschet, *A Migration Legend of the Creek Indians* 2:11.

56. Swanton, *Religious Beliefs*, p. 655.

57. Speck, *Ceremonial Songs of the Creek and Yuchi Indians*, p. 220.

58. In Henry R. Schoolcraft, *Historical annd Statistical Information respecting the History, Conditions, and Prospects of the Indian Tribes of the United States* 1(1851):274.

59. Swanton, *Social and Religious Beliefs*, pp. 266, 268.

60. Swanton, *Religious Beliefs*, p. 659.

61. Swanton, *Religious Beliefs*, p. 668.

62. Frank G. Speck, "A List of Plant Curatives Obtained from the Houma Indians of Louisiana," p. 60.

63. Frank G. Speck, "Catawba Herbals and Curing Practices," p. 44.

64. Greenlee, "Medicine and Curing Practices," p. 323.

65. Charles Fairbanks, *The Function of Black Drink Among the Creeks*, p. 140.

66. Vogel, *American Indian Medicine*, p. 201.

67. Swanton, *Religious Beliefs*, pp. 648, 656, 665.

68. Speck, "A List of Plant Curatives," p. 65.

69. Frank G. Speck, Royal B. Hassrick, and Edmund S. Carpenter, "Rappahanock Herbals, Folk-Lore, and Science of Cures."

70. Vogel, *American Indian Medicine*, p. 342.

71. Speck, *Ceremonial Songs*, p. 233.

72. Swanton, *Religious Beliefs*, p. 267.

73. Swanton, *Social and Religious Beliefs*, p. 267.

74. John Lawson, *The History of Carolina*, p. 103.

75. James Mooney, *The Swimmer Manuscript*, p. 275.

76. W.E.S. Folsom-Dickerson, *The White Path*, p. 72.

77. Speck, "Catawba Herbals," p. 46.

78. Swanton, *Religious Beliefs*, p. 665.

79. Barton, *Collections* 1:30; *Collections* 2:41–43, 56.

80. Swanton, *Religious Beliefs*, p. 668.

81. Speck, "Catawba Herbals," p. 44.

82. Claus, Gathercoal, and Wirth, *Pharmacognosy*, p. 220.

83. Swanton, *Religious Beliefs*, p. 267.

84. Milligan, *Indian Way: The Chickasaws*, pp. 72, 136.

85. Swanton, *Social and Religious Beliefs*, p. 267.

86. D. I. Bushnell, *The Choctaw of Bayou Lacomb*, p. 24.

87. Milligan, *Indian Way: The Chickasaws*, p. 72.

88. Folsom-Dickerson, *The White Path*, p. 72.

89. Hawkins, *A Sketch of the Creek Country*, p. 77.

90. Speck, *Ceremonial Songs*, pp. 225–26.

91. Swanton, *Religious Beliefs*, p. 657.

92. Folsom-Dickerson, *The White Path*, p. 75.

93. Speck, "Catawba Herbals," p. 45.
94. Speck, *Ceremonial Songs*, pp. 222–24.
95. Swanton, *Religious Beliefs*, p. 660.
96. Folsom-Dickerson, *The White Path*, p. 66.
97. Swanton, *Religious Beliefs*, p. 658.
98. Vogel, *American Indian Medicine*, p. 365.
99. Greenlee, "Medicine and Curing Practices," p. 323.
100. Speck, *Ceremonial Songs*, pp. 232–233.
101. Swanton, *Religious Beliefs*, p. 641.
102. Swanton, *Religious Beliefs*, p. 642.
103. Folsom-Dickerson, *The White Path*, p. 64.
104. Bushnell, *The Choctaw of Bayou Lacomb*, p. 23.
105. Speck, "Catawba Herbals," p. 66.
106. Vogel, *American Indian Medicine*, p. 365.
107. Gatschet, *A Migration Legend of the Creek Indians* 2:11.
108. Hawkins, *A Sketch of the Creek Country*, p. 77.
109. Hawkins, *A Sketch of the Creek Country*, p. 78.
110. Swanton, *Religious Beliefs*, p. 662.
111. Swanton, *Religious Beliefs*, p. 509.
112. Hawkins, *A Sketch of the Creek Country*, p. 77.
113. Swanton, *Religious Beliefs*, p. 657.
114. R. M. Loughridge and D. M. Hodge, *English and Muskokee Dictionary*, p. 151.
115. Hudson, *The Southeastern Indians*, p. 34.
116. William Bartram, *Travels of William Bartram*, p. 267.
117. Bartram, *Observations*, p. 47.
118. Swanton, *Religious Beliefs*, p. 657.
119. Louis Capron, *The Medicine Bundles of the Florida Seminole and the Green Corn Dance*, p. 202.
120. Speck, *Ceremonial Songs*, pp. 227–28.
121. Swanton, *Religious Beliefs*, p. 648.
122. Swanton, *Religious Beliefs*, p. 656.
123. Swanton, *Religious Beliefs*, p. 656.
124. Adair, *The History of the American Indian*, p. 363.
125. Swanton, *Religious Beliefs*, p. 665.
126. Folsom-Dickerson, *The White Path*, p. 68.
127. Speck, "A List of Plant Curatives," p. 61.
128. Mooney, *The Sacred Formulas*, p. 326.
129. Swanton, *Religious Beliefs*, p. 665.
130. Hudson, *The Southeastern Indians*, p. 342.

CHAPTER 4 MAGIC AND WITCHCRAFT

1. John R. Swanton, *Religious Beliefs and Medical Practices of the Creek*

Indians, pp. 498–501; James H. Howard and James Shaffer, "Medicines and Medicine Headdresses of the Yamasee," pp. 125–26.

2. Swanton, *Religious Beliefs*, p. 502.

3. Benjamin Hawkins, *A Sketch of the Creek Country in the Years 1798 and 1799*, pp. 79–80.

4. Hawkins, *A Sketch of the Creek Country*, pp. 79–80.

CHAPTER 5   CEREMONIALISM, GENERAL CONSIDERATIONS

1. John R. Swanton, *Indians of the Southeastern United States*, p. 217.

2. Benjamin Hawkins, *A Sketch of the Creek Country in the Years 1798 and 1799*, p. 45.

3. John R. Swanton, *Religious Beliefs and Medical Practices of the Creek Indians*, pp. 232–35, 241.

4. Hawkins, *A Sketch of the Creek Country*, p. 49.

5. Alexander Spoehr, *Kinship System of the Seminole*, p. 52.

6. Spoehr, *Kinship System of the Seminole*, p. 52–53.

7. Spoehr, *Kinship System of the Seminole*, p. 53.

8. Swanton, *Religious Beliefs*, pp. 283–95.

9. Swanton, *Religious Beliefs*, p. 286.

10. Swanton, *Religious Beliefs*, p. 286.

11. Frank G. Speck, *Ceremonial Songs of the Creek and Yuchi Indians*, p. 163.

12. Swanton, *Religious Beliefs*, p. 522.

13. Swanton, *Religious Beliefs*, Plate 13a.

14. Swanton, *Religious Beliefs*, p. 521.

15. Speck, *Ceremonial Songs*, p. 163; Swanton, *Religious Beliefs*, p. 521.

16. Swanton, *Religious Beliefs*, pp. 526–27.

CHAPTER 6   CEREMONIALISM, THE GREEN CORN

1. John R. Swanton, *Religious Beliefs and Medical Practices of the Creek Indians*, p. 609.

2. General E. A. Hitchcock, quoted in Swanton, *Religious Beliefs*, pp. 573–74.

3. Louis Capron, *The Medicine Bundles of the Florida Seminole and the Green Corn Dance*; William C. Sturtevant, "The Medicine Bundles and Busks of the Florida Seminole."

4. Capron, *Medicine Bundles of the Florida Seminole*, pp. 168–69.

5. James H. Howard, *Shawnee! The Ceremonialism of a Native American Tribe and Its Cultural Background*, pp. 273–85.

CHAPTER 7   CEREMONIALISM, THE NIGHTTIME DANCES

1. Raymond Harjo, one of my Creek informants, insists that the *Opvnka hajo* was originally the Creek and Seminole War Dance, and that most of the really old Stomp Dance songs refer to incidents in battle.

2. James H. Howard, *Shawnee! The Ceremonialism of a Native American Tribe and Its Cultural Background*, pp. 322–24.

3. John R. Swanton, *Religious Beliefs and Medical Practices of the Creek Indians*, p. 532.

4. Swanton, *Religious Beliefs*, p. 529.

5. Swanton, *Religious Beliefs*, p. 528.

6. Frank G. Speck, Leonard Broom, and Will West Long, *Cherokee Dance and Drama*, pp. 65–68.

7. Swanton, *Religious Beliefs*, p. 530.

8. Frank G. Speck, *Ceremonial Songs of the Creek and Yuchi Indians*, p. 204.

9. Howard, *Shawnee!*, pp. 325–26.

10. Swanton, *Religious Beliefs*, p. 534.

11. Swanton, *Religious Beliefs*, pp. 523–24.

12. Claude Medford, Jr., *Songs of the Muskogee Creek*, Pt. 2.

CHAPTER 8   SPORTS AND GAMES

1. James H. Howard, *The Southeastern Ceremonial Complex and Its Interpretation*, pp. 142–48.

2. Stewart Culin, *Games of the North American Indians*, p. 148.

CHAPTER 9   SUPERNATURALS

1. John R. Swanton, *Religious Beliefs and Medical Practices of the Creek Indians*, p. 497.

2. Swanton, *Religious Beliefs*, p. 497.

3. Swanton, *Religious Beliefs*, p. 497.

4. Swanton, *Religious Beliefs*, p. 497.

5. Swanton, *Religious Beliefs*, p. 497.

6. Swanton, *Religious Beliefs*, p. 499.

CHAPTER 10   THE SEMINOLE WORLD

1. Alexander Spoehr, *Kinship System of the Seminole*, p. 77.

2. Albert S. Gatschet, *A Migration Legend of the Creek Indians* 2:4.

3. Henry R. Schoolcraft, *Historical and Statistical Information Respecting*

the History, Conditions and Prospects of the Indian Tribes of the United States 1:273.

4. James Adair, *The History of the American Indians*, p. 75.

CHAPTER 11   MORTUARY PRACTICES

1. Frank G. Speck, *Ceremonial Songs of the Creek and Yuchi Indians*, p. 236.

BIBLIOGRAPHY

Adair, James
    1775   *The History of the American Indians.* London: Edward
          and Charles Dilly.
Barton, Benjamin Smith
    1810   *Collections for an Essay Towards a Materia Medica of the*
          United States. 3d ed., with add. Philadelphia: Edward
          Earle & Co.
Bartram, William
    1791   *Travels of William Bartram.* Philadelphia: James &
          Johnson.
    1853   *Observations on the Creek and Cherokee Indians, 1789.*
          Prefatory and sup. notes by E. G. Squier, American Ethno-
          logical Society *Transactions*, Vol. 3, pt. 1, New York.
Bushnell, D. I.
    1909   *The Choctaw of Bayou Lacomb.* Bureau of American
          Ethnology *Bulletin 48*, pp. 1–37. Washington, D.C.
Capron, Louis
    1953   *The Medicine Bundles of the Florida Seminole and the*
          Green Corn Dance. Bureau of American Ethnology *Bulle-*
          tin 151, pp. 155–210. Washington, D.C.
Claus, Edward P., Gathercoal [Edmund Norris], and Wirth [Elmer
          Hauser].
    1961   *Pharmacognosy*, 3d. ed., rev. Philadelphia: Lea & Febiger.

Cline, Howard F.
    1964   "Colonial Indians in Florida, 1700–1823." (manuscript in
                its author's possession, quoted in William C. Sturtevant
                "Creek into Seminole," 1971).
Coe, Charles H.
    1898   *Red Patriots: the Story of the Seminoles.* Cincinnati: The
                Editor Publishing Co.
Culin, Stewart
    1907   *Games of the North American Indians.* Bureau of Amer-
                ican Ethnology *24th Annual Report*, 1902–1903, Wash-
                ington, D.C.
Fairbanks, Charles H.
    1957   "Ethnohistorical Report of the Florida Indian." De-
                fendant's Exhibit No. 141, Before the Indian Claims Com-
                mission, Docket Nos. 73 and 151 (mimeographed).
    1973   *The Florida Seminole People.* Phoenix: Indian Tribal Ser-
                ies.
    1979   "The Function of Black Drink Among the Creeks." In
                Black Drink, A Native American Tea, Charles M. Hud-
                son, ed. Athens: University of Georgia Press, pp. 120–49.
Folsom-Dickerson, W. E. S.
    1965   *The White Path.* San Antonio: The Naylor Company.
Gatschet, Albert S.
    1884   *A Migration Legend of the Creek Indians.* Vol. 1. Phil-
                adelphia: D. G. Brinton.
    1888   *A Migration Legend of the Creek Indians.* Vol. 2. St.
                Louis: Printed for the author.
Gilmore, Melvin R.
    1919   *Uses of Plants by the Indians of the Missouri River Region.*
                Bureau of American Ethnology *33rd Annual Report*, pp.
                43–154. Washington, D.C.
Greenlee, Robert F.
    1944   "Medicine annd Curing Practices of the Modern Florida
                Seminole," *American Anthropologist* 46:317–28.
Haas, Mary P.
    1940   "Creek Inter-town Relations," *American Anthropologist*
                42 (No. 3):479–89.
Hawkins, Benjamin
    1848   *A Sketch of the Creek Country in the years 1798 and*

1799, Georgia Historical Society *Collections* 3, (pt. 1):19–85, Savannah.

Hewitt, J. N. B. (John R. Swanton, editor)
1939 *Notes on the Creek Indians*, Bureau of American Ethnology *Bulletin 123*, pp. 119–59. Washington, D.C.

Hitchcock, General E. A.
n.d. Manuscript notes in possession of Mrs. W. H. Croffut, Washington, D.C., In *Creek Religion and Medicine* by John R. Swanton. Bureau of American Ethnology *42nd Annual Report*, pp. 473–672. Washington, D.C., 1928.

Howard, James H.
1968 *The Southeastern Ceremonial Complex and Its Interpretation*, Columbia: Missouri Archaeological Society *Memoir Number 6*.
1981 *Shawnee! The Ceremonialism of a Native American Tribe and Its Cultural Background*. Athens and London: Ohio University Press.

Howard, James H. and James Shaffer
1962 "Medicines and Medicine Headdresses of the Yamasee," *American Indian Tradition* (Alton, Ill.) 8 (No. 3):125–26.

Hudson, Charles
1976 *The Southeastern Indians*. Knoxville: University of Tennessee Press.

Lawson John
1860 *The History of Carolina*. Raleigh, N.C.

Loughridge, R. M. and D. M. Hodge
1964 *English and Muskokee Dictionary* (reprint of St. Louis, 1890, edition). Okmulgee, Oklahoma: Baptist Home Mission Board.

MacCauley, Clay
1887 *The Seminole Indians of Florida*, Bureau of American Ethnology *5th Annual Report*, 1883–1884, pp. 469–532. Washington, D.C.

McReynolds, Edwin C.
1957 *The Seminoles*. Norman: University of Oklahoma Press.

Medford, Claude, Jr.
1970 *Songs of the Muskogee Creek* (in two parts). Jacket notes for Indian House records 3001 and 3002 of the same name. Taos, New Mexico.

Milligan, Dorothy
  1976   *The Indian Way: The Chickasaws.* Quanah, Texas: Nor-
            tex Press.
Mooney, James
  1890   "Cherokee Theory and Practice of Medicine," *Journal of
            American Folklore* 3:44–50.
  1891   *The Sacred Formulas of the Cherokees.* Bureau of Amer-
            ican Ethnology, *7th Annual Report,* 1885–1886. Wash-
            ington, D.C.
Mooney, James
  1932   *The Swimmer Manuscript: Cherokee Sacred Formulas and
            Medicinal Prescriptions,* Frans M. Olbrechts, ed. Bureau
            of American Ethnology *Bulletin 99,* pp. 1–319. Washing-
            ton, D.C.
Murdock, George P., and Timothy J. O'Leary, eds.
  1975   *Ethnographic Bibliography of North America,* 4th rev.
            ed., vol. 4, *Eastern United States,* Behavior Science
            Bibliographies Series. New Haven: Human Relations Area
            Files Press.
Peters, Virginia B.
  1979   *The Florida Wars.* Hamden, Connecticut: The Shoe
            String Press.
Pope, John
  1792   *Tour through the Northern and Western Territories of the
            United States.* Richmond.
Porter, Kenneth W.
  1967   "Billy Bowlegs (Holata Micco) in the Seminole Wars,"
            Florida Historical Quarterly 45 (no. 3):219–42.
Schoolcraft, Henry R.
  1851–57   *Historical and Statistical Information respecting the His-
            tory, Conditions, and Prospects of the Indian Tribes of the
            United States.* Parts 1–6. Philadelphia.
Speck, Frank G.
  1904   "Choctaw-Creek Medicines." MS, American Philo-
            sophical Society.
  1911   *Ceremonial Songs of the Creek and Yuchi Indians.* An-
            thropological Publications of the University of Pennsylva-
            nia Museum, vol. 1, no. 2. Philadelphia: University
            Museum.

1937   "Catawba Medicines and Curative Practices." *Publica-
            tions of the Philadelphia Anthropological Society*, no. 1,
            pp. 179–97.
1941   "A List of Plant Curatives Obtained from the Houma
            Indians of Louisiana." *Primitive Man* 14, no. 4 (October
            1941).
1944   "Catawba Herbals and Curing Practices," *Journal of
            American Folklore* 52, no. 223 (January-March 1944).
Speck, Frank G., Leonard Broom, and Will West Long
1951   *Cherokee Dance and Drama*, Berkeley and Los Angeles:
            University of California Press. Reprint with added index
            and new preface by Leonard Broom, Norman: University
            of Oklahoma Press, 1983.
Speck, Frank G., Royal B. Hassrick, and Edmund S. Carpenter
1947   "Rappahannock Herbals, Folk-Lore and Science of
            Cures," *Proceedings of the Delaware County Institute of
            Science* 10, no. 1 (November 1, 1947), Media, Pennsyl-
            vania.
Spoehr, Alexander
1942   *Kinship System of the Seminole*. Field Museum of Natural
            History Anthropological Series, vol. 23, no. 2, pp. 29–
            113. Chicago.
Sturtevant, William C.
1962   "The Medicine Bundles and Busks of the Florida Semi-
            nole." *Florida Anthropologist* 15: 73–82.
1971   "Creek Into Seminole." In *North American Indians in
            Historical Perspective*, Eleanor Burke Leacock and Nancy
            Oestreich Lurie eds., New York: Random House, pp. 92–
            128.
Swan, Caleb
1857   "Position and State of Manners and Arts in the Creek or
            Muskogee Nation in 1791." In *Historical and Statistical
            Information Respecting the History, Conditions, and Pros-
            pects of the Indian Tribes of the United States*, Parts 1–6,
            Philadelphia, 1851–1857, vol. 5, pp. 251–83.
Swanton, John R.
1922   *Early History of the Creek Indians and their Neighbors*.
            Bureau of American Ethnology *Bulletin 73*. Washington,
            D.C.

1928a   "Religious Beliefs and Medical Practices of the Creek Indians." Bureau of American Ethnology *42nd Annual Report*, pp. 473–672. Washington, D.C.

1928b   "Social and Religious Beliefs and Usages of the Chickasaw Indians." Bureau of American Ethnology *44th Annual Report*, pp. 169–273. Washington, D.C.

1946   *The Indians of the Southeastern United States.* Bureau of American Ethnology *Bulletin 137.* Washington, D.C.

Vogel, Virgil J.

1970   *American Indian Medicine.* Norman: University of Oklahoma Press.

Wright, Muriel H.

1951   *A Guide to the Indian Tribes of Oklahoma*, Norman: University of Oklahoma Press.

INDEX